THE MICROSTRUCTURE OF SECURITIES MARKETS

THE MICROSTRUCTURE OF SECURITIES MARKETS

Kalman J. Cohen
Duke University

Steven F. Maier
UAI Technology, Inc., and Duke University

Robert A. Schwartz
New York University

David K. Whitcomb
Rutgers University

Prentice-Hall, Englewood Cliffs, New Jersey 07632

Library of Congress Cataloging-in-Publication Data

Main entry under title:

The Microstructure of securities markets.

Bibliography: p. 233
Includes index.
1. Securities. 2. Securities—United States.
3. Stock exchange. 4. Stock exchange—United States.
I. Cohen, Kalman J.
HG4661.M53 1985 332.64 85-28265
ISBN 0-13-581794-3

Cover design: Edsal Enterprises
Manufacturing buyer: Ed O'Dougherty

Printed in the United States of America

10 9 8 7 6 5 4 3 2 1

Prentice-Hall International (UK) Limited, *London*
Prentice-Hall of Australia Pty. Limited, *Sydney*
Prentice-Hall Canada Inc., *Toronto*
Prentice-Hall Hispanoamericana, S.A., *Mexico*
Prentice-Hall of India Private Limited, *New Delhi*
Prentice-Hall of Japan, Inc., *Tokyo*
Prentice-Hall of Southeast Asia Pte. Ltd., *Singapore*
Editora Prentice-Hall do Brasil, Ltda., *Rio de Janeiro*
Whitehall Books Limited, *Wellington, New Zealand*

CONTENTS

PREFACE

Two events with far-reaching consequences for the securities industry occurred in 1975 with the passage by Congress of the Securities Act Amendments: the era of fixed commissions ended, and the development of a national market system was mandated. These events propelled the industry toward a new era of enhanced competition, greater integration, and dramatic growth.

Two other major changes have occurred since 1975: a virtual explosion of the order flow has placed demands on the market centers that could not possibly have been met a decade ago, and the increasing application of computer technology has vastly expanded the capacity of the market centers to handle this larger order flow. The new computer technology has further provided the electronic linkages among the stock exchanges, the OTC market makers, and the brokerage houses that would seem to make a truly national (and eventually international) system possible.

The accelerated rate of change has been matched by a remarkable increase of interest on the part of practitioners, government regulators, and academicians in the operations of the securities markets. As a consequence, a new field within the area of financial economics has emerged: security market microstructure. Microstructure analysis considers the interplay among market participants, trading mechanisms, and the dynamic behavior of security prices when trading is impeded by friction (i.e., information, decision, and transaction costs).

For the past decade, we have been part of a growing number of academicians who have been concerned with the workings of the securities markets. The purpose of this book is to integrate our observations, our theoretical and empirical findings, and the policy proposals we have developed. The structure of this book reflects our four-part interest.

In Part I, "How Securities Markets Work," we present both a conceptual and an institutional overview of the markets. We begin with the conceptual. Chapter 1 reviews the microstructure literature and the fundamental issues with which it has dealt. Chapter 2 next presents a comparison of existing stock exchange trading arrangements. The striking diversity of systems observed around the world highlights the wide range of viable alternatives, and the complex trade-offs they involve. The development of the institutional foundations of our work is continued in Chapter 3, where we examine more closely the most striking change currently occurring: automation of the trading process.

Part II, "Analysis of the Auction Market Process," deals with fundamental issues concerning trading and price determination. Chapter 4 first presents a model of the returns generation process. We use this model to show that when friction impedes trading, returns variance is greater (all else equal) for thinner issues. We then use this variance-thinness relationship to assess empirically the impact of stock exchange specialists (the primary market makers in the agency/auction markets of the United States). Chapter 5 next presents a model of an investor's order-placement strategy. This model is used to explain two further attributes of price determination: nontrivial bid-ask spreads are an equilibrium property of asset markets, and equilibrium spreads are larger for thinner issues. The analysis presented in Chapter 5 completes the microstructure foundation that we use in the remainder of the book.

In Part III, "Implications for Empirical Research in Finance," we link the microstructure attributes of friction (inflated returns variance for thinner issues, and the existence of an equilibrium bid-ask spread which is larger for thinner issues) to the dynamic behavior of security prices. To this end, Chapter 6 first presents a model of the price-adjustment delays that are embedded in actual (nonfrictionless) trading. This model is then used to explain various empirical findings involving correlation in stock and market index returns, and bias in the estimation of beta coefficients. Chapter 7 next presents two approaches to adjusting for the bias in short-period beta estimates; tests are reported for U.S. and French data. The significance of our findings concerning correlation patterns and beta bias underscores the need for empirical research in finance to take account of the real-world processes by which returns are generated.

In Part IV, "Implications for Market Architecture," we turn to one further topic of central importance in microstructure analysis—the design of market trading arrangements. Our attention focuses on two major issues: consolidation of the order flow and the stabilization of price movements. With regard to consolidation, Chapter 8 addresses the question of whether regulation should require that all trades in a stock be executed on the exchange that serves as the primary market for that stock, or whether orders should be allowed to execute on different exchanges or in in-house markets made by brokerage firms. Turning to stabilization, Chapter 9 considers the argument that stabilization will be undersupplied in competitive equilibrium (given the current legal framework) and therefore that supplementary stabilization should be provided by the exchanges (primarily through specialist operations). In this chapter, we also use simulation to analyze further the role and impact of the specialist, and present policy proposals for creating an efficient market in stabilization.

The conclusion, which summarizes our study, highlights the common elements in our microstructure analyses, and points out important directions for future research.

ACKNOWLEDGMENTS

We are indebted to our colleagues, Ernest Bloch, Robert M. Conroy, William K. H. Fung, Gabriel A. Hawawini, Thomas S. Y. Ho, Walter L. Ness, Jr., Hitoshi Okuda, and Paul S. Schreiber, who have joined us in coauthoring some of our previous research in microstructure.

Various aspects of the research were partially supported by grants from the Duke University Research Council, The New York Stock Exchange, and The Nomura Research Institute. The Fuqua School of Business at Duke University, The Salomon Brothers Center for the Study of Financial Institutions at New York University, and UAI Technology, Inc., also provided a wide range of support facilities, without which the research could not have been undertaken and the manuscript could not have been prepared.

We are particularly grateful to Barbara Webb at UAI Technology, Inc., for performing a wide variety of essential production tasks. Throughout, she did so with competence, good cheer, and never-ending optimism.

Nancy H. Carlson, Robert A. Metzger, and James J. Oddo, while MBA students at Duke University, were of great assistance in helping to edit and proofread the manuscript for this book. A number of research assistants at Duke University's Fuqua School of Business also provided support; we thank Raymond A. Cebold, Gregory A. Torski, and Mark W. Whalen. Christopher D. Piros has also made helpful comments on portions of the manuscript.

Last, but most important of all, we thank our wives, Joan, Laura, Christine, and Henrietta, for the encouragement that they have given us throughout our work.

Note to the Reader

In references to previous work in which the coauthors of this book have collaborated, we use the following abbreviations:

Abbreviation	Authors
CHMSW	Cohen, Hawawini, Maier, Schwartz, and Whitcomb
CMSW	Cohen, Maier, Schwartz, and Whitcomb
CMNOSW	Cohen, Maier, Ness, Okuda, Schwartz, and Whitcomb
CNOSW	Cohen, Ness, Okuda, Schwartz, and Whitcomb

THE MICROSTRUCTURE OF SECURITIES MARKETS

1

SECURITY MARKET MICROSTRUCTURE: THE ISSUES AND THE LITERATURE

The *practical* impetus for the analysis of security market microstructure has been the tremendous structural change in securities markets since 1975. The *intellectual* impetus for market microstructure analysis has been the striking fact that actual markets deviate in important ways from the models of classical price theory. In securities markets, prices are not set by a process resembling the classic Walrasian auction. More important, by much recent evidence, they do not behave as if they were. Serial correlation patterns in security and index returns, biases in ordinary least squares (OLS) beta estimates, the existence of a bid-ask spread, and unresolved anomalies in the behavior of the returns on small firms (especially in certain months) all suggest that trading does not take place at equilibrium prices.

The beginnings of an answer to this puzzle lie, as usual, in classical price theory. Competitive market prices will behave like prices set in a Walrasian auction only if no frictions (information, decision, and transaction costs) impede the trading process. Before microstructure analysis, the major body of literature in financial economies has assumed a frictionless trading process (much as in physics Newtonian mechanics modeled the movement of point masses in a perfect vacuum). Such analyses directly address the underlying processes in their pure forms. However, to develop a better understanding of the behavior of actual markets (or the flight of a feather dropped from the Leaning Tower of Pisa), the effects of friction must be modeled. Doing so is the primary thrust of microstructure analysis.

To this end, the microstructure literature examines the elements of the security trading process: the arrival and dissemination of information; the generation and arrival of orders; and the market architecture which determines how orders are transformed into trades. The analysis also explicitly takes into account the behavior of specific types of market participants: nonprofessional investors, institutional investors, speculators, dealers, and specialists. Of concern are such issues as what the actions of profit-motivated market makers might be, what the role of regulated specialists should be, how trading is affected by the market's organization, how such trading in turn affects prices, and how the system's performance affects investors.

Because of the fundamental nature of the analysis and its concern with the effects of friction, security market microstructure has strong public policy implications for the organization of securities markets and the institutions operating within them. Simultaneously, it gives insight and direction to the empirical study of stock price movements and risk-return relationships.

Within the broader microstructure context, the central focus of this book is on the interaction between investor trading strategy, market architecture, and the resulting returns generation process. Major implications of our analysis concern the measurement of systematic risk and the design of trading systems. We begin our study by presenting, in this chapter, an overview of the relevant literature and of the major structural issues concerning systems design.[1]

1.1 MARKET MAKERS AND THE BID-ASK SPREAD

First and foremost, the microstructure literature has focused on one design feature of a trading system: the operations of the dealer qua market maker. The first modern academic studies of market makers to appear in the literature actually predated the events of 1975. These are Stigler (1964), Demsetz (1968), and the U.S. Securities and Exchange Commission (1971). Stigler focused attention on the role of the specialist as a market maker. He showed how such a market maker, in his speculative trading, provides liquidity to the market, and stated that in competitive equilibrium, the spread between bid and ask prices will just cover the specialist's unit costs. In his analysis, Stigler raised an issue that has been discussed in much of the ensuing literature: the existence of economies of scale in market making.

Demsetz presented the first formal model of the bid-ask spread as a "markup that is paid for predictable immediacy of exchange in organized markets" (p. 36). Consistent with Stigler, Demsetz viewed the bid-ask spread as a return to the providers of immediacy. He reasoned that with sufficient competition between the various immediacy providers, the spread will just equal the cost of offering the service.

We have argued [see CMSW (1979a)] that Demsetz's formal model holds only when all buy-sell orders for a given security are routed to one dealer with whom each investor must trade, and who alone can set the market quotes. Demsetz's verbal discussion, however, does properly reflect the fact that specialists on the organized U.S. stock exchanges (he wrote with regard to the New York Stock Exchange) do not have monopoly dealer positions, but rather face competition from other dealers, competing markets, public-limit-order traders, and floor traders who can bypass him completely. Because the security markets comprise the dynamic interaction of a large and diverse group, it is clear that the nature of competition and the process of price formation in these markets are indeed highly complex matters.

Demsetz's paper inspired further analyses on the provision of marketability services. The primary studies were by Tinic (1972) and Tinic-West (1972, 1974). Interest in the supply of dealer services was also stimulated by the Institutional Investor Study [see U.S. Securities and Exchange Commission (1971)]. The study itself yielded a number of articles on market structure and market maker profitability; these include Farrar (1971), Feuerstein (1972), and Smidt (1971).

Along with its almost exclusive focus on the role of market makers qua dealers, primary emphasis was first given in the microstructure literature to the size of the bid-ask spread. Contributions in this area were made by Bagehot (1971), Benston-Hagerman (1974), Santomero (1974), Logue (1975), and Hamilton (1976, 1978). These papers were mainly concerned with the economic function performed by a market maker, and with explaining how the market maker is compensated for services he provides to a continuous, double-auction trading system such as the New York Stock Exchange (NYSE). Major concepts discussed included the distinction between informationally motivated trading and liquidity-motivated trading [see Bagehot (1971)], and the existence of scale economies in market making [see Benston-Hagerman (1974), Hamilton (1976), and Branch-Freed (1977)]. For a recent review of this literature, see Stoll (1985).

The various analyses of the bid-ask spread have generated several alternative views of the specialist's role in relation to the spread. As discussed by Barnea-Logue (1975), these include: setter of the spread but passive provider of immediacy (Demsetz, Tinic, and West), aggressive trader making money from liquidity transactors and losing to inside information transactors [Bagehot (1971) and later Copeland-Galai (1983)], and active adjustor of spreads in response to changes in his inventory position [Smidt (1971)]. This body of literature has had a substantial impact upon academicians' thoughts concerning why spreads exist in asset markets. Throughout, the impression is forcefully given that dealers and stock exchange specialists account for and control the size of the spread, and that they are the major (if not the sole) providers of liquidity to the market.

Starting with Garman (1976) and Stoll (1978a), attention shifted to building more rigorous models of the determinants of individual dealer bid-ask spreads, and to the specification of optimal dealer quotes. The essence of Stoll's model is that to supply immediacy, the dealer must move away from his desired investment portfolio and hence must be compensated for the utility loss by setting a spread between his buying and selling prices. In this analysis, Stoll does not assume a monopoly dealer; but neither does he treat interactions among dealers or between dealers and ordinary investors, and investors are assumed to trade only by market order (i.e., they must buy from and sell to dealers and may not enter limit orders on their own). This basic focus is retained in the dealer models of Amihud-Mendelson (1980), Mildenstein-Schleef (1983), Ho-Stoll (1981), and Copeland-Galai (1983).

Our own approach to the subject has taken a different tack. In CMSW (1981), we explicitly recognized the distinction between the individual dealer bid-ask spreads and the market spread (the difference between the lowest ask price and highest bid price across all traders). This is because on organized exchanges such as the NYSE, customer limit orders are placed on specialist limit-order books and the market quotes are frequently set on one or both sides by these *public* limit orders. Hence the observed spread is commonly not the specialist's personal bid-ask spread, and quite clearly the specialist is not the sole provider of liquidity.

Our analysis shows that in competitive markets, existence of the market spread can be attributed to the impact of optimal investor order-placement strategy, and that spreads will tend to be larger in markets for thinner issues. That is, we show that in the neighborhood of an established counterpart quote, the attractiveness of transacting with certainty causes a "gravitational pull" effect (if a trader's price is close enough to a counterpart offer, he will "jump" his price and transact with certainty via a market order). It is this gravitational pull that causes the spread to be preserved under market aggregation.

Ho-Stoll (1980, 1983) have utilized this conceptual approach in their analyses of the quotes placed by competing dealers. They too find that when competitive dealers have nonidentical quotes, the market spread will exist because of the dealers' use of optimal trading strategies. They specify conditions under which a dealer would trade immediately with another dealer rather than wait for an incoming order, and define an equilibrium spread as the absence of interdealer trading demand. Ho-Stoll (1983) [as well as Glosten (1981), Kahn (1982), and Conroy-Winkler (1985)] represent a convergence of the dealer literature toward our CMSW (1979a, 1981) view that competing limit-order traders interact to set the spread (although the dealer literature remains within a pure-dealer-market framework).

In a somewhat different context, recognition that spreads exist because of investor order-placement strategy, has introduced the notion of order-placement strategy into the literature. As a result, recognition is now developing that the order flow to a market is not entirely exogenous to the market's trading system and to traders' expectations concerning likely market clearing prices. This view has recently been formalized by Ho-Schwartz-Whitcomb (1985).

1.2 OTHER MARKET PERFORMANCE CHARACTERISTICS

Although the strong focus in the literature on the supply of market maker services and on the bid-ask spread as an important transaction cost has led to much attention being given to the spread, consideration has also been given to three other market performance characteristics: the volatility of security prices, the difference at any moment of time between a security's actual price and its "true" (frictionless market) equilibrium price, and the existence of intertemporal correlation patterns in security returns. We now consider each of these performance characteristics in turn.

1.2.1 The Volatility of Security Prices

Barnea (1974) and Silber (1975) were among the first to recognize that the volatility of a security's price depends in part on the quality of the market for that security. Barnea (1974) attempted to detect the specialist's impact on a stock's price movements by relating very short period price volatility to longer-period volatility. While we believe that such an analysis is obscured by the impact of other factors [see the discussion by Schwartz-Whitcomb (1976) and Barnea's reply (1976)], it is clear that the paper by Barnea pointed the way to a broader assessment of a security's trading characteristics and to an enhanced understanding of the impact of market makers. In his empirical examination of the Tel Aviv Stock Exchange, Silber (1975) considered the price volatility–thinness relationship. His results suggest that volatility is substantially greater for thinner issues.

Our own analysis [CMSW (1978a)] has shown that price volatility is expected to be greater for thinner issues [a conclusion that Kahn (1982) also reaches in a rather different model]. We have presented empirical tests of the volatility-thinness relationship and evidence on the impact of specialists on stock price movements [CMNOSW (1977)]. In addition, we have argued that intervention by specialists to reduce price volatility may be desirable because the variance reduction that results from the placement of limit orders on the market is a public good–type externality that would be undersupplied in a nonstabilized market [CMSW (1977)].

1.2.2 Differences between Actual and True Prices

Because of its orientation, the microstructure literature recognizes that prices observed in security markets differ from the true assessments of value that would prevail if trading were a frictionless process. This is apparent in the early bid-ask model of Demsetz where, because buy and sell orders are assumed to arrive at the market sporadically, the intersection of the fundamental demand

and supply functions of investors establishes a price at which no one could actually transact. With this as a starting point, Demsetz shows that a dealer can enable buyers and sellers to transact by offering to buy at a bid below his underlying price and to sell at an ask above it.

The notion of a true price has been incorporated into the various dealer decision models of, for example, Mildenstein-Schleef (1983), Amihud-Mendelson (1980), Ho-Stoll (1981, 1983), and Copeland-Galai (1983). These analyses have not, however, focused per se on the distinction between true and actual prices. This distinction is, on the other hand, a primary subject in the analyses of Beja-Hakansson (1979) and Hakansson-Beja-Kale (HBK) (1985). These authors do not view the specialist function as primarily the supply of immediacy but rather as one of keeping actual prices as close as possible to true prices. HBK (1985) use simulation analysis to show that effective rules for specialist intervention can be specified, and hence that this aspect of the specialist's function could be automated.

Ho-Schwartz-Whitcomb (1985) show that actual prices will deviate from true prices in markets composed of a large number of atomistic traders. This demonstration involves the solution of an investor's optimal trading strategy: the price and size of an order, given his underlying demand curve to hold shares, the design of the trading system, and his expectation of the clearing price. The demonstration also involves the development of an aggregation model that contrasts the aggregation of individual orders with the aggregation of the underlying buy-sell functions (in the analysis, investors are taken to be distributed according to their propensities to hold shares). Following Ho-Schwartz-Whitcomb, Schreiber-Schwartz (1985, 1986) argue that efficient price discovery in a securities market is a major, and implementable, objective of system design and market regulation.

1.2.3 Serial Correlation Patterns in Security Returns

The last market performance characteristic that we consider is the presence of serial correlation patterns in security returns. Of chief interest is not autocorrelation in the returns for individual securities, but rather cross-serial correlation between security returns or, equivalently, between each security and the market (that is, the correlation between the return on one security in one period and the return on other securities or the market as a whole in some *other* period).

Here the microstructure research has followed a larger literature on tests of random walk and the efficient market hypothesis, which demonstrated that serial correlation patterns in individual returns are very weak (see, e.g., Fama (1970)]. The patterns are believed to be weak enough so that given transaction costs, they cannot be profitably exploited by the use of properly designed trading rules. However, evidence continues to appear in the literature [see, e.g., Fisher

(1966) and Schwartz-Whitcomb (1977a, 1977b)] that serial correlation is nonetheless present in index returns and in market model residuals. That this serial correlation is largely due to cross-serial correlation was not apparent until (1) shorter-period (i.e., daily and weekly instead of monthly) data were used to estimate beta [Schwartz-Whitcomb (1974)], (2) it was documented that short-period beta estimates are biased [Scholes-Williams (1977), Hawawini (1977), and Dimson (1979)], and (3) it was demonstrated that cross-serial correlation accounts for the bias [CHMSW (1980, 1983b) and Hawawini (1980)].

One other way of looking at the data has reinforced the observation that serial correlation patterns are pervasive and statistically significant: whereas for individual securities and for each security paired with the market, the observed serial and cross-serial correlations are weak, when a set of securities is arrayed according to some measure of their market size (i.e., the value of shares outstanding), the individual correlations show a strong, monotonic relationship with market size [CHMSW (1983a)]. Quite clearly, something meaningful is being exhibited by the data.

We have argued [CHMSW (1980)] that the pattern of serial and cross-serial correlation results from new information not being instantaneously or simultaneously reflected in security prices. Rather, due to (1) the processes by which new information generates orders to trade, and (2) the institutional arrangements for translating orders into trades and transaction prices, an intricate pattern of lags and nonsynchronous trading exists. However, the complex pattern of serial cross-correlation need not be expected to allow the formulation of profitable trading rules. The reason is that when a stock's price does not fully adjust to new information, there may be no basis for determining whether the price has over- or underadjusted, or for knowing when the total adjustment will be completed. Hence, in the original meaning of the term, the market may still be informationally efficient even though there is substantial intertemporal dependency in the returns data.

What the presence of cross-serial correlation calls attention to, however, is efficiency in a different meaning of the term—operational efficiency. The more efficient the organization of the market system, the less friction there will be in the trading process, the more rapid will be the flow of orders to the market, the faster will orders be transformed into trades, and hence the more quickly will information be fully reflected in stock prices. Hence, the more operationally efficient the system, the weaker should be the pattern of serial cross-correlation, and the less biased should be short-period betas (for a given distribution of market values outstanding). Alternatively viewed, an indirect test of the degree of operational efficiency of a trading system can be provided by an empirical examination (which holds constant the distribution of market values of individual stocks) of correlation patterns in returns and the bias in unadjusted (OLS) beta.

Relatively little consideration has been given to the implications of serial cross-correlation patterns for the operational efficiency of markets. However, a number of papers [Schwartz-Whitcomb (1974), Scholes-Williams (1977), Dimson (1979), Saniga-McInish-Gouldey (1981), CHMSW (1983a, 1983b), Fowler-Rorke-Jog (1984), and Ord-McInish-Wood (1984)] have been concerned with the problem of obtaining unbiased beta estimates from short-period data. Scholes-Williams, Dimson, and CHMSW (1983b) present alternative methods of adjusting OLS beta estimates; the Scholes-Williams and CHMSW adjustments are compared on the same data set by Fung-Schwartz-Whitcomb (1985) and by McInish-Wood (1985a).

1.3 THE IMPACT OF INFORMATION ON TRADING VOLUME AND PRICE

Another major issue addressed by the microstructure literature is the generation of new information and its reflection in trading volume and price. Copeland (1976) models the demand shifts and resulting trades that accompany the sequential arrival of identical information to a group of homogeneous traders. When all traders agree on their interpretation of the information, Copeland shows trading volume to be a logarithmically increasing function of the number of traders and the strength of the information. In the more general case where traders disagree and are subject to a short-sales constraint, Copeland uses a simulation to demonstrate that the largest volume occurs when traders are most in agreement.

A distinguishing characteristic of much of the literature on security market microstructure is its attempt to model trading out of equilibrium. The reason for this focus is that in security markets information arrives with great frequency; an attempt to delay trading (until a frictionless market clearing price can be found by successive iterations in real time) would deny traders the rapidity of execution which they demand. If we were to assume a Walrasian or other equilibrium-price-formation model, then we would be unable to explain various observed phenomena (such as market orders, bid-ask spreads, and serial correlation of returns).

Beja-Hakansson (B-H) (1977) present alternative equilibrium and nonequilibrium trading models which satisfy certain feasibility and market-clearing properties, and compare them according to allocational efficiency, communication requirements, and distributional effects. They show that a nonequilibrium tâtonnement with intermediate trading is Pareto efficient. B-H show that the informed trader with up-to-date information about future prices or about the rationing scheme gains from the substitution of nonequilibrium prices for Walrasian tâtonnement prices (he profits from the intermediate trading). This explains the value of both a seat on the exchange and expenditures for information (security analysis). B-H argue that in a world of frequently changing preferences and real-time interactions, Walrasian tâtonnement will not converge, and the refusal to trade except at equilibrium prices precludes possible Pareto improvements.

An implication of non-Walrasian price adjustment processes is that there may exist an opportunity for speculation on price trends somewhat akin to "technical" analysis (as opposed to the assessment of securities' "fundamental" prospects). Beja-Goldman (B-G) (1980) study speculation in this vein. They present a differential equations model of price adjustment where the adjustment rate is based on two factors: the excess demand that would exist at the current price if traders were to submit their orders to a Walrasian auctioneer, and the additional demand generated by disequilibrium speculation. The speculative demand is assumed to be based on adaptive estimates of the price trend similar to exponential smoothing; this is not unlike certain "chartist" behavior. B-G show that this speculative demand may cause endogenously generated price oscillations, and derive conditions under which the oscillations will have decreasing amplitude converging to zero.

The revelation of inside information through the trading process is explored in a paper by Glosten (1981), which also exemplifies a growing tendency in the microstructure literature to specify more completely the structure of the trading mechanism. Glosten assumes a pure limit-order-book market (e.g., the NYSE without the specialist's dealership function) and two classes of traders: the informed insiders and the uninformed. If insider information is held monopolistically, an insider will trade off his gains from trading against the probability that his trades will reveal the information. On the other hand, competition among insiders will drive up their collective rate of order arrival and the information will be revealed immediately. In this context, informational efficiency is defined as the probability that information is revealed in the sequence of transaction prices before it is announced explicitly. One of the more interesting aspects of this research is that like the work on the serial correlation phenomena discussed earlier, it provides a link between microstructure and the efficient market hypothesis.

1.4 MAJOR CONSIDERATIONS IN THE DESIGN OF TRADING SYSTEMS

As we noted above, one factor is present in virtually all of the microstructure literature: friction in the trading process drives all of the problems addressed. This is implicit in the early bid-ask model of Demsetz, it is an essential part of the later work of Garman, it provides a basis for the ensuing literature on the supply of dealer services, and it ultimately explains why actual prices differ from the underlying values we have here referred to as the true prices [see Ho-Schwartz-Whitcomb (1985)]. In our own work, we have shown how information, decision, and transaction costs keep individual investors from trading continuously, and so prevent new information from being instantaneously reflected in stock prices [CHMSW (1980)]. We show further how this friction causes a stock's price volatility to be inversely related to the size of its market [CMSW (1978a)], accounts for the existence of the market bid-ask spread [CMSW (1981)], and accounts for the serial cross-correlation patterns that cause beta estimates obtained from short-period returns data to be biased [CHMSW (1983a, 1983b)].

Because of its inherent relationship with the realities of nonfrictionless market systems, microstructure analysis has generated a number of implications for the design of a trading system, several of which we examine in this section. Although most researchers have concentrated on the design aspects themselves, Silber (1981) has considered how the competitive structure of the market can itself induce innovation with regard to one aspect of trading: the specification of futures contracts.

1.4.1 Competition in the Provision of Market-Making Services

Smidt (1971) and Logue (1975) were among the first microstructure researchers to focus on whether or not the market-making function should be monopolized; they strongly favor competition. In support of this conclusion, the empirical findings of Benston-Hagerman (1974), Hamilton (1976), and Branch-Freed (1977) suggest that market making is not a natural monopoly. Tinic-West's (1974) comparative Toronto Stock Exchange, New York Stock Exchange, and over-the-counter (OTC) study indicates that spreads are affected by market structure. The empirical studies of Santomero (1974) and Hamilton (1978) have shown that the advent of the National Association of Security Dealers' Automated Quotation (NASDAQ) system lowered spreads in the OTC. Stoll's (1978a) dealer model suggests that dealer services will be forthcoming under competition even for the riskier securities and that for a number of reasons a competitive organization is preferable to having a regulated, monopolistic dealer.

By and large, however, the dealer/specialist-oriented studies have been relatively limited in their ability to generate public policy implications. This is primarily because these studies, being too exclusively concerned with the magnitude of dealer-specialist costs and with the degree of competition between the various dealer-specialist groups, have attributed too little importance to the fact that the limit orders of ordinary traders also provide immediacy to the market. Nonetheless, the very fact that many dealer-specialist-oriented studies have (incorrectly in our opinion) viewed dealers-specialists as *imposing* a spread on the market has had a strong impact on the public policy debate concerning the role of designated market makers in a restructured national market system.

1.4.2 Integration of the Marketplace

One of the most crucial and protracted debates concerning the development of a national market system is whether or not to allow brokerage firms having seats on organized exchanges to execute customer orders in-house. Currently, NYSE Rule 390 and American Stock Exchange (AMEX) Rule 5 require (subject to important exceptions) member firms to bring their principal orders for listed securities to an exchange. In recent years, the Securities and Exchange Commission (SEC) has felt the rule to be anticompetitive.

In June 1977, the SEC announced that Rule 390 was to be removed by the end of that year. A widespread cry of alarm was heard from most segments of the industry, various members of Congress, and certain academicians. The forcefulness of the response caused the SEC to back off and to let 390 stand for the time being. Then, in 1980, SEC Rule 19c-3 was instituted. This rule stipulated that effective July 18, 1980, exchange members must be allowed to trade off-board all stocks listed subsequent to April 26, 1979. Currently, the SEC is considering extending 19c-3 to cover all stocks. That is, Rule 390 may be totally eliminated.

The complexity and longevity of the debate reflect the difficulty of understanding the nature of competition in the securities industry. Part of the problem is that as discussed in Bloch-Schwartz (1978b), the industry encompasses two types of markets: the market for trading services and the markets for the securities that are traded. By pushing for in-house execution, the SEC is seeking to strengthen competition in the market for trading services; concomitantly, it is feared, removal of the prohibition against in-house executions would fragment the markets for the securities that are traded, thereby rendering these markets less competitive and less effective.[2]

The scope of the consolidation issue is far greater, however, and issues concerning competition in the markets for the securities that are traded are more intricate than the off-board trading debate might suggest. Even without in-house executions by member firms, the market is not fully consolidated: many securities listed on the national exchanges (AMEX and NYSE) are cross-listed on one or more of the regionals (Cincinnati, Boston, Midwest, Pacific, and Philadelphia); exchange-listed stocks are traded OTC in the so-called third market by nonmember firms; and large block trades are typically negotiated "upstairs" before being executed on the trading floor. Does this complex structure represent a desirable balance between competition among broker-dealers and market centers, and consolidation of the order flow? The answer depends on the benefits of strengthening competition in the provision of broker-dealer services [see, e.g., Hamilton (1976)]; on the value of enforcing time and other reasonable secondary trading priority rules [see Bloch-Schwartz (1978b) and Cohen-Conroy-Maier (1985)]; on the benefits of consolidating the information flow so as to increase the efficiency of price discovery [see Schreiber-Schwartz (1985)]; on the public good aspects of trading that are provided by an exchange [see CMSW (1982)]; and on the impetus that might be given to the development of superior trading systems by competition among the alternative market centers [see Silber (1981)].

1.4.3 Continuous Markets versus Periodic Calls

Another major structural issue is whether trading should be continuous or whether orders should be batched for simultaneous execution at periodic calls. Trading is continuous on many exchanges (e.g., in the United States, the Far East, Britain, and Canada). That is, orders are executed any time they cross during the trading day. In contrast, on other exchanges (e.g., in France, Belgium, Israel, and at the opening of "continuous" double-auction markets such as the NYSE), trades are executed when the market for a stock is called, and all trades that execute at the call are cleared at the same price.

Garbade-Silber's (1979a) analysis of a call market considered the impact of a market's clearing frequency on its performance characteristics. Ho-Schwartz-Whitcomb (1985) have shown that the price and quantity (of shares traded) decisions of market participants are affected by the call market arrangements, and their analysis implies that the performance characteristics of a stock will therefore depend on the structural design of the market where it is traded. We do not pursue the issue of call versus continuous trading in this book, but leave it as a subject that should clearly be given more attention since these two alternative systems present traders with significantly different trading opportunities and market information. To date, little attention has been given in the microstructure literature to contrasting these two very different types of market architecture.

1.4.4 Automation of the Trading Process

Another major structural characteristic of a trading system is the degree to which the process is automated. To the casual visitor, there seems to be a lot of electronic equipment on most major exchanges, especially those in the United States, Toronto, and Tokyo. However, the equipment has been used primarily for routing orders, displaying quotes, reporting transactions, and handling post-trade clearing procedures. There has been resistance to automating the most crucial part of the process: trade execution itself. [The major exception is the Computer Assisted Trading Systems (CATS), which Toronto and Tokyo use to provide automatic execution of all orders for their thinner issues.]

Why is this so? Why do traders resist entrusting their orders to a machine which they call a black box? After all, the airlines industry long ago used computers successfully to process a far more complex set of information (concerning flights and seat availability) than the type of information characteristic of the securities industry. Why can we not submit buy-sell orders with the same ease that we can make flight reservations for anywhere from just about anywhere around the world?

The major difference between securities markets and most other markets is that in securities markets, the setting of prices is an integral part of the execution of trades. When orders for airlines tickets are submitted, the prices of the seats have already been established and so the reservations are being made at known prices. Not so for stocks. The trader of securities always faces some uncertainty concerning the price at which his order will or could have executed, and the actual timing and handling of the order will affect the price of the transaction in which he participates. For larger traders, there is the fear that an exposed order will signal valuable price information to others and that their own market power will cause prices to move away from them if they do not work their orders carefully over time.

Because the academic literature has only recently dealt with the fact that traders will use strategy in submitting their trading orders, we academicians have largely ignored the problems and opportunities of automated trading. Following the rather straightforward proposals of Mendelson (1972) and Mendelson-Peake-Williams (1979) for a fully automated trade execution system (which served mainly to raise the hackles of professional traders and exchange officials), little has been heard from academia on this topic [for a recent discussion, however, see Amihud-Mendelson (1985)].

Nonetheless, automated trading is coming quickly, and it does not appear to be willing to bow to the prescriptions of academicians or to the gripes of professional traders. We feel that it is desirable to analyze this change in the context of our existing securities markets and in light of the security market microstructure view of the world. We do this in Chapter 3.

1.4.5 Stabilization of Price Movements

The final structural issue to be highlighted concerns the means by which price movements are stabilized. Most exchanges have at least some procedure for preventing unacceptably large price changes. Call markets, for instance, often do not allow trades to go through at prices that deviate by more than a given proportion from prices struck at preceding calls. The very batching of orders for periodic execution at a call is, ceteris paribus, a way of reducing the volatility of prices. In continuous markets, trading is commonly suspended when the market suddenly changes too fast. In some continuous auction markets, such as the Toronto and Montreal exchanges, market makers are required to set quotes within a prescribed range around previous transaction prices. On the major U.S. exchanges, the trading of each stock is assigned to a specialist who has the affirmative obligation of making a fair and orderly market (where ''fair and orderly'' primarily means that transaction price changes are not too erratic over relatively brief intervals of time).

In CMNOSW (1977) and CMSW (1977, 1983), we consider in more detail the operations of the specialist. It is not at all obvious, however, that the free movement of prices should be impeded by specialist intervention or by any other procedure for stabilizing the market. Most academicians, in fact, have been in favor of laissez-faire with regard to this issue, and feel that markets should be left free to stabilize themselves as they will, according to the natural responses of speculators, liquidity traders, and informational traders.

We take exception. In brief, our reasons are twofold: (1) As noted above, we believe that the stabilization provided by limit-order traders and unregulated dealers creates a public good–type externality for others, so the stabilization they supply in competitive equilibrium is suboptimal. (2) Because actual prices deviate from true prices, the stabilization of price in the very short run may enable traders more fully to achieve Pareto-optimal trades [see Ho-Schwartz-Whitcomb (1985)]. Once again, however, the arguments are quite complex, and the conclusions reached remain subject to debate.

1.5 CONCLUSION

Momentous changes are taking place in the securities markets, and many further changes can be foreseen. We hope that the microstructure literature will continue to develop so as to give direction to these changes. There is no substitute for fundamental theoretical analysis in studying policy issues concerning the design of trading arrangements. The changes that are occurring are global, not marginal; data and experience collected from the past can have relatively little value for predicting the behavior of the market when the system is altered; and much of the change will be irreversible: an effective system that is dismantled may never be rebuilt.

NOTES

1. For further discussion of the literature, see West-Tinic (1971), CMSW (1979a), Garbade (1982), and Stoll (1985).
2. See Garbade-Silber (1976) for an analysis of the search behavior of traders in a fragmented market, and Garbade-Silber (1979b) for a study of the performance behavior of dually traded securities.

2

AN INTERNATIONAL COMPARISON OF STOCK EXCHANGE OPERATIONS*

This chapter brings together in a comparative framework some of the observations from our visits to 14 foreign and two U.S. stock exchanges.[1] Foreign stock exchanges get much of our attention here because we suspect many of our readers will be less familiar with them. The U.S. exchanges (and the OTC market) get a lot more attention in Chapter 3, when we talk about electronic trading and the stock exchange of the future. A major theme of Section 2.1 is the structure of exchange trading systems; we classify and compare exchange trading structures, with a primary classification by whether they are batch (i.e., orders collected over time for a multilateral trade, or "call") or continuous (i.e., bilateral trades conducted whenever two orders cross). Two other important themes (exchange services and trading in multiple markets) comprise Sections 2.2 and 2.3.

Throughout, we describe our observations on these themes and note the perceptions of market participants. We also offer our own explanations as to why things are done in certain ways and discuss whether these approaches make sense. Section 2.4 contains our conclusions concerning the interaction between the basic trading structure and the services provided by exchanges, and our speculations regarding the reasons for the differences among trading structures. Table 1 summarizes the features of the trading systems of the stock exchanges studied, along with information about trading hours, price reporting, settlement, stabilization, and off-exchange trading.

2.1 FUNDAMENTAL TYPES OF EXCHANGE TRADING SYSTEMS

Our observations on the exchanges we visited reveal a bewildering variety of trading systems. To bring order to this chaos, it is necessary to devise a classification scheme for different types of trading systems. We have chosen to classify trading systems primarily by whether they are batch or continuous; this is in part due to the analytical focus in some of our ongoing work.[2] We further classify continuous trading systems by whether they are matching systems or dealer systems, and then we finally classify both batch and continuous systems by their trading technology.

2.1.1 Batch (Periodic Call) Systems

In batch trading systems, orders coming in over an interval of time are not transacted immediately, but rather are stored and transacted together in a multilateral transaction. We subdivide batch trading systems by whether they are verbal or written, although the real distinction relates not to the technology of order entry but instead to whether or not traders (some or all) are able to observe the market forming and to modify their orders accordingly. Verbal systems permit this, but written systems by and large do not.

2.1.1.1 À la criée. The classic example of a verbal call auction is *à la criée* trading in the Paris forward market, where the most important shares and government bonds are traded. In Paris, while 70% of client trading orders originate with banks, all orders must be transacted on the floor of the exchange by a broker or his clerk. The trading is done at seven posts. The issues listed at a particular post are called in alphabetical order by an auctioneer who opens trading in an issue by naming it and stating yesterday's closing price. Traders then shout "I have" (for sell orders) or "I take" (for buy orders) and state the quantity to be traded. The auctioneer adjusts the price until a supply-demand balance (or the smallest imbalance possible given the minimum price change unit) is reached. If demand and supply do not exactly balance, the auctioneer will fully satisfy all market orders and all limit orders placed at a price better than the batch price. He will then partially fulfill those limit orders placed at exactly the batch price on the heavier side of the market.

The interactive *à la criée* process allows floor traders (trading for their own account or holding a large customer's discretionary order) to revise their bids and offers in light of the market information being revealed by the trial prices called by the auctioneer. It is for this reason that the *à la criée* process is used for the most actively traded stocks. The Paris Stock Exchange also allows for a high activity rate in its *à la criée* issues by permitting callbacks. That is, any broker can request a second price fixing at any time after an issue has opened, even while another share is being called for the first time. However, the second and all subsequent prices are unlikely to be batch prices since usually just one counterparty is found for the broker requesting the callback. Thus the callback is, in effect, a switch to continuous trading by a matching system with bilateral bargains in the "crowd" (Section 2.1.2.4).

Other exchanges having a verbal call for some issues include Brussels and Tel Aviv.[3] All except Tel Aviv allow callbacks, but most of the volume is concentrated at the batch trades.[4]

2.1.1.2 Written order entry (par cassiers). The essence of a written order entry system (called *par cassiers* in French) is that trading orders are accumulated in an order "book," but the system provides no "indicated" price (the price at which the orders on hand would transact were the call to occur at the given moment). Hence there is no meaningful opportunity for modifying orders before the orders are transacted.

Par cassiers trading is used in the Paris cash market for securities not listed in the forward market. Trading is organized by a market maker (a broker who has been assigned certain securities to handle). The market maker accepts orders in writing from other brokers as well as his own firm's orders, and establishes a price that equates supply and demand. If supply and demand do not exactly balance, the market maker can allocate or reduce the larger side, or he can make up the balance from his own firm's account (but only to reduce the size of a potential price change). Unexecuted orders are held in an order book and can be executed later if they have not been designated call only.

The Amsterdam, Frankfurt, and Vienna markets for infrequently traded stocks also use the *par cassiers* method. In Vienna, traders may modify their orders if the auctioneer judges that the trial price would result in an excessive price change, and in Amsterdam, the market maker (but not other traders) may enter balancing orders for his own account.

The difference in the technology of order entry between *à la criée* and *par cassiers* is not really as important as the extent of opportunities to modify the orders. The *à la criée* system gives the greatest opportunities for modifying orders, and approximates the Walrasian tâtonnement of economic theory.

2.1.1.3 Openings, some continuous markets. Continuous markets with matching systems and order books [U.S. exchanges, Toronto CATS, Japanese exchanges, and the frequently traded stocks in Amsterdam, Frankfurt, and Vienna (see Section 2.1.2.1)] open via batch trading. The method is similar to *par cassiers* with written (or computer) order entry, sometimes modified in writing, or *à la criée* by the crowd around the trading post. Whoever holds the order book finds the price at which supply and demand are most nearly balanced and announces this as the opening price, provided that it satisfies the maximum price change limits (if any) of the exchange. The batching occurs because orders have been coming in to the brokers or banks overnight and during the morning prior to opening. For this reason, and perhaps because of the perception that volatility is lower and that it is easier to deal a medium-sized block at the opening, order-book trading systems frequently see 20 to 40% of their volume traded at the opening.

We would expect on theoretical grounds (see Chapter 5) that the nature of trading would be rather different and the volume rate substantially higher in the period immediately after the opening as compared to later in the day. The reason is that if the opening is conducted somewhat in the dark with limited ability by market participants to revise orders, there will be many unexecuted limit orders on the books with prices very close to the opening price. Thus immediately after the opening when the opening price becomes known, customers may jump their limit-order prices to hit the nearby counterpart limit orders; this could explain the higher volume of trading that is observed for a short period after the market opens. If all order placers could see the market forming in real time and revise (e.g., as in the CATS or *à la criée* systems), there would be somewhat greater volume at the opening and no excess of volume immediately thereafter. To the extent that floor traders can get a reasonable estimate of the likely opening price, then the special-handling orders which they hold have an advantage over ordinary orders in that they can jump to hit their counterparts at the opening rather than after.

2.1.1.4 Allocation of excess supply or demand at the batch price. Most exchanges provide for the allocation of excess supply or demand. The need for allocation arises from three causes: (1) price is not a continuous variable (i.e., because of the minimum price-change units, such as 1/8 of a dollar in the United States, there may be no allowed price where supply exactly equals demand); (2) quantity is not a continuous variable (most trades are in multiples of round lots); and (3) a fortiori, when the batch price is set to avoid violating a maximum price-change limit rather than where supply equals demand (Section 2.2.3.1).

Allocation is often done by random selection of those orders on the "heavy" side that are not to be satisfied, though some exchanges specify that market orders and all limit orders better than the batch price will be filled and that heavy-side orders at the batch price will be filled proportionally. The exchange usually sets a minimum fulfillment proportion (e.g., 25%). Several encourage market makers or floor traders to enter additional orders on the "light" side before making the batch price final. Frankfurt and Vienna go even further: they do not allow any trading in their batched systems unless supply exactly equals demand. This puts pressure on traders to enter additional orders so as the balance supply and demand (but a transaction does not always result).

2.1.2 Continuous Market Systems

The use of the word "continuous" does not mean that transactions literally occur all the time, only that transactions can occur whenever the orders of two traders cross. The major distinction we shall make here is between dealer systems, where an intermediary "makes the market" by satisfying the ultimate customer's order from the intermediary's own account, and matching systems, where traders act as agents for the ultimate customers. We have further classified matching systems by the technology of order entry as order book, board trading, and crowd systems. Most continuous markets are in fact neither pure matching systems nor pure dealer systems, but allow customers to compete with official market makers by entering limit orders; we have classified these under the various matching categories.

2.1.2.1 Dealer systems. The most important examples of a dealer stock market are the London Stock Exchange and the U.S. OTC market. In London, the dealers (called jobbers) stand at a post on the trading floor (or sometimes operate by telephone) and write on a chalkboard the names of the stocks handled and the midspread prices (i.e., prices halfway between their bids and asks). Floor brokers holding customer orders walk around to competing jobbers and get bid-ask quotations (but without quantity offers) from each jobber without disclosing whether they wish to buy or sell or are "just looking." The broker selects the best counterpart jobber quotation for his customer.[5] The chosen jobber will normally take the full amount of the broker's order at the quoted price so long as the order is not a large block (about $500,000 for major issues). If the broker has a relatively large order, he asks the jobber to state the amount he will deal on each side of his quotation.

In London, as in other dealer markets, there is no special opening procedure. Jobbers just post their quotations, and brokers start circulating with their orders. There is no opening auction or batching, although a somewhat higher volume would normally be observed in the first hour.[6]

Characteristic of pure dealer systems is the near-complete absence of public limit orders. In London, for example, a customer limit order will normally result only if the jobber cannot take the whole of a large block. The broker then puts a limit on the remainder and leaves it with the jobber. The jobber may then find other jobbers who are willing to take the rest of the block, or he may ask another broker to find a counterparty. Presumably, a smaller customer can also leave a limit order with a jobber (but the jobber is unlikely to exert himself to deal a small lot); thus the offer may remain poorly exposed to the market for a long time.

A similar situation exists in the U.S. OTC market. There, only dealers can expose orders to the market by displaying quotes on the National Association of Security Dealers' Automated Quotation (NASDAQ) system. A dealer will generally not alter his quotes on NASDAQ as a result of a customer limit order unless the dealer is also a broker making a market in the stock and the customer is his own. Even then, the broker-dealer is not obligated to expose his customer's order, and may not do so.[7]

2.1.2.2 Matching systems: order book. The purest example of an order-book system is the trading on the First and Second Sections of the Tokyo Stock Exchange. For the 250 actively traded stocks not in Tokyo's automated trading system, orders come into the brokerage firm back office (usually on a computer system) and are then delivered to the floor brokers by hand. Large orders and the firm's own-account orders are phoned directly to the floor. Floor brokers give their orders verbally to the exchange order-book clerk, who writes them in his order book. When a floor trader comes to the order-book clerk with a market order, the clerk effects the trade and reports it to an exchange staff member at his post, who then enters it in the exchange computer.

We classify the Tokyo system as a "pure" order-book matching system because the order-book clerk does not act as a dealer trading for his own account but is merely the keeper of the order book and the enforcer of its rules. Similarly pure order-book systems exist in Frankfurt and in Vienna. Order-book systems with market makers exist in Amsterdam, the United States, and Toronto's CATS.[8] In the U.S. exchanges (NYSE, AMEX, and the regional exchanges), an official market maker (called a specialist) maintains the order book and also acts as a dealer. Thus the price quotations (i.e., lowest ask and highest bid) may be those of either the specialist or public (private investors', institutions', or brokers' own-account) limit orders. Besides the competition in market making facing the NYSE or AMEX specialist from public limit orders and the crowd at some trading posts, the regional exchanges cross-list and quote many of the same stocks, and many are quoted as well by OTC dealers. This potential competition is enhanced by the Intermarket Trading System (ITS), a quotation information and order-routing system discussed in Section 2.3.1. Hence specialists can be called monopolists only in limit-order-book information to which they have sole access.[9]

The Tokyo book is much "thicker" than the NYSE book for a comparable stock. The reason for this is that nearly all orders must go on the book because interbroker trading on the floor is allowed only for orders that are between the quotes; this greatly limits crowd trading.[10]

A key issue in any order-book system is whether the order book is open to anyone other than its keeper, and if so to whom. In Tokyo, the order book is open to anyone on the floor, but it is not readily available to anyone off the floor (although large customers can often get quotes by special request to their broker). Thus the order-book information is useful only to members of the exchange and to those large traders whose patronage is sufficiently important. On the other hand, the Toronto CATS order book is open to anyone possessing a terminal, except that any trader may conceal that part of his order which exceeds 100 shares. The penalty for so concealing part of an order is to lose time priority (i.e., the concealed part of the order goes automatically to the end of the queue of orders at that price). During the period before the opening of trading, CATS displays an indicated opening price (i.e., the price at which the opening orders would transact if the opening were to occur at the given moment). In contrast, the Frankfurt order-book clerk gives very little information about the order book to floor traders, and the U.S. specialist and Vienna clerk give some information on an informal basis so as to give traders a better feeling for the market.

2.1.2.3 Matching systems: board trading. The Hong Kong Stock Exchange is the purest example of a board trading system because no exchange personnel are involved in order entry, floor information transmission, or price setting. It illustrates both the economy of the board trading system and its technical problems. The members have seats arranged in rows across the trading hall facing a long curved chalk board. Each member has at his seat telephones for communicating with his office and television monitors with which he can see sections of the board not readily visible from his seat. Also, television monitors show the trading boards on the two other important Hong Kong stock exchanges.

The brokers themselves enter the offers to buy and sell on the trading board by writing their customers' offer prices and giving their firms' initials. All securities are traded in board lots (normally 1000 shares at typical Hong Kong prices). Only the two best bid prices and the two best ask prices may appear on the board; thus when a member is able to better the price offered by other members, he erases the worst price and substitutes his own price at the head of the queue. If there are several offers at the same price, they are listed in order of time priority. If an order is larger than 12 board lots, the amount in excess of 12 lots receives the lowest time priority at the common price. All bids and offers on the board must be firm for one board lot. It is possible to back away from a larger offer without anyone knowing, since the quantities are never written on the board prior to the transaction.

With the exception of direct business and special lots,[11] all trading is supposed to take place on the board. Once a buy or sell offer has been placed on the board, another member may shout "I give" or "I take" to signify that he accepts the offer that has just been put out on the board. If an offer has been on the board for some time, the counterparty must come to the board to make the deal.

When a deal has been consumated, the member making the deal notes the price and quantity on the chalkboard (in the below-the-line "transactions" section), and the seller makes a triplicate copy of the contract notes. In this entire process, the exchange itself takes no direct part except to make the facilities of the trading room and the television monitors available, and to engage in a limited amount of surveillance.

Montreal and Toronto operate essentially similar board trading systems with the following minor exceptions: (1) an exchange official posts the prices; (2) brokers stand in sections of the floor rather than having seats, and trades are always consumated by walking to the broker's position; and (3) market makers compete with customers' orders entered on the board. Sydney and Singapore also have board trading systems, and Tel Aviv experimented with the Sydney system for a subset of actively traded stocks but went back to batch trading.

All of the board trading systems we have observed have the following important characteristics in common (although none of these characteristics is strictly necessary to the technology of board training): (1) traders do not reveal the sizes of their orders and they are responsible for honoring only one board lot; (2) there are time priorities but only for the first and second best prices on each side; (3) large orders are discriminated against in the time priorities; and (4) there is no special procedure for opening the market (brokers merely begin posting their bids and offers on the board). The board trading system is economical to operate and is capable of accommodating at least moderate trading volume.

2.1.2.4 Matching systems: crowd. While the term "crowd" calls to mind the crowd trading *à la criée* in Paris, the crowd is also a means of conducting the bilateral bargains that characterize continuous market trading. In fact, if a trade is allowed to occur whenever two traders agree on the price and no better offer is made by any other trader, you have a continuous market, but with the special characteristic that all orders are held (i.e., are "discretionary" or "worked") by floor traders. In such a system, there are no time priorities.

The Zurich Stock Exchange (and most commodity exchanges) does all its trading by means of the crowd. In Zurich, each security is assigned to one of three trading rings. Traders come to the ring at the beginning of trading, with the orders "in their pockets." The Official Clerk opens trading in an issue by calling its name, but does not call out prices or otherwise attempt to reach a supply-demand balance. This is done by the traders themselves, who call out bids and asks. Each deal is essentially bilateral, although a trader wishing, for example, to sell an amount larger than one lot may have to find two or more buyers. However, there is no attempt to find a common price at the opening, and the first two or three deals may be done at differing prices. There is likely to be a greater volume of transactions at the beginning of trading, but the completely free off-exchange trading that is allowed in Zurich reduces the batching effect substantially.

In Zurich, as in most other crowd trading systems, there is a provision for a call back. The issues traded at a particular ring are divided into groups, and while one group is being called by the Official Clerk, any trader can call back any security in the group which has already opened. However, once trading in a group is over, traders cannot call back a stock in that group until the second call of the group. The reason for this procedure is to prevent the chaos that would ensue if, for example, all issues were traded together in one large group.

By dividing the issues among three rings and further dividing them at a ring into groups, the callback procedure is kept under reasonable control. When it has become clear over time that trading is too active in the issues in a group, the group is further split up. This has the further effect of promoting batching since all orders for an issue must be processed only when that issue's group is being called. The use of a second call permits orders to be processed at more than one time interval. Thus we see that the crowd trading system has some elements of batching, although, technically, trading proceeds continuously for an issue during the (relatively brief) interval that its group is trading.

A "pure" crowd trading system is not feasible when there are a large number of active issues such as in the NYSE and Tokyo exchanges. However, when there are a relatively small number of active issues (as we see in the commodity exchanges and in a number of stock exchanges such as Zurich, where on-floor volume is limited), the crowd trading system is feasible.

2.1.3 Perceptions of Desirability of Alternative Trading Systems

This issue is becoming a major focus of microstructure and we shall have more to say about it in Chapters 8 and 9. Here we simply report views of foreign stock exchange and bank personnel, and conclusions that may be drawn directly from our observations.

2.1.3.1 Batch versus continuous trading. The advantages of batch trading cited by practically every exchange that uses it for some or all of its transactions are: (1) The batching of orders provides stabilization of prices; this is especially important for infrequently traded issues, and many of the exchanges that use batching use it as the only method of trading thin issues and as the method of opening frequently traded issues. (2) The costs of execution and settlement are substantially lower. (3) The single price per day (or in the case of Amsterdam the single price per segment of the day) reduces settlement errors.

The advantages of continuous trading vis-à-vis batching are: (1) Continuous trading provides immediacy in that a customer need not wait a full day to buy or sell an issue. (2) Continuous trading provides substantially better market price information during the day than any existing batch trading system. In Paris, Brussels, or Tel Aviv, for example, it is virtually impossible for anyone not physically present in the market to know or to estimate the batch price before the trade has occurred; after the trade it is too late to use the information.[12] (3) The advantage that a batch trading system has in stabilization may be eliminated if the market is not "transparent," and if order revision is not sufficiently provided for. That is, if there is no provision for entering speculative stabilizing orders to reduce an extreme price movement resulting from a simple imbalance of buy and sell orders, a batch trading market can have substantial volatility.

The Paris Stock Exchange has tentatively decided to switch from once-a-day batch trading to semicontinuous trading for a few of its most active issues. This decision is consistent with the views of many other observers on the nature of the securities that should be traded by batch versus continuous systems. However, Tel Aviv recently abandoned an experiment with continuous (board) trading of active issues.

Both batch and continuous systems normally offer means by which professional traders can take advantage of their presence in the market and by which medium-sized blocks can be traded with a minimal price impact on the market. In the continuous market system, the method of dealing with these problems is the on-line transmission of price information. In addition, the observation on the floor of frequent transaction prices enables professional traders to get a feeling for the market and react before others; also, block traders can observe the effect of putting orders on the market seriatim over the course of a day or perhaps several days. In batch trading systems, *à la criée* trading gives the professional on the floor substantially better market information than a trader off the floor can obtain, and it gives the block trader the opportunity to observe via a trial price (and without a transaction) the effect of part of his block before he commits more of it in the final rounds of the call. Both types of market are commonly used by professional traders in the manner we have described, but block traders typically do the largest part of their business off-exchange when they can.

2.1.3.2 Matching versus dealer. A well-managed dealer system with sufficient dealer capital (such as London's) provides immediacy and considerable capacity to absorb a great volume of orders and blocks ranging up to at least medium size. However, it is clearly possible to achieve the same goal in a matching system if it provides for a class of market makers with special advantages (such as lower transaction costs and access to the order flow) sufficient to ensure their participation.

The disadvantage of a dealer system is that public limit orders are not allowed to compete with market maker bids and offers. Without considering the fairness of this, it is enough to note that this creates an incentive for brokerage firms or banks handling public orders to create-in-house limit-order books and matching systems or to act as dealers, and it requires the force of law to prevent this. The most important issue examined in the U.K. Restrictive Practices case settled in the summer of 1983 was whether the London Stock Exchange would be allowed to continue the "single-capacity" rule by which brokers are prevented from creating in-house markets or acting as dealers. Given the economic incentives to do otherwise and the advantage that many investors perceive in being able to trade by means of limit order, it was doubtful that the stock exchange could have long maintained the single-capacity system even if the exchange's rules had been allowed to remain in force. Hence their agreement to end fixed commission rates, which will in turn lead to dual capacity, is only bowing to reality.

2.1.3.3 Order book versus board trading versus crowd trading. The order-book system is the most expensive to establish and maintain (and requires a surveillance function if the book is held by a member rather than an exchange official), but it is capable of handling a huge volume of trading in many issues and can be open and fair to all investors (including those not on the trading floor).

The board trading system is inexpensive and capable of dealing with a substantial volume of trading. This system provides considerable advantages to floor traders and to investors large enough to be represented by a floor trader willing to handle a discretionary order. However, while limit orders are provided for in such a system, it is of the essence in a board trading system not to have an open limit-order book; to do otherwise would be to become an order-book system with merely a board display of the order book. Thus arguments which might be advanced for an open limit-order book would be arguments against board trading.

The crowd trading system is adapted well only to a small number of issues where the natural chaos of callbacks and multilateral competition for bilateral bargains may be kept to a minimum. In a crowd system, there are no time priorities and all orders must be handled as discretionary orders; the latter may result in poor execution of small orders unless they can be batched so as to be handled efficiently.

2.2 EXCHANGE SERVICES

In this section, we classify and discuss the various ancillary services provided by an exchange. These include special arrangements for both large and small orders, stabilization, surveillance, and price-volume information. In some of the service areas, the extent and nature of the services provided differ as much across exchanges as do the fundamental trading systems discussed in Section 2.1. In a number of service areas (especially surveillance and price-volume information), the U.S. and Canadian exchanges provide a level of service far above that of most foreign stock exchanges; in other areas, however (such as special arrangements for infrequently traded issues), foreign exchanges provide services that are not provided by the U.S exchange.

2.2.1 Special Arrangements for Thinly Traded Issues and Small Orders

Many foreign stock exchanges list a large number of very infrequently traded issues and often accept a considerable number of small trading orders. To make this business profitable to an exchange and at the same time to overcome the potential diseconomies of small scale which might drive trading of this sort off an exchange and onto an OTC or other specialized market, exchanges offer a variety of special arrangements designed to make trading less expensive. These include the use of batch trading for both infrequently traded issues and odd-lot orders, and the use of an unlisted securities market.

2.2.1.1 Batch trading. Amsterdam, Brussels, Frankfurt, Luxembourg, Paris, and Vienna all use batch trading for infrequently traded issues, and those exchanges which also use batch trading for frequently traded stocks invariably provide a somewhat different system for the infrequently traded stocks. Usually that system consists of a once-a-day batching without callback; this may be done primarily for reasons of economy. In addition, the proposition is widely accepted that batching reduces price volatility; of course, this is especially important for infrequently traded issues whose natural volatility is substantially higher than frequently traded issues (see Chapter 4). Frankfurt also uses batch trading for small orders of frequently traded issues. This makes it unnecessary to have a special odd-lots dealer and consequently reduces the transaction cost on small orders.

2.2.1.2 Unlisted securities markets. Whereas some exchanges, such as Tokyo, have two sets of listing standards, with the lesser standards facilitating listing of smaller issues, London's Unlisted Securities Market (USM) goes all the way and permits trading of unlisted securities. In London, any jobber who wishes to make a market in any domestic issue may do so under the USM rules. The trading system is essentially the same as London's regular jobber system. If there is a viable market for a company's shares, they will be traded whether or not the company initiates listing. The division of trading into a listed market and the USM is seen by London as sufficient warning to investors that the strict capital, profitability, and disclosure requirements of the stock exchange may not be met.[13]

In the United States, the exchanges leave the unlisted securities market to the OTC dealers. Now that the exchanges and the OTC dealers have been connected through the ITS system, we wonder whether an exchange might be able profitably to offer its order-book services to those customers who wish to use limit orders (and in effect to compete with OTC dealers). It would seem that the customer could never lose from this arrangement because his order can always be routed to the best counterpart either on the exchange limit-order book or among OTC dealers. The main operational question would seem to be whether a cheap enough order-handling and order-routing system can be designed to make the operation effective at low trading volume. This issue will be considered in Chapter 3.

2.2.2 Special Arrangements for On-Exchange Block Trading

The basic problem with block trading, from the point of view of the trader, is the trader's fear that a large block suddenly dropped on the market could push price in an unfavorable direction. Since, as we shall see in Section 2.3.3, there are natural attractions to block traders in going off-exchange, the growth of institutional trading and the ability of more concentrated brokerage firms or bank securities departments to batch smaller customer orders poses a profound challenge to the existence and health of the exchanges. Whenever it is in the economic interest of block traders to go off-exchange, and it is only exchange rules that keep some of the trading on exchange, the exchanges stand in perpetual danger of losing their order flow. Thus the exchanges seek to facilitate on-exchange block trading by various special arrangements.

2.2.2.1 Facilitating market transparency and discretionary order handling. An example of the various ways in which a block order may be handled when on-exchange trading is required comes from Frankfurt.[14] Normally, the bank trading a block order will break up the order and spread it around among floor brokers. This helps the bank to maintain its anonymity and avoid creating the impression that a large order has been dropped on the market. Because Germany has eight regional exchanges, the order may also be broken up geographically. In addition, if the customer has given the bank the freedom to exercise the order on or off the floor (and the banks frequently advise this), the bank can also search for a counterpart in the telephone market (Section 2.3.3) and if one is found, do a "put-through" (Section 2.2.2.2).

In Tel Aviv, it is also customary for those large orders going through the exchange to be broken into several parts. This is facilitated by the practice of some large traders of effectively entering their offer curves rather than a single-price "take it or leave it" offer. That is, the seller of 3000 shares might price the first 1000 shares at 50 and the next 2000 shares at 51. This poses no special difficulties for the banks handling the trading, since they customarily provide their floor traders with a computer order-summary sheet, which lists the net supply or demand at each price. Thus in the case of our customer, if the batch price happens to be 50, he will sell 1000 shares, whereas if it is 51 he will sell 3000.

Toronto's CATS system has no special rules for large orders, but two of its rules appear designed to make the task of handling large orders somewhat easier. The first is the rule allowing partial disclosure of an order for more than one board lot. By this rule, it is possible for a large trader to enter his order, have it sitting in the system, but to disclose only a portion of it. The price he pays for this anonymity is that the undisclosed portion goes to the end of the time priority queue below any disclosed order at the same price. Once the disclosed portion trades, the block trader is automatically informed; he is then able, if he wishes, to disclose more of the order or improve on its price so as to move it up in the queue. The second CATS device that helps block traders is the open book with a preopening "indicated" price. With the open book, if the market is deep on the counterpart side, the trader can know this and place his order; if the counterpart market is not deep, the trader may place only part of his order, hoping to elicit additional counterpart orders.

A number of other markets also use some form of indicated prices to enable floor traders to respond appropriately to market conditions and to learn the effect on the market of large discretionary orders which they may hold. As we noted, the *à la criée* system seems to be designed for this purpose and removes what would otherwise be a major disadvantage of batch trading. However, only traders present on the floor can take advantage of the transparency of the *à la criée* market.

2.2.2.2 Put-throughs. Many exchanges have rules allowing specified large-block transactions to be negotiated off the floor and then brought to the floor for a formal transaction. For example, in London, a broker handling a large-block transaction, after first getting quotes from jobbers, may find a counterparty through his phone contacts with institutions. Then he must offer both sides of the transaction to a jobber who can (1) take part of one side himself at a price previously agreed between the two principals, or (2) do a put-through—buy from one seller and sell to one buyer. The jobber's turn for this two-way transaction is lower than his usual spread because there is no risk to the jobber.[15] A similar put-through rule in Amsterdam requires that the market maker be allowed to take up to 25% of either side of the block.

The equivalent of the dealer market put-through in a matching system is illustrated by Tokyo's rule. As in London, large-block transactions may be negotiated off the floor by a brokerage firm, which must then bring the crossed transaction to the book, where the transaction is put through the market. In an order-book market, this means that limit orders at a price equal to or superior to one side of the block transactions will receive priority over the inferior block offer.[16]

The purpose of the put-through rules in both dealer markets and order-book markets is to tie the on- and off-exchange markets together. The Tokyo example illustrates how this works; note that the on-exchange market price and the off-exchange market price must come together in the process. In Amsterdam, if there are limit orders on the book, the put-through rule brings these orders into the block transaction, since the market maker will take enough of the block to satisfy these orders.

2.2.2.3 Special lots trading. In the Hong Kong board trading system, an order larger than $HK 1,000,000 may be negotiated off-board at any price and is simply recorded on the special lots trading board. This procedure does not tie the markets together to any extent, but it does inform the main market about the prices at which business is being done off-exchange. A smaller block order must be entered as a quotation on the special lots trading board. In this case, the broker for the order must first offer the block to counterparts on the main board in price–time priority order. Should they reject the parcel, the broker may then go to the special lots board, stating the quantity of shares and name of the company and the price per share for the whole parcel. At this point, of course, the broker may cross the special lots order with a counterpart which he has found by telephone negotiation. The latter rule would appear partially to tie the markets together; note, however, that since the main board counterparts must take the full block rather than only parts of it, the consolidation effect is limited, and prices can differ in the two parts of the market.

2.2.3 Stabilization

The 14 foreign exchanges we studied offer a variety of stabilization techniques, some of which are not seen in the United States. Although the stated rationales for the different stabilization techniques are quite varied, there is a frequently unstated rationale common to many of them: this is the attempt to concentrate (or batch) orders, especially in times of market stress. For example, while fixed maximum-price-change limits are often justified as an attempt to protect market-order traders from their own folly, they also serve to advise the market of possible speculating stabilization opportunities and to batch trading orders over a period of anywhere from a few minutes to several days.

2.2.3.1 Maximum price-change limits. This is the most common stabilization method and it is used by over half of the exchanges we visited (although the U.S. and Canadian exchanges, Frankfurt, London, Hong Kong, Zurich, and the Brussels forward market do not). Frequently, however, the maximum price-change allowance is not hard and fast, but is rather a judgment call by an exchange official.

The maximum price-change limits work in the following way. Suppose that there is unusually brisk demand for stock X, and the maximum price-change limit is 10%. If the batch clearing price for X today would exceed 1.10 times the previous day's price, the auctioneer will halt trading and announce the excess demand situation. If, after a 10- or 15-minute wait for incoming selling orders, the market clearing price still exceeds the limit, no trade is allowed and the exchange publishes today's price as 1.10 times yesterday's price (along with some notation that no trading was allowed). This then becomes tomorrow's base price from which a further 10% movement upward or downward is allowed. Thus, over the course of two or three days, there can be a large price change in such a system. A good example of this occurred following the Sunday, May 10, 1981, presidential victory of French Socialist François Mitterand. On Monday, the first day following the election, virtually no shares were traded, and all were marked down 10% below their Friday levels. This became the base price for Tuesday, and most shares were then marked down an additional 10 to 20% before an equilibrium price was finally found on Wednesday.

Usually the maximum price-change limits are lower proportionately for bonds, and Tokyo even differentiates among stocks by price, setting more liberal limits for lower-priced stocks. This is consistent with the empirical evidence of Chapter 4 that lower-priced shares have greater natural volatility.

The stated reason for maximum price-change limits is to protect market-order traders who may have entered a market order to sell (buy) and without the rule would find themselves selling at perhaps a 20 or 30% discount (premium).

We see two other reasons for the maximum price-change rules and the way they are administered. First, publication of a "buyers only" or "sellers only" price serves to advertise a market imbalance, and balancing orders may come in on the following day. A second purpose is to pool orders over time, in effect extending the normal batching process from one day to several. This mechanism does not prevent a one-directional price movement, but may serve to reduce the frequency with which a big movement on one day is followed by a further large movement (continuation or reversal) on the next. None of these rationales implies an improvement in efficiency; any argument must be made on equity grounds.

2.2.3.2 Trading halts with indicated prices. A few exchanges (the Brussels forward market and Zurich) take the less drastic step of halting trading temporarily when an excessive price would otherwise occur, letting stabilizing orders come in if they will, and then resuming trading after 10 or 20 minutes with no price limit. A variant on this procedure is the preopening indicated price disseminated by the Amsterdam and Frankfurt exchanges. This allows traders to observe the projected price, to decide if it is justified by fundamental facts, and if not to enter stabilizing orders.

2.2.3.3 Refusal to accept destabilizing orders. There are several variants of this stabilizing procedure: (1) The U.S. and Canadian exchanges require their official market makers to satisfy the "tick test"; they cannot buy on an up tick (i.e., following a price increase over the last two previous transactions) or sell on a down tick. (2) In Brussels, if the trial price that comes closest to balancing the written buy and sell orders exceeds the previous day's close, the auctioneer will accept only sell orders. (3) In Tell Aviv, when the official broker is conducting the auction and increases the price, no member can increase his buy order.

2.2.3.4 Stabilizing speculation by market makers. All exchanges have individuals who are frequent or full-time traders and who act at times as speculating stabilizers to reduce what they see as random demand-supply fluctuations. (See Chapter 9 for simulation results on the feasibility and profitability of stabilizing speculation.) Some markets (Amsterdam, Brussels, London, Montreal, Toronto, and the U.S. exchanges) encourage this activity by giving some participants a trading advantage: lower trading costs and/or preferred or exclusive access to some market information. In some markets, the encouragement takes the form of an exclusive monopoly on trading, but it is interesting to note that in Amsterdam, where this is the case for most stocks, the five largest domestic issues give the market makers sufficient incentive to be present without having a trading monopoly. In all of these markets (except the U.S.), the market maker is not *required* to intervene to stabilize.

A number of exchanges have informal market makers who are not given any special privileges, but whose economic power and regular trading activities may make stabilizing speculation more profitable for them than others. Most notable are Japan's Big Four securities firms and Israel's major banks. The Israeli banks have frequently intervened on a major scale to prevent large fluctuations in the prices of their stocks and to force those stock prices upward as necessary to keep pace with the rapid Israeli inflation. Their motive for doing this has been that their frequent new issues of equity can sell at a higher price if the price volatility of their shares in the secondary market is kept low. In the fall of 1983, the Israeli banks used up vast amounts of liquid capital in a vain attempt to prevent a price downturn and had to be bailed out by the government. The lesson would appear to be the same one drawn from the experience of governments "managing" their exchange rates: you can stabilize, but you cannot "peg."

2.2.3.5 "Affirmative obligation" stabilization. U.S. specialists and, to a much lesser extent, Toronto's "registered traders," have an obligation to stabilize: the U.S. specialists are expected to keep transaction-to-transaction price changes or price changes over each 1000 shares traded within certain limits (which may vary from stock to stock according to its "natural" volatility); Toronto's registered market makers to do not face this obligation, but instead must keep the bid-ask spread within stated limits. Chapter 9 demonstrates that the specialists' efforts to reduce the spread must also reduce transaction-to-transaction and day-to-day price changes. The specialists' and registered traders' stabilization activities are expected to cause them losses for which they are compensated by being given commissions and/or exclusive access to information.

Affirmative obligation stabilizers are the subject of substantial surveillance activities by the U.S. and Toronto exchanges. These activities are intended in part to assure that the market maker does not take advantage of his special position. In addition, a purpose of surveillance on the U.S. and Toronto exchanges is to ensure that the specialist or registered trader is performing his stabilization functions; since these functions are inherently unprofitable, the natural inclination would be to do as little as possible. For this reason, the exchanges must (1) examine at least a sample of trades to determine if the stabilizer has been exercising his influence properly, and (2) reassign or threaten to reassign stocks away from stabilizers who do not stabilize.[17] The cost, complexity, and inherent difficulties of this sort of surveillance represent the greatest disadvantage of affirmative obligation stabilization. We shall examine the merits of and possible alternative forms of affirmative obligation stabilization in Chapter 9.

2.2.3.6 Temporal and spatial concentration of orders. In general, one of the most powerful and subtle means of stabilizing is not through direct stabilization rules, but rather through the fundamental market structure or market architecture. In this context, batch trading and short exchange hours may be viewed as an attempt to concentrate orders temporally.[18] Similarly, rules such as the NYSE's Rule 390 which require member-customer trades to go through the exchange may be viewed as an attempt to concentrate orders spatially and thus to prevent market fragmentation. An analysis of the effect of off-exchange trading is given in Chapter 8.

2.2.4 Surveillance

In general, most exchanges abroad do substantially less surveillance of trading activities than is done in the United States. The major exception is Tokyo, which, like the U.S. major exchanges, has both an on-floor stock watch and an "exception principle" examination of completed transactions. Like the NYSE and AMEX, Tokyo's stock watch is done initially by a computer which triggers an examination by an investigator under any of the following four situations: (1) a large price movement, (2) unusual trading volume in an issue, (3) unusual activity over a period of time in an issue by a single broker; or (4) unusual trading volume at the end of the session.

The reasons why other exchanges do less surveillance are: (1) their smaller size compared to the U.S. exchanges and Tokyo, which causes costs per unit to be greater; (2) a European tradition, most strongly expressed in Britain and Germany, that brokers and bankers are "gentlemen"; (3) the fact that affirmative obligation stabilization, which requires more elaborate surveillance, is not offered abroad; and (4) the fact that many of the stock exchange trading systems (such as those in Hong Kong, Luxembourg, and Zurich) are simply arrangements facilitating bilateral trading among members.

2.2.5 Price and Volume Information

Table 1 summarizes the price and volume information offered by the various exchanges. We identify several different types of information, together with some indication of how rapidly or how broadly it is disseminated. One form of rather complete information is what we call an on-line transaction record (T in Table 1), where prices and volumes are transmitted on-line over a ticker or to commercial information vendors. Table 1 does not indicate how widely this information is transmitted, but the widest dissemination is usually achieved by selling the information to a commercial vendor such as Dow Jones Information Service, Reuters, or Telekurs. An on-line transaction record is much less valuable to investors in those trading systems where most of the volume is concentrated at the opening or where there is only one batch transaction per day (T-). Some exchanges (such as Frankfurt) report on-line prices only but not volume

TABLE 1A Summary of Exchange Trading Systems and Services[a]

	Trading System								
	Batch				Continuous				
					Matching				
	Criée	Written	At Opening	No. of Calls/Day	Order Bk.	Board	Crowd	Dealer	Hours
AMEX			Y	1	Y				9:30–16:00
Amsterdam									
Bonds and frequently traded stocks			Y+	2	Y				10:00–12:15 12:45–16:30
Infrequently traded stocks		Y		2					11:30–12:15 12:45–13:30
Brussels									
Forward	Y+	Y+		1		Y	Y*		12:30–Irr.
Cash:corbeille		Y+		1		Y	Y*		12:50–Irr.
Cash:parquet		Y		1					13:10–Irr.
Frankfurt									
Frequently traded			Y	1	Y				11:30–13:30
Infrequently traded		Y		1					12:00–12:15
Hong Kong						Y			9:30–12:30
London								Y	9:30–15:30 Phone: 15:30–17:30
Luxembourg	Y			1			Y		Stocks: 12:00–13:00 Bonds: 11:00–13:00
Montreal			Y	1		Y			10:00–16:00
NYSE			Y	1	Y				9:30–16:00
Paris									
Forward	Y+			1			Y		12:30–14:30

(continued)

TABLE 1A *(continued)*

	Trading System								
	Batch				Continuous				
					Matching				
	Criée	Written	At Opening	No. of Calls/ Day	Order Bk.	Board	Crowd	Dealer	Hours
Paris *(continued)*									16:00–17:00 U.S. stocks
Cash: par opposition	Y	Y		1	Y		Y		12:30–14:30
Cash: par cassiers		Y		1	Y				Bonds: 11:30–12:30 Stocks: 12:30–14:30
Unlisted		Y		1					12:30–14:30
Sydney						Y			10:00–12:00 14:00–15:00
Tel-Aviv	Y	Y+		1					13:00–Irr.
Tokyo			Y+	2	Y				9:00–11:00 13:00–15:00 Foreign Sec. opens 10:30
Toronto									
Floor trading			Y	1		Y			10:00–16:00
CATS			Y+	1	Y				10:00–16:00
Vienna									
Frequently traded			Y	1	Y				10:30–12:45
Infrequently traded		Y+		1					12:15–12:45
Zurich							Y		9:30–10:00 (Unlisted) 10:00–Irr. (Listed)

TABLE 1A *(continued)*

	Stabilization					Settlement			Off-Exch. Trading	
	Max. Price-Chg. Lim.	Indi-cation	Batch Trading	Official Mkt. Maker	Type of P/V Info. Avail.	Cash or Fwd.	Period	Bk. Entry Transfer	In-House	Blocks
AMEX	N	Y	N	AO	T, BA, NPV	C	5 d.	N	Y, 19c.3	L
Amsterdam										
Bonds and frequently traded stocks	10%	Y	N	Y	P, I, NPV	C	5 d.	Y	N	PT
Infrequently traded stocks	10%	Y	Y	Y	P, NPV	C	5 d.	Y	N	PT
Brussels										
Forward	N	Y	N	N	T-, NPV	F	≤2 w.	Y	N	L
Cash:corbeille	10%	Y	Y	Y	T-, NPV	C	1 d.	Y	N	L
Cash:parquet	2-5%	N	Y	Y	T-, NPV	C	1 d.	Y	N	L
Frankfurt										L (stocks)
Frequently traded	N	Y	N	N	P, BA, NPV	C	2 d.	Y	Y (bonds)	Y (bonds)
Infrequently traded	N	Y	Y	N	P-, NPV	C	2 d.	Y	Y (bonds)	Y (bonds)
Hong Kong	N	N	N	N	T, BA, NPV	C	1 d.	N	N	L
London	N	N	N	Y	MS, NP	F	≤2 w.	N	N	PT
Luxembourg	2-10%	Y	Y	N	NPV	C	1-6 d.	Y	Y	Y
Montreal	N	N	N	Y	T, BA, NPV	C	5 d.	N	N	L
NYSE	N	Y	N	AO	T, BA, NPV	C	5 d.	N	Y, 19c.3	L
Paris										
Forward	5-10%	Y	Y	N	T-, NPV	F	≤3 w. + Contango	Y, 80%	N	N
Cash: par opposition	5-10%	N	Y	Y	T-, NPV	C	1 d.	Y, 80%	N	N
Cash: par cassiers	5-10%	N	Y	Y	T-, NPV	C	1 d.	Y, 80%	N	N
Unlisted	5-10%	N	Y	Y	T-, NPV	C	1 d.	Y, 80%	N	N

(continued)

TABLE 1A *(continued)*

	Stabilization					Settlement			Off-Exch. Trading	
	Max. Price-Chg. Lim.	Indi-cation	Batch Trading	Official Mkt. Maker	Type of P/V Info. Avail.	Cash or Fwd.	Period	Bk. Entry Transfer	In-House	Blocks
Sydney	N	N	N	N	T, BA, NPV	F	≤2 w.	N	N	L
Tel-Aviv	5-10%	Y	Y	N	T-, NPV	C	1 d.	Y	NOB	L
Tokyo	20%	Y	N	N	T, O, NPV	C	3 d.	N	N	PT
Toronto										
Floor trading	N	N	N	AO	T, BA, NPV	C	5 d.	N	N	L
CATS	N	Y	N	AO	T, I, O, NPV	C	5 d.	N	N	L
Vienna										
Frequently traded	5%	Y	N	N	P, I, BA, NP	F	≤7 d.	N	Y	L
Infrequently traded	5%	Y	Y	N	P, I, BA, NP	F	≤7 d.	N	Y	L
Zurich	N	Y	N	N	P, BA, NPV	C	5 d.	BSO	Y	L
						F	≤2 m.	BSO		

[a] See Table 1B for the key to this table.

TABLE 1B Key to Table 1A

Y	Yes	BA	Bid-ask quotes available
Y+	Orders may be modified after trial price given	I	Preopening indication price
Y*	Orders may be labeled "opening only"	NPV	Newspaper price and volume report
N	No	NP	Newspaper price report, no volume
Irr.	Closing hours irregular; closes when last issue called and no further orders received	MS	On-line midspread quotation
AO	Market makers with "affirmative obligation"	O	Open limit-order book
NA	Not available	C	Cash
T	On-line transaction record	F	Forward
T-	On-line transaction record, most volume at opening	BSO	Book entry transfer for bearer shares only
P	On-line transaction prices	NOB	Netting orders before opening/call only
P-	On-line prices only, most volume at opening	L	Limited off-exchange block trading (very large size or other special conditions)
		PT	Put-throughs

(P). Nearly all exchanges report price and volume at the end of a day via an exchange-published newspaper, parts of which inevitably get reprinted by the major dailies in the exchange's city (NPV), while a few report price but not volume in that manner (NP).

A few exchanges (the U.S. and Canadian exchanges, Frankfurt, Hong Kong, Sydney, Vienna, and Zurich) report bid and ask prices on-line (BA). London, by contrast, reports on-line only the average of the bid and ask prices of a representative jobber, the midspread quote (MS). Several exchanges report preopening indication prices (I), but only Amsterdam and Toronto CATS systematically disseminate this information beyond the trading floor. Finally, Tokyo's nonautomated trading and its CATS and Toronto's CATS have open limit-order books (O), but in Tokyo's nonautomated trading this information is not readily available beyond the exchange floor.[19]

In general, outside the United States and Canada, on-line market information is much less available, and nearly every foreign exchange has some "hole" in its price-volume reporting system. Perhaps the worst offender is London (prior to 1986, when it will institute a NASDAQ type of system). The reason for giving only the midspread price is that jobbers fear that competing jobbers and brokers could infer their inventory positions if the price and volume of each transaction were reported, even if the jobber making the transaction were not identified. In addition, no jobber would want to be committed to a single bid-ask quotation at a given moment, since a jobber may give different quotations to different brokers depending on his assessment of the broker's likely position and eagerness to trade.

2.3 TRADING IN MULTIPLE MARKETS

Some of the most important issues faced by securities exchanges concern trading of the same securities in multiple markets. This trading takes two forms: (1) trading of securities cross-listed on two or more exchanges, and (2) off-exchange trading. The major issues involved concern whether the linkages among markets permit unimpeded arbitrage and which market will capture the order flow.

In this section, we look first at domestic and international linkages among exchanges, next at in-house retail trading in the United States and abroad, and then at block trading off-exchange.

2.3.1 Domestic Linkages among Exchanges

Most countries have more than one exchange, but usually one dominates. Only in Germany, Hong Kong, and Switzerland are there two or more exchanges of approximately equal size. Even in Germany, trading in any one stock tends to gravitate to one of the two major exchanges; thus the steel and mining stocks trade mainly on the Dusseldorf exchange, and the motor car companies and foreign issues trade mainly on the Frankfurt exchange. In France, not only does Paris dominate, but by law there is no cross-listing of stocks; hence the regional exchanges get only the regional issues.

The U.S. Intermarket Trading System (ITS) uses a computer to accept the bid-ask quotations of each of the regional and national exchanges and to display these on television monitors on the floors of the exchanges. If an order comes to one exchange to buy, for example, and a lower ask is available at another exchange, the order may be routed to the other exchange through ITS and a response received through ITS.

Only the United States has such a regional linkage system, but in both Canada and Japan, serious consideration is being given to adopting the principle. In both countries, it is the smaller regional exchanges (Montreal in Canada and Osaka in Japan) which seem to feel that they have the most to gain from an ITS type of system. However, in the United States, the introduction of ITS has not materially changed the market shares of the regional and national exchanges.[20]

The ITS system does not provide a complete linkage among exchanges. In theory, ITS should satisfy price priority, but not time or other secondary priorities. That is, there is nothing to guarantee that a buy order that arrives in Philadelphia before a buy order at the same price arrives at the AMEX will in fact transact earlier. In practice, even price priority may sometimes be violated by "trade-throughs." The major reason for the trade-throughs would appear to be that an order larger than 100 shares is less likely to be satisfied at a regional exchange than at a national exchange and thus may be left at the national exchange even if the regional exchange appears to have a superior price on ITS. In addition, ITS is not instantaneous, although its response time is normally measured in seconds, and ITS quotations may occasionally be stale.[21]

2.3.2 International Linkages among Exchanges

The most dynamic market for international issues is in London. A number of foreign issues (largely from the Commonwealth and other former colonies, like the United States) are listed, but a growing number are traded on the unlisted market, and volume is heavy in many issues. Here, any jobber wishing to make a market in any foreign security listed on any exchange anywhere (including "window dressing" listings in Luxembourg and elsewhere) may do so without formalities but under stock exchange rules of behavior. This leaves the listing decision up to members of the stock exchange, rather than to the issuing corporation. Investors are warned by the unlisted nature of the securities that conventional disclosure requirements may not be satisfied, and that extraordinary risks may be present.

A number of other European exchanges list substantial numbers of foreign securities relative to domestic listings; most notable are those in the Benelux countries, Switzerland, and Frankfurt. Most of these exchanges have relatively simple listing requirements and firms are assisted in the listing application by sponsoring banks; perhaps more important are the relatively mild disclosure requirements in force, even under the new European Community (EC) "harmonization" directives. This asymmetry of listing and disclosure requirements, along with the European netting arrangement (Section 2.3.3) gives rise to an asymmetrical order flow between the United States and Europe and threatens New York's preeminence as the international financial capital. If international diversification continues to grow, this "balance of trade deficit" in securities trading will increase and become an important factor limiting the growth of U.S. exchanges.

Our observation, confirmed by exchange officials, bankers, and brokers at every exchange with important linkages to other exchanges, is that as communications between distant places improve, the exchange which benefits most tends to be the exchange already having the greatest share of the order flow in a particular issue. Thus, for example, the ITS system has not diverted order flow away from the NYSE (except in the small-order category), and the Tokyo Stock Exchange has substantially increased its share of the total order flow despite the Japanese government's efforts to preserve the regional exchanges. In addition, few foreign exchanges have been really successful in capturing more than a small share of their nationals' orders for international issues whose primary markets are elsewhere. A theoretical explanation for this is offered in Chapter 8.

There is no international ITS (although the EC has a European price information system[22]). The principal mechanism in place or in prospect which works to equilibrate prices for a cross-listed security is arbitrage by specialized arbitrage firms trading own-account and by brokers-banks trading own-account and routing customer orders. In the international securities market, as in the foreign exchange market, this is done largely by the major international banks. Because of the time difference between the United States and Europe, most of the arbitrage is not simultaneous ("pure") arbitrage, but rather a matter of adjusting prices in the foreign market to those in the home market at the close of the previous day's trading.[23] Some simultaneous arbitrage occurs between the U.S. exchange market and the after-hours off-exchange European market. More of the arbitrage between Europe and America occurs during the regular working day in Europe and is a matter of netting European orders among the major banks (Section 2.3.3). This is largely a telephone market among large traders.

Arbitrage operations within Europe are assisted by the commercial price information systems of Reuters and Telekurs, a Swiss firm. Telekurs disseminates on-line price information for 110,000 issues (largely bonds and money market instruments, including Eurobonds) to a large number of technologically sophisticated terminals with query capabilities and to other less sophisticated television screen monitors throughout Europe. A feature available on their terminal systems assists arbitrage by searching all exchanges for prices that exceed limits specified by the user in his own currency. Telekurs officials assure us that most of their new services, such as the arbitrage search software just mentioned, can be readily adopted by bank arbitrageurs once they are properly explained. One might conclude from this that the market, by its revealed choices, feels the need for additional linkages beyond those that now exist.

One thing which all markets trading international securities have in common is the fact that they do not apply the usual stabilization techniques to foreign securities. The maximum price-change limits that most exchanges apply to domestic securities are invariably lacking for international securities trading; of all the stabilization devices we have identified, only the temporal concentration of orders by batching and short trading hours are applied to foreign securities. The reason is straightforward: if maximum price-change limits, or even a temporary halt and indication, were applied to an international security, most order volume would simply flow to the home market for the period during which the trading halt applied. If a specialist were to stabilize foreign securities by direct intervention, he would probably end up stabilizing the entire world's trading in the security since traders in other markets would be free riders on his stabilization. The lesson is that an exchange wishing to attract order volume in international securities by providing a stabilized market must do so only by structural design rather than by active stabilization measures.

2.3.3. In-House and Off-Exchange Trading

In-house trading is a major issue in the United States because of SEC Rule 19c-3, which allows brokerage firms to make an in-house market in all securities listed since April 1979. In this subsection, we characterize the different types of in-house and off-exchange trading and describe the process.

2.3.3.1 Netting of orders before opening/batch trading. In Frankfurt (bonds only), Luxembourg, Tel Aviv, Vienna, and Zurich, the banks (which in each of these exchanges handle practically all trading) are allowed to "net" their customers' market and limit orders before the opening, or the daily call, as the case may be. The bank simply brings to the market the net demand or supply at each potential price, and this net forms the basis of the bank floor traders' offers. In Tel Aviv, the banks facilitate their floor traders' handling of the orders by presenting them with a computer printout giving the net demand or supply at each price. The netting process is facilitated at all five exchanges by short trading hours and late openings, which give the banks time to accumulate orders.

In international trading, a potential asymmetry in the NYSE's order flow exists because of the European netting arrangement. A group of major German, Swiss, and (reportedly) French banks nets their U.S. market orders in-house and to some extent among banks prior to the NYSE opening each day. The banks bring their net-net volume to the United States and trade it at the market opening, accounting for the netted transactions at this opening price. The netting is incomplete, but a substantial reduction of order flow does occur, and it is not matched by a corresponding net netting of American orders for European stocks.

Netting orders before batch trading has no effect on the price that is ultimately set in the market. The only effect is a reduction of the exchange's revenue, if that revenue depends on the trading volume on the floor. In this connection, it is interesting to note that the Zurich Stock Exchange's commission revenue depends on all trades by members rather than just floor trades. The rationale for this may be that the exchange's price making and price dissemination services benefit all traders wherever their particular transaction occurs.

2.3.3.2 Separate in-house order book. When the stock exchange is a continuous market, a brokerage firm or banker may, if allowed, also cross customer limit orders and market orders in-house. Banks in Luxembourg and Zurich are free to do this, but it is not clear that they do it to any considerable extent since the transaction cost which they pay to the exchange is the same whether a transaction occurs on or off the exchange; thus they have no particular cost incentive to cross in-house.

In the United States, the NYSE's Rule 390 prevents its member brokers from "making a market in-house" in all stocks listed on the NYSE before April 1979. (SEC Rule 19c-3 voided Rule 390 for stocks listed after April 1979). That is, members may not act as *principal* in filling a customer's order except on *an* exchange. This rule and the continuous-trading nature of the NYSE effectively prevents member brokers even from crossing customer orders in-house, because the broker cannot guarantee his limit-order customer that if a trade occurs in the primary (exchange) market at the limit price, the limit order will filled. Only if the broker could act as dealer off-exchange could it guarantee such primary market protection.[24]

Merrill Lynch sought to outflank Rule 390 by using what was almost a captive stock exchange, the Cincinnati Stock Exchange (of Jersey City). The Cincinnati is automated and does not have specialists (stocks traded on it are stabilized free, in effect, by the NYSE specialists), so Merrill hoped to reduce its transaction costs. The operations and degree of success of the Cincinnati will be discussed in Section 3.2.4.

2.3.3.3 Broker/bank off-exchange dealer activities. Several exchanges (Frankfurt for bonds, Hong Kong for after-hours trading, Luxembourg, Vienna, Zurich, and, for 19c-3 stocks, the U.S. exchanges) allow brokers or banks to act as off-exchange dealers. This is a threat to exchange operations and market consolidation, because it permits a potentially profitable in-house market to be created.

Merrill's in-house market (operated from 1980 to 1983) serves as an example. While Merrill sometimes satisfied its in-house customer by crossing his limit order with another customer's order, it normally satisfied such orders by buying or selling from inventory. If Merrill chose, it satisfied the customer's order as dealer; if not, Merrill purchased or sold at an exchange as principal. The latter operation enabled Merrill to batch its customer orders and to gain an economy of scale in execution by giving its floor traders a discretionary order so as to execute at a better price than if each small-customer order were executed directly. Merrill's choice of whether to act as dealer or simply to collect a few customer orders, meet them from inventory, and then reverse the position on the exchange depended on its assessment of the market. Its ability to go to the exchange for processing its customer orders rather than always having to act as dealer enabled it to use the exchange as the market of last resort. That is, if Merrill felt that the market in a stock was likely to decline and it had several customer sell orders to satisfy, it could simply lay these off at the exchange without having to take a risky dealer position. On such transactions Merrill did not realize its primary goal in the in-house market—that of saving commission costs.

Despite these attractions, Merrill and the other large brokerage firms that started formal in-house markets have dropped or curtailed them. The reasons are complicated and we think the issue is far from settled, so we shall pick it up again in Chapters 3 and 8.

2.3.3.4 Off-exchange block trading in the telephone market. We observed block trading in many markets, and the block trading in Eurobonds in the back offices of Kredietbank in Luxembourg is typical. With the demise of EUREX (an automated Euroband trading system; see Section 3.2.2), the Eurobond market is for all practical purposes a telephone market only. The usual method of dealing is for the block trader to be in frequent phone contact with institutional investors and portfolio managers so as to know their general trading posture (i.e., whether at a particular time they wish to buy short maturities, sell long maturities, or whatever). Thus, when a block is to be placed, the block trader knows whom to call to find a likely counterpart. Frequently, only one or two calls need to be made to effect a trade. We see two principal advantages in this method of dealing: (1) the telephone calls to potential counterparts serve to advertise the block trader's services as agent, and (2) the ability to place most blocks with only one or a few phone calls makes it possible to deal a large block without showing your hand to the entire market.

2.4 CONCLUSION

This chapter has examined the different fundamental trading structures and the basic services offered by stock exchanges around the world. There are interactions between trading structures and services and there are reasons (other than historical) for the existence of the particular structures and services. We summarize these reasons in this section.

Perhaps the most important interaction is that between the trading system and the amount and value of price-volume information provided. Nowhere is this interaction more telling than in a dealer market. If the dealer market is oligopolistic, there is a strong incentive to disseminate little information on-line because, with a price-volume record, each dealer can estimate his rivals' inventory positions and devise trading strategies.[25] As the number of dealers in a security increases, the advertising value of firm quotes and a transaction record begins to outweigh the diminishing value of inferences about competitor's activities. Thus it is no surprise that the U.S. OTC market offers much more price information than the London Stock Exchange or that an exchange market where a specialist competes against the limit orders of other dealers and the public provides extensive information.

Another trading structure-price information interaction hinges on the information provided in a batch trade in a call market or at the opening in a continuous order-book market. Where it is critical and worth the cost to an important class of traders to obtain indicated prices before the batch trade, an arrangement like Paris's verbal auction or the NYSE's informal sharing of information between the specialist and the crowd occurs. Where the value of an indicated price does not overcome the cost of obtaining it (as with thin stocks) and the reluctance of the order-book holder to give up his information monopoly, the batch trade is done in the dark. Along the same line, because sole access to order book information may yield trading profits (see Chapter 9), a completely open book is made available only in markets where the order-book holder may not trade for his own account.[26]

There is also interaction between the types of stabilization offered and the fundamental trading structure. Batch trading systems (if they do not disseminate indicated prices before the call) are the main users of daily price-change limits; this is in part because the price information they provide is after the fact and does not enable all investors to respond rapidly to price movements. Batch systems also concentrate the order flow temporally, reducing the role of professional market markers as speculating stabilizers and providers of counterpart liquidity.

Market makers have a greater role in continuous-trading markets, but the nature of that role depends on the trading structure. An affirmative obligation to stabilize can exist only when market makers have an exclusive franchise on the stocks they handle, because the individual output of multiple stabilizers cannot be measured and compensated. Affirmative obligation stabilization also exists only in exchanges where off-exchange trading is restricted. This is because, unless stabilization is paid for by all shareholders, trading off-exchange deprives the stabilizer of compensation for his activities. We will consider the design of stabilization systems in Chapter 9.

There is one issue, which relates to fundamental trading structure and to the services performed by exchanges, that we have not considered here. This is automation. There is so much happening and so much that we can reasonably forecast will happen relating to automation that we devote a separate chapter to automation and its implications for trading structures.

NOTES

*Some of the observations, speculations, and conclusions reported in this chapter were summarized in much briefer form in D. K. Whitcomb, "An International Comparison of Stock Exchange Trading Structures," in Y. Amihud, T. Ho, and R. A. Schwartz, ed. *Market Making and the Changing Structure of the Securities Industry* (Reading, Mass: Lexington Books, 1985).

1. These visits were funded by a grant from the New York Stock Exchange to Thomas S. Y. Ho, Robert A. Schwartz, and David K. Whitcomb and were carried out during the period 1980–1983. We are grateful to Dr. William Freund of the NYSE for introductions and to the executives of the exchanges visited for their time and insights.
2. See Ho-Schwartz-Whitcomb (1985). An alternative classification scheme could be based on whether trading is effected by brokers or bankers. The countries where brokers handle all security trading are the United States, Canada, Japan, the United Kingdom, Hong Kong, France, and Belgium. Countries where bankers dominate trading are Germany, Austria, Switzerland, Luxembourg, and Israel; and in Holland both brokers and bankers are active in trading. Typically in bank-dominated trading systems, off-exchange trading is relatively important and the stock exchange is relatively less important in the financial sector than in otherwise similar broker-trading countries.
3. Until the end of 1982, Tokyo had a four-times-a-day call for a few large stocks. It was unusual in that the auctioneer did not allow a batch transaction unless a price had been reached where supply and demand were *exactly* equal. The rationale for this rule and alternatives to it are discussed in Section 2.1.1.4.

4. Several European exchanges have a system that seems like an *à la criée* system but is not. In Luxembourg and Zurich, the official auctioneer names the issues at the opening of trading, but neither states prices nor tries to reach an equilibrium; trading there is "continuous market" matching by bilateral bargains within a crowd.
5. By the time you read this, an automated quotation system may already be in place in London (it is scheduled for mid-1986). Like the OTC market's NASDAQ, it will display each dealer's bid and ask price. As a result of the negotiated settlement to the Restrictive Practices court action brought by the government (and of competitive pressures from British banks and foreign brokers and banks), brokers as well as jobbers will be able to make markets, and commission rates will no longer be fixed. (See "London Stock Plan Set," *The New York Times*, July 20, 1984, p. D11.) The result is likely to be a substantial increase in competition among dealers and a market with characteristics more like the U.S. OTC market. See Section 3.3.4 for a discussion of possible implications for international trading.
6. In London, the long trading hours (see Table 1) substantially reduce the batching effect at the opening.
7. Possible trends toward creating a limit-order "book" for OTC stocks are discussed in Section 3.3.1.
8. CATS (Computer Assisted Trading System) provides fully automated order entry (from remote terminals) and execution for about 700 inactively traded issues. An essentially similar CATS was instituted in 1982 for Tokyo's Second Section (thinner) stocks, and it was extended in 1985 to all but 250 First Section stocks. These and other automated trading systems will be discussed in Chapter 3.
9. Specialists choose to give some order-book information to floor brokers, and many orders are held by brokers in the "crowd" (at the trading posts for major stocks), so even the information monopoly cannot be said to be complete. Its effect is discussed and modeled in Section 9.2.
10. This observation may explain the finding, reported in Chapter 8, that thick Japanese stocks have lower variance, all else equal, than comparable U.S. stocks, whereas thin U.S. stocks, which are effectively stabilized by the specialist, have relatively lower variance than their Japanese counterparts.
11. See Section 2.2.2.3.
12. Floor information is necessary even to the trading strategy of a small trader who can establish a limit price independently of the market since his quantity offer depends on the equilibrium price [see Ho-Schwartz-Whitcomb (1985)]. It is even more important for traders who would expect to have a price effect on the market from their own transactions or for those who cannot set a limit price independently of what is happening in the market. The Toronto CATS and the Amsterdam Stock Exchange both seem to offer solutions which enable a batch trading system to be as "transparent" as a continuous market. In both, "indicated" prices, reflecting the orders presently on hand, are disseminated prior to the opening. This enables a trader to fine-tune his order.
13. The British Companies Act guarantees certain standards of financial practice and disclosure even among unlisted securities.
14. While bond trading in Frankfurt may be done off-exchange, a gentlemen's agreement between the banks and the stock exchange requires that the share trading be done on-exchange unless the customer specifically orders otherwise.

15. Schmidt (1977, p. 64) states that in the mid-1970s, put-throughs amounted to about 10% of London transactions by value and were growing in their use for medium-sized transactions because brokers can reduce the jobber's turn by substituting their own agent services. This is one of the natural economic factors contributing to the gradual breakdown of the once hard-and-fast distinction between jobbers and brokers.
16. Thus, for example, if the block transaction is 10,000 shares at an agreed price of 98 and there are buy limit orders on the book at 98, 99, and 100, these must be filled before the block purchase order can be filled at 98. In the United States, limit-order protection also applies among exchanges, due to ITS.
17. See New York Stock Exchange (1976).
18. Batch trading can be a stabilization device in a continuous market if traders can specify "opening only" on their trading orders so as to gain voluntarily the stabilization effects of batching (as is done in Brussels, for example).
19. We describe the situation at this writing. Soon, however, London will disseminate dealer quotes on-line, and Tokyo's CATS will probably be extended to all or nearly all First Section stocks, making it technically possible to distribute limit-order-book information off-floor.
20. On the other hand, ITS accounted for 13 to 44% of the 1983 trading volume of the regional exchanges (versus 2.4% of the NYSE's volume), so it might be said that ITS has prevented an erosion of the regional exchanges' market shares [see Davis (1985, Table II)].
21. The proportion of trade-throughs has apparently been shrinking since the ITS participant exchanges adopted an anti-trade-through rule. A recent AMEX study estimates that no more than two AMEX limit orders a day suffer this fate, on average [see Williams (1985)].
22. The EC system (called IDIS—Interbourse Data Interchange System) was scheduled to be operating by the end of 1984 with about 400 securities and eventual connections among the London, Amsterdam, Brussels, Paris, Copenhagen, Madrid, Milan, and Dublin exchanges. However, there are no plans for order routing, and the prices transmitted mean different things in different markets, as we have noted (see Lim, "Trading Stocks across Frontiers," *Euromoney*, May 1984, pp. 110–112).
23. Only in Paris are the trading hours adjusted for international securities; there, the exchange reopens at 4:00 P.M. Paris time to trade American securities during the first hour that the NYSE is open. Elsewhere in Europe, local exchange trading in American and Japanese securities occurs during the hours when the home exchanges are closed, and in Japan, trading in American and European securities likewise occurs during the dark period in the home market.
24. If the broker could not act as dealer, it could guarantee primary market protection by putting its customer's order on both the NYSE order book and its own in-house order book, withdrawing the order from the NYSE if a counterpart in-house order were received and a crossing could be made. This would be technically feasible if both broker and NYSE had fully automated order books (which would make it possible instantaneously to withdraw a duplicate order), but it would be quite expensive. The broker's gain from operating such an in-house order book would be the saving it would realize from not paying the NYSE specialist commission and facilities fee.
25. Ho-Stoll (1983) note that a dealer can estimate his rivals' "reservation fees" from

their inventory positions. Their model uses these estimates in setting the dealer's quotes.

26. In some exchanges, the order book is so thin relative to total order flow that its informational value is slight. Thus there does not appear to be substantial specialist resistance to the NYSE's planned limit-order information system.

3

ELECTRONIC TRADING AND THE STOCK EXCHANGE OF THE FUTURE

Nobody has a good track record predicting changes in the securities industry, and nobody (since Jules Verne) has done very well in guessing at technological change and its effect on society. Nevertheless, so much is happening and so much is about to happen in the securities industry that we cannot avoid discussing the technological innovations and competitive pressures that will alter the structure of stock exchanges in the future.

We are not going to describe the stock exchange of 2001. Rather, we will examine the steps toward automation that have been taken recently and seek to forecast the changes that we believe will happen sooner than many people can imagine. Our focus remains on the structure of trading systems and on the interaction between structure, technological innovation, and competitive pressure. We classify the types of automation being implemented and discuss the reasons for resistance on the part of some participants (Section 3.1), describe the major existing (and late lamented) automated trading and trade-assistance systems (Section 3.2), and consider the shape of things to come (Section 3.3).

3.1 NATURE AND LIMITATIONS OF AUTOMATION

Most exchanges use computers for on-line transaction reporting and quote dissemination (see Chapter 2), and major brokerage firms and banks use computers for securities order handling. In this chapter, we concentrate on automation in the trading process: order handling on the floor, assistance in price setting by the auctioneer or specialist, and fully automated trading. In this section, we describe these three types of automation and discuss the reasons why market participants accept or resist them.

3.1.1 Automated Order Handling on the Exchange Floor

The major securities firms in the United States and abroad have well-developed automated order-handling systems, but these generally stop at the securities firms' back offices at the exchange. Besides the fully automated CATS in Toronto and Tokyo (see Sections 3.1.3 and 3.2.1), only the U.S. exchanges have automated order-handling systems, and these are only for small orders.[1] In the U.S. systems (described in more detail in Section 3.2.3), small orders are routed electronically to the specialist's post and displayed on a screen. The specialist can then cross them against orders from his book, from the crowd, from the ITS system, or from his own account as dealer.

The various U.S. systems were created largely in response to a flood of small orders that threatened to engulf specialists, brokers, and settlement systems in a sea of clerical work and settlement errors (the so-called back-office problem). Electronic small-order routing was ultimately accepted because these orders (often called no-brain orders) were already handled in a routine manner by floor traders and because no major participant's market position was threatened by the development. The specialists retained their sole franchise on the order book and their role as dealers, the independent floor brokers kept their role as handlers of large discretionary orders, and the brokerage firms were cured of an immense headache.

By contrast, direct routing of orders from bank computers to an exchange computer is opposed by many members of the Paris Stock Exchange because it would threaten the role of the brokers who now have an exclusive franchise on floor trading.[2] Similarly, in exchanges like Frankfurt, those members who act as order clerks have a largely clerical role (unlike U.S. specialists, who also have dealership and stabilizer roles), and oppose systems that could eliminate that role.

3.1.2 Assistance in Price Setting

Several exchanges use computers to assist the auctioneer or specialist in the price-setting activity at the opening or the daily call. These systems summarize the limit orders at each price and balance them against the market orders. At the NYSE, the OARS system does this for small orders to reduce the specialist's burden at the opening. At the call in Tel Aviv, the bank traders give those orders which they have at yesterday's price to exchange keypunch operators who enter this information into the exchange computer. It is used to produce a printout which tells the official auctioneer the net balance at this price. He then calls out price adjustments and accepts additional orders verbally and takes them down by hand. Brussels goes a little further by using its computer to summarize the *par cassiers* orders at each price so as to assist the auctioneer in conducting the *à la criée* trading which modifies the written orders and arrives at the final opening price.

In general, the orders committed to these various systems are market orders and relatively small nondiscretionary limit orders which traders need not conceal or modify. Larger orders continue to be "worked" in the *à la criée* process or in the crowd.

3.1.3 Fully Automated Trading Systems

Relatively few fully automated trading systems are currently in operation. They include Toronto's and Tokyo's CATS (see Section 3.2.1 for details), the United Kingdom's ARIEL and Bermuda's INTEX (Section 3.2.2), some of the U.S. exchanges' small-order trading systems (Section 3.2.3),[3] the Cincinnati Stock Exchange's NSTS (Section 3.2.4), the NASD's SOES (Section 3.2.5), and Instinet (Section 3.2.6).

All these systems integrate order entry, price setting, and trade execution, but only the CATS concentrate all trading in a group of securities on the computer system. The others operate at the periphery of a nonautomated market, and none presently accounts for more than a fraction of the trading volume on its "primary market."

Both CATS were instituted by the stock exchanges themselves, largely in response to a severe lack of space on the exchange floors. Both have been limited to the relatively thinly traded securities listed on the exchange's "Second Section" (though Tokyo has just expanded its CATS to trade all but 250 First Section securities, and in Toronto's volatile market a CATS stock will occasionally be the daily volume leader). Each illustrates the reasons for acceptance of or resistance to automation.

Toronto's floor space problem and decision to limit CATS to thin securities led to its acceptance by floor traders and brokers, but there has been some grumbling since. Floor traders complain that entering an order on CATS is slower than it would have been on the floor. Floor traders do not complain publicly about it, but CATS has also created an open limit-order book. What this means is that CATS equalizes the access to price information and the access to the market among traders at and away from the floor. This is a common effect of automation, and it is quite natural for those losing a favored position (which they may have purchased with money and hard work) to object.

Tokyo's CATS, on the other hand, has caused negligible structural change because the order book was already open and because trading is so thin on the Second Section that presence on the floor conveyed little advantage. The only potential losers were the *saitori* (order-book clerks) and they were "bought off" by being allowed to retain a make-work role (see Section 3.2.1).

ARIEL, Instinet, INTEXT, and NSTS are entrepreneurial responses to competitive opportunity rather than the creation of a stock exchange. Because participation in each is voluntary (traders can enter and transact orders for a stock on either an automated or a nonautomated system), they offer an object lesson in the effect of system design and market forces on the attractiveness of automation. The issue faced by each is how to capture order flow in competition with a primary market and in the face of the old maxim, "order flow attracts order flow." ARIEL and NSTS have apparently not succeeded (for reasons we discuss in the next section), and it is too early to conclude anything about INTEX, but Instinet is attracting order flow (from brokerage firms and institutions) and may be poised to become a major factor in both the OTC and listed-stock markets (Section 3.3).

3.2 AUTOMATION TODAY

In this section, we discuss the alphabet soup of automated order handling and trading systems that exist today (along with one defunct system, EUREX). We take each system in turn so as to give some detail on how it works, what market(s) it aims at, and, in the case of struggling or defunct systems, what went wrong.

3.2.1 CATS

Toronto's Computer Assisted Trading System (CATS) deserves pride of place because it was the first fully automated stock exchange. Operating since 1977, CATS conducts all the Toronto Stock Exchange's trading in about 700 generally less actively traded listed issues.[4]

Structurally, CATS is a continuous-auction, order-book type of exchange (which is in some contrast to the Toronto Stock Exchange's board trading system for larger stocks). The most important details of CATS' operations are:

1. CATS trading orders (market orders, limit orders, stop-loss orders, or short-sell orders) are entered via keyboard on a CANDAT II terminal at member-firm brokerage offices or on the trading floor at the TSE. The same terminal provides a display of the limit-order book, of the history of recent trades in the issue being considered, and private information about the present order and all other orders from this terminal for the issue in question. The order-status information may also be produced in hard copy. Quite a few pieces of information must be entered and edited before the order goes into the system. Changes in an order must also go through the edit procedure. CATS is slower than verbal order entry on the exchange floor, but faster from the retail brokerage office than the usual

telephone order transmittal. Thus professional traders may lose some of their speed advantage. The fact that CATS provides the same information simultaneously to any person possessing a CANDAT II terminal further reduces professional traders' advantages.

2. A key feature of CATS is the open limit-order book, whereby anyone with a Level II terminal can see the entire limit-order book (but without trader identification). A short-form display summarizes this information, but it is also available in detail on request. A large trader may conceal any part of his order beyond 100 shares (a "board lot") at the cost that the nondisclosed part of the order goes to the end of the time priority trading queue at that price.
3. At the morning opening and following any system failure or trading halt that requires a reopening, the CATS system has a warm-up period (normally 45 minutes but shorter on occasion) during which (1) orders may be entered, and (2) the book plus an up-to-the-minute indicated price are displayed, but (3) trading is not conducted. The prices on buy orders above the current crossing price and sell orders below the current crossing price are not identified so as to preserve the anonymity of orders and to disguise the extent of acceptable deviation from the current crossing price. Time priorities are not used at the opening, so there is an incentive to wait until about the last 15 minutes before the opening before placing an order. At the opening, excess supply or demand is allocated proportionally across those orders at the opening price on the "heavy" side of the market. Around 25% of the trading occurs at the opening and about 35% during the first trading hour.
4. Following the opening, CATS goes to a continuous market-order-book transaction mode, with strict price and time priorities. The limit-order book remains open and large orders may continue to elect nondisclosure. Once the disclosed portion of a large order is executed, the trader is informed and reminded via a message on his CRT screen that the rest of the order remains undisclosed.

Since 1982, Tokyo's Second Section trading has been done on a CATS similar to Toronto's. The main difference between the two systems lies in a "Japanese solution" to the potential unemployment problem caused by automation. The *saitori* (members of the exchange who act as order-book clerks) have no role in the fully automated system, so they are given the make-work role of monitoring potential transactions for price changes exceeding the exchange's limits. In normal operation, CATS notifies the order-book clerk that it is holding up a transaction that would violate the limits, and the clerk then tells the system whether or not to permit the transaction.

Tokyo extended CATS to all but 250 of its First Section (more heavily traded) stocks in mid-1985. This gives Tokyo the greatest volume of fully automated trading of any market. There appears to be less resistance to computer trading in Japan than there is in the United States or in Toronto (so long as employment is maintained). This is probably because all orders must already go to the *saitori's* book, and mechanization does not alter anything fundamental in the trading process. The large security firms favor mechanization because they can reduce costs and use the sophisticated computer systems which they already have.

CATS may be about to spread to a third continent. The Zurich Stock Exchange is seriously studying a CATS-type system for its bond trading, and might eventually apply it to equity trading as well. Zurich bond trading generates very low on-exchange volume, so CATS will operate more as an information system at first. It is probable that Zurich's version of CATS will give best quotation prices but will not provide an open book.

3.2.2 EUREX, ARIEL, and INTEX

EUREX was an automated international Eurobond trading system that was started in 1978 in Luxembourg and went out of business at the beginning of 1981. In brief, EUREX was a market maker system. Dealers entered their bids and asks in a computer system which executed the trades. Traders (largely institutional investors or banks acting as agents on their behalf) were not allowed to have EUREX terminals and entered their limit orders (market orders were not permitted) by telex. The limit orders would execute against the best counterpart market maker quotation, if any.

Several structural aspects of EUREX are of particular interest:

1. EUREX was not an open limit-order book. Bid-ask quotations and depth information were not available to traders, who had to put in their limit orders without knowledge of whether they would execute. The interesting feature of this is that a trader could get a better price than his limit price since the market makers also operated in the dark and could not see the traders' limit prices. This would appear to be an attempt to mimic some aspects of the telephone system.
2. Market makers' orders were put in only when a quotation was requested rather than being put in and left until altered or canceled.
3. There was a complex procedure for large orders: the market maker with the best quotation received confirmation data (i.e., the identification of the limit-order maker and the quantity of the order) when his quotation "crossed" a block limit order, and he could then revise his quotation away from the market or make a deal for one round lot only. He would "win" the full order so long as he continued to satisfy the limit price on the block order and his own quotation remained better than the average of the other market makers' quotations.[5]

The reasons cited for the failure of EUREX are: (1) There were too few market makers (banks) outside of Luxembourg willing to take part. (2) Unlike CATS, EUREX was not part of an exchange and had to capture its order flow from a competing telephone market. (3) EUREX was designed to work best with small orders, but there were not enough small orders. We would add: (4) The order entry procedure was inefficient, probably eliminating much of the potential advantage of automation. (5) The system provided poor price information to subscribers. (6) Aiming a computer system at a telephone market is a tough nut to crack and probably accounts for (1). It appears to be better to start with a guaranteed flow of small orders, and try to capture some large orders as well, rather than to focus exclusively on large orders.

ARIEL is a London-based computer block-trading system started by several major institutional investors in 1974. ARIEL is registered as a "licensed dealer in securities" to trade any issue traded on the stock exchange that justifies ARIEL trading by its volume and institutional interest; its share of the total London volume in those securities traded on ARIEL is about 2%. ARIEL was founded in part for the purpose of bluffing the stock exchange into lowering its commissions. The bluff worked, but it was too late; the stock exchange waited until ARIEL had bought its computer and installed its software and then lowered its commissions so as to reduce ARIEL's potential market share.

ARIEL commissions are lower than stock exchange commissions and there is no jobber's turn. However, no market makers operate in ARIEL (although they can), the stock exchange does not allow its members to use ARIEL, and the Bank of England does not permit ARIEL to be used for government-bond transactions. On balance, the negative factors outweigh the positive, and ARIEL's effect on the London securities market has been minor.

The latest entry in the automation sweepstakes is Bermuda's International Futures Exchange, INTEX, which opened in October 1984. INTEX is the world's first fully automated futures exchange. Instead of a trading pit, a Vax computer in Bermuda (assisted by others in London and Virginia) crosses orders sent from terminals in subscribers' offices in the United States and elsewhere. The terminals display the current bid-ask prices and unfilled limit orders within a range around the bid and ask (e.g., $2 for the gold contract).

Bermuda was chosen as much for its relaxed regulatory climate as for its international location partway between the two main centers of futures trading. INTEX is not without its problems. As of the end of 1984, only about 200 to 300 contracts per day were trading on INTEX, and the commission rate was higher than on many traditional futures exchanges. However, execution (when counterpart demand is sufficient for it to occur) is very rapid, and the total cost of a transaction may compare favorably with that on traditional exchanges. It is too early to write off the claim of INTEX chairman, George Grummer: "Everybody in the industry knows that the traditional system of trading futures by open outcry and hand signal is growing increasingly unworkable and that sooner or later the exchanges will have to move into the Twentieth Century or face a complete breakdown."[6]

3.2.3 Automation in the U.S. Stock Exchanges

In recent years, the U.S. stock exchanges have introduced a variety of electronic order-routing and information systems with acronyms that would make the DOD (Department of Defense) proud: OARS, DOT, R4, AUTOPER, SCOREX, MAX, PACE, LOIS (now known, less poetically, as the display book), and ITS. The reason for the variety lies in the unspoken strategy of the exchanges: Don't try to automate the entire trading process at once (à la CATS), because that would inevitably alter the trading structure (and probably hurt some important member constituencies). Rather, automate small-order (round lots under about 1000 shares) routing, quotation display, and trade reporting/settlement, because these are the areas where automation will reduce costs and errors without altering the roles of floor traders and specialists.

Consistent with this strategy, the NYSE has three separate small-order routing systems. OARS has already been introduced; it assembles small market orders before the opening, letting the specialist work with just the net in setting the opening price. DOT (Designated Order Turnaround) further reduces the specialist's burden by routing small orders to his post during the trading day and handling most details of order execution with minimal specialist input. R4 (Registered Representative Rapid Response) allows brokers to give their clients immediate execution at the consolidated (ITS) quotes on small market orders up to 599 shares of certain stocks. Once an order is entered on a broker's terminal, execution at the counterpart quote is guaranteed (although reporting of the counterpart's execution may have to be initiated manually).[7] R4 may be viewed as a competitive response by the NYSE to similar systems initiated by the regional exchanges and Instinet.

Perhaps the most interesting exchange-based automation system is the Pacific Stock Exchange's SCOREX. A market order sent to the Pacific for a stock included in SCOREX is guaranteed execution within 30 seconds at the consolidated inside quotes on ITS (the lowest asked or the highest bid on any of the U.S. exchanges or OTC). SCOREX also automatically reports the trade and initiates clearance, imposes no specialist or floor brokerage fees, and will be linked to a broker's computer system free of charge. SCOREX is an attempt by the Pacific to attract order flow from the NYSE by offering fast, error-free execution at a price that can never be worse.[8] It has induced other exchanges to respond with similar systems (the NYSE's R4, Philadelphia's PACE, and Midwestern's MAX). It is an antidote to Autoquote (which enables regional specialists to link their quotes to primary market quotes and avoid competition by setting their own quotes "away"). On the other hand, although the regional exchanges do offer competition to the NYSE, only small orders are transacted (for example, PACE accepts only orders for less than 600 shares), and the regional exchange specialist frequently "lays off" any resulting order imbalance by making a trade on the NYSE via ITS.

The AMEX has recently entered the high-tech sweepstakes with its own small-order routing and semiautomatic execution system, AUTOPER. An order routed to the specialist's post via AUTOPER is displayed on a touch screen and triggers an acoustic signal. The system guesses the most likely transaction price, and the specialist touches the screen to confirm or correct the price and initiate execution. As with the NYSE's systems, reporting the counterpart execution must be initiated manually (since the counterpart may be the specialist, an order on the book, or an order in the crowd), and a mark sense card must be filled out to report the transaction to the tape and the settlement system.

One area where automation has been slow in coming is the limit-order book. The NYSE has had a limit-order-book information system, LOIS, on the drawing boards for some years, and a pilot version, called the display book, is now operational for a few heavily traded stocks. In the current version, orders coming to the specialist on the NYSE's various automated systems and orders delivered to him by hand are displayed on a screen at the specialist's post. The specialist can execute a displayed order against his own account or for a floor trader by making a keyboard entry. This is the forerunner of a possible open limit-order book, although presently the information is available only to the specialist and orders held by members of the crowd are not included. Like SCOREX, an open limit-order book has the capacity to bring about real structural change.

We have discussed ITS in some detail in Chapter 2. Here we need only add that, while ITS routes orders from the originating exchange to the market with the best price, its interface with any exchange's own order-handling systems is strictly manual. This severely limits the ability of ITS to network the markets and gives impetus to approaches like SCOREX and Instinet's Designated Market Maker (Section 3.2.6).

3.2.4 The Cincinnati Stock Exchange of Jersey City

As one of the smaller regional stock exchanges, the Cincinnati had only one thing going for it: members of the NYSE could cross agency orders against their dealer inventory on the Cincinnati without violating NYSE Rule 390. In order to parley this modest advantage into something really useful to the major broker-dealer firms, the Cincinnati started an experiment in fully automated trading, called the National Securities Trading System (NSTS) in 1978. This experiment has not strictly failed, but neither has it exactly succeeded. NSTS's share of consolidated volume in the stocks it handles fell from 2 to 0.6% between 1978 and 1983 and Merrill Lynch, its major backer and source of order flow, backed out in April 1983.[9] The reasons are subtle and instructive.

NSTS is much like CATS in its basic design. A central computer (located in Jersey City, New Jersey) maintains the limit-order book, and remote terminals are used by brokers and dealers to enter orders and receive trade reports. Like CATS, price and time priorities are in force, and the order book is completely open. Unlike CATS, however, NSTS operates at the periphery of a primary market, trying to attract order flow away from that market.

Why has NSTS failed to attract increasing order flow? Part of the answer lies in ITS. It should be a major source of order flow for NSTS since dealer or agency limit orders on the NSTS book are exposed on ITS (and now that Merrill Lynch has left NSTS, ITS does account for about 40% of NSTS orders). However, even the "black box" NSTS has a manual linkage to ITS. Because NSTS has a small order book compared to the NYSE, an order sent to NSTS will probably have to be routed (manually) through ITS to the NYSE or another market. Most brokers, even those with NSTS terminals, apparently feel that it is easier and surer to route the order to the NYSE in the first place; there, if the order is small and the NYSE makes the market, as is likely, the order will be executed rapidly in the NYSE's semiautomated systems. Large orders are even less likely to be routed to NSTS. If you are not sitting at an NSTS terminal, you cannot get "size away from market" (number of shares for which counterpart demand exists at prices other than the particular marketplace's best bid or ask) information from ITS, so you would almost certainly send your large order to the NYSE.

Another part of the answer may lie in the fact that although NSTS is (in part) a dealer market, it effectively discriminates against dealer orders, since agency orders are given priority over dealer orders at the same price. This may have contributed to Merrill's decision to withdraw.

Finally, NSTS has been unable to overcome the inherent disadvantage faced by a small order pool competing in a (somewhat) fragmented market against a large pool. As we discuss in Chapter 8, if a small and a large order pool exist side by side without a linkage that satisfies price *and time* priorities, the probability of execution for a limit order coming into the small pool is lower. Unless the small pool can offer compensating advantages or a creative solution to the pool-size problem, it will remain a small pool.

3.2.5 SOES, Son of CAES, Out of NASDAQ by NASD

Paradoxically, the OTC market has benefited the most by automation, but it is still the least automated of the U.S. stock markets. The benefit comes from the National Association of Securities Dealers' (NASD) Automated Quotation (AQ) system, which deserves most of the credit for the rapid rise of the OTC to the second spot among U.S. stock markets.[10] What NASDAQ has done is to create a single market where before there was fragmentation. OTC dealers enter their quotes on a NASDAQ level III terminal, the quotes are ordered by a central computer, and are displayed to brokers (with dealer ID) on a level II terminal.[11]

This process makes it easy for brokers to find the best quote. However, brokers still have to make the transaction by telephone (except in SOES), there is no public-limit-order book, and size is not generally disclosed.

Since 1982, the most actively traded and heavily capitalized OTC stocks have been labeled NASDAQ-NMS (National Market System). Unlike regular OTC stocks, the dealer must report the price and transaction size within 90 seconds of a transaction. Thus, an on-line transaction record is created, which can be accessed from NASDAQ and other terminals. In late 1984, it was expected that the SEC would approve an NASD proposal to increase the number of securities eligible for NMS status to more than 2200 (despite vociferous objections by the exchanges to the NASD's use of the phrase "National Market System").[12]

For Rule 19c-3 NMS stocks (stocks listed on an exchange after April 1979 and also traded OTC), the NASD has created CAES (Computer Assisted Execution System). CAES allows orders to be transmitted to dealers directly through NASDAQ terminals with confirmations printed out at each end. It is not fully automated, because the dealer must accept the transaction, and volume is presently small (the NYSE gets most 19c-3 order flow).

And now comes SOES, son of CAES, etc. The Small Order Execution System started up in December 1984 with 25 actively traded NMS stocks and expanded to around 1900 issues by mid-1985. Unlike CAES, which requires the dealer to accept each transaction, SOES automatically executes orders up to 500 shares. This requires dealers to guarantee to buy or sell at least 500 shares (rather than the usual 100) at their quotes, a change they would have had to make anyway as a competitive response to SCOREX and Instinet.

3.2.6 Instinet

For the past 15 years, Institutional Networks, Inc., as its name implies, has operated an electronic block-trading system for institutions (mutual funds, pension funds, and bank trust departments). Like ARIEL (which uses Instinet's software, under licensing agreement), Instinet limped along, neither succeeding nor failing. However, starting in 1983, Instinet introduced a series of innovations which will greatly strengthen its position and which will likely lead the stock exchanges and the OTC market into competitive responses that will transform the structure of trading.

To understand Instinet's operations, it helps to have a look at one of its terminals. The screen is divided into five segments. Across the top run updated system trade reports and messages relating to negotiations under way from the terminal. Immediately below is another strip reporting the most recent limit orders entered into the system and last sale data for the stocks the user is currently following. At the bottom of the screen is another strip reporting general market information (e.g., indexes). The main part of the screen is divided into the market montage (left) and the Instinet order book (right), each for whichever security the user selects among the 4700 currently in the system. The market montage gives on-line the inside quotes and size in each of the eight U.S. markets on which a stock might be traded and the time since the quote was last updated. The Instinet order book gives the price, size, and time entered (but *not* the maker) of each limit order consigned to Instinet and arrays them in decreasing price order. Instinet terminals are in use at about 80 financial institutions and about 200 broker-dealers and regional exchange specialists.[13]

The most striking innovation at Instinet is automated small-order execution via Instinet Designated Market Makers. These are specialists at the Pacific and Boston stock exchanges and OTC market makers who are willing to guarantee execution within 30 seconds at the best inside spread on any market for orders up to 1000 shares (for about 1700 exchange-listed and 3000 NASDAQ-quoted securities).[14] Thus, a brokerage firm can offer its client guaranteed execution (and get an immediate printed confirmation) on orders larger than will be accepted by the small-order execution systems of the exchanges and the NASD, and at prices that can be better.

This innovation has led four major retail brokerage firms, Merrill Lynch, E.F. Hutton, Dean Witter Reynolds, and Shearson/American Express to become major shareholders in Instinet, to use it as a conduit for retail orders, and to use it to make a market for OTC and 19c-3 stocks.[15] In addition, a number of banks have begun using Instinet as a discount broker in their retail stock brokerage ventures, largely for reasons of cost and execution speed, and the CBOE has begun using instinet as a route for its market makers to place their stock trading orders and obtain pricing information.[16]

It is important to note that the small-order execution service is a completely new role for Instinet. It is no longer solely an alternative stock exchange for institutions; now it is also a broker's broker, routing orders efficiently to the best market and enlivening the competition among markets. In Section 3.3, we examine how the two roles may interact in the future, strengthening the alternative stock exchange role and changing the way some markets (particularly the OTC) operate.

3.3 THE SHAPE OF THINGS TO COME

A pattern seems to be emerging from the developments we surveyed in Section 3.2. In a nutshell it is (1) complete and integrated automation of small-order trading; (2) transformation of the structure of the OTC market and possibly of the exchange markets; (3) automated, round-the-clock international trading; and (4) after these other developments have occurred, much more use of automation (but still of the interactive kind) in block trading.

The greatest uncertainty in this emerging pattern relates to the competitive responses of market participants. The nature of these responses will determine the basic structure of trading, as we shall point out. What is certain is that the structure is changing, and changing fast.

3.3.1 An Automated and Transformed OTC Market

The most immediate effect of the NASD's SOES and of Instinet's small-order execution service is to increase the apparent size at the inside spread (from 100 shares to 1000 and soon to more as competing market makers respond to the Instinet Designated Market Maker). This can increase the total order flow to the OTC market (as the introduction of NASDAQ has done so spectacularly). Nearly as immediate is a diversion of order flow from telephone lines to automated order entry-display-execution systems such as Instinet.[17]

Now consider the effect an increased flow of OTC market orders has on the automated system's internal limit-order book. Each market order routed through the automated system passes by this limit-order book, and if a limit order equals or betters the inside quote on the external market, it captures the market order. Thus is created a limit-order book for OTC stocks. Investors who trade listed stocks by limit order but who hitherto could not effectively use limit orders on the OTC market (because only dealer orders are exposed on NASDAQ) now find that their limit orders can be exposed to a significant and growing portion of OTC order flow and can be advertised (via terminals) to potential investors.[18] This enables individuals and institutions to compete with dealers in making the market, just as they do with listed stocks.

There is more. The OTC market now has so much volume that the lack of an organized opening bothers brokers. It would be a simple matter to use an electronic book to open the OTC market the way CATS does in Toronto or Tokyo: assemble preopening limit orders and market orders, include market maker quotes (treated just like any other limit order), and transmit on-line the indicated opening price (or the whole limit-order book) right up to the opening. This would let investors know the prices at which their orders are likely to be executed[19] and make it possible to "work" large orders (i.e., put them onto the market in pieces to discover if counterpart demand exists). Such an opening procedure would greatly increase the volume that can be handled and that would be offered at the opening.

This sounds very much like a stock exchange, and it raises another possibility: Might an existing stock exchange (particularly one struggling for survival in a very competitive environment) not find it desirable to trade OTC stocks in a second-tier unlisted market? A stock exchange has certain competitive advantages, namely an opening procedure and a limit-order book. If these were combined with automated trading, guaranteed execution of small orders at the quotes, and participation of specialists as market makers (but not as affirmative obligation stabilizers—see Chapter 9), a "hungry" exchange might give the NASD a run for its money. We know of no exchange *planning* this, but they *are* aware of the possibility.[20]

Will the other OTC dealers sit back and let a stock exchange or the dealers acting as Designated Marker Makers in a system such as Instinet capture the order flow? Probably not. Dealers will respond by disclosing their own size so that brokers using NASDAQ will know the price at which their telephone orders for more than 100 shares will be transacted. Some dealers may join competing systems (such as those announced by Troster Singer Stevens Rothchild and Transactions Services). Quotes will be forced nearer the market as investors increasingly refuse to let a broker-dealer execute at his "off the market" quote.[21] The NASD has already responded with SOES and may have to respond further. The point is that there will be competitive responses in the OTC market, though no one can predict their exact nature.

Will a limit-order book of critical mass result? The answer depends on how competition develops among automated order entry-display-execution systems. If a single system with an internal limit-order book emerges, there will be a large enough flow of orders past the book to make it attractive for many traders to use limit orders. If multiple systems coexist (or if SOES, with no limit-order book, dominates), only dealer quotations will be exposed to the entire market. Essentially, the issue is one of fragmentation: once OTC limit orders become technically feasible, it matters (for reasons we develop in Chapter 8) whether they enter a common pool or multiple pools. In the long run, if multiple systems do emerge and survive, there will likely be competitive and regulatory pressures for them to link their limit-order books so as to eliminate fragmentation.

We cannot predict the outcome of the competitive struggle over OTC order flow and we cannot be sure that an integrated limit-order book of critical mass will develop quickly. However, it does seem certain that the OTC market will rapidly become highly automated and, in the long run, more like a stock exchange.

3.3.2 A Network of Stock Exchanges or an Empty Shell?

A few years ago, Wall Street was all in a dither about Rule 19c-3, and we [CMSW (1982)] were among those who feared that in-house trading might fragment the listed-stock markets before it replaced the exchanges with a network of broker-dealer automated trading systems. Now we know that multiple in-house order queues exact too high a price of participants (see Chapter 8) and that most of the integrated broker-dealer firms that once made an in-house market using their own computer systems or the Cincinnati Stock Exchange's NSTS no longer do so.

Some of these broker-dealers may have found a better way. As we reported in Section 3.2.6, four major retail brokers have begun using Instinet to make a market for 19-c3 stocks. Why are they willing, in effect, to put their own-account (principal) limit orders on a book so much smaller than that of the NYSE or the AMEX? The reason would seem to be that they expect Instinet to be successful in attracting a large flow of market orders passing its limit-order book on the way to regional exchanges or upstairs market makers; hence orders at the market on that book could execute quickly.[22] This market-order flow is likely to be especially heavy for 19c-3 stocks because its source would be integrated broker-dealers. Thus the threat that 19c-3 poses to the exchanges has not been eliminated by the NSTS's lack of success; it has just been moved to a newer and more dangerous arena. No longer is the linkage to the rest of the market a manual connection to an ITS unable to guarantee execution in size. Now the broker who wants to cross agency orders in-house or against his principal inventory can offer his market-order customer guaranteed execution at the inside market and his limit-order customer faster and more likely execution.

Under this scenario, the NYSE could lose substantial market-order flow to the regional exchanges for non-19c-3 stocks and to its own members using an automated order entry-display-execution system such as Instinet to make a market in 19c-3 stocks. (Over time, the balance will shift as more issues become subject to 19c-3.) Then it could find its limit-order book losing attractiveness to that of the competing automated system. The same would be happening to the AMEX (if the OTC does not get it first!). Next the specialists would lack the commission revenues and whatever information value they derive from the limit-order book to justify affirmative obligation stabilization (see Chapter 9), and they would shed that role. The exchanges would be left as an arena for crowd trading to the extent that this is an effective way of handling discretionary orders (for blocks, etc.; see Section 3.3.5).

How likely is this scenario? The exchanges, and particularly the NYSE, have a lot more going for them in the struggle for order flow than do OTC dealers. The exchanges already have an opening procedure, they have experience in automated small-order handling, and they offer a limit-order book. A lot depends on whether multiple automated order entry-display-execution systems end up coexisting (without linked order books). If so, the NYSE will probably retain its advantage of faster limit-order execution, and the integrated broker-dealers' 19c-3 trading experiments will have failed again.

3.3.3 Are Home Computers Just for Video Games?

Ever since the home computer became the hottest ticket on the current scene, observers have been predicting that it would revolutionize stock trading. Let us examine the possibilities.

Already personal computers (PCs) routinely access real-time quotations and "fundamental" information banks, and (in some cases) route orders to brokers through software programs marketed by discount brokers (e.g., Fidelity and C.D. Anderson & Co.[23]) and information services (e.g., Dow Jones). It is by connecting home order entry with an automated order entry-display-execution system that the home computer will have its greatest impact. Simply delivering orders to a broker is not enough; accessing all market information and executing trades instantaneously (or entering limit orders) where *and when* you want is the name of the game.

When is important, because the home computer will help catalyze the demand for an off-hours market. Elements of the demand already exist: Market makers often end the trading day with a considerable (long or short) inventory which they would like to lay off (and sometimes do in the informal overnight market).[24] Asian and European investors do their local market trading in U.S. stocks when our markets are dark; U.S. share prices on foreign markets depend heavily on what the U.S. market did or is expected to do, and an off-hours U.S. market would generate a real arbitrage flow. And there is a whole universe of foreign securities out there trading in their primary markets while we are sleeping or brushing our teeth in the morning.[25]

Key questions are: Who will use the home computer? Will there be a role for brokers? and Will exchanges or off-exchange trading system get the business?

To the first question, the answer is probably the market pros, bringing their work home with them. Most traders would really like to trade 25 hours a day, especially if anyone else out there might be stealing a march on them. There may also be a market among business people who find it less disruptive to check the market and trade from a terminal than from a phone.

The *minimum* role for brokers is one of reducing agency costs by providing a credit check and a trading limit so that counterparts can count on a quote being firm and a transaction being honored. Advice, custody, and the execution of discretionary orders are optional services that will continue to be unbundled. Whether all these services will be performed by the current brokerage firms or by banks is a question people in the financial services industry are betting billions on.

Whether the exchanges will get the order flow depends on its timing (as well as on the issues we discussed in Section 3.3.2). Off-hours trading of domestic and foreign stocks is much more likely to develop as a computer-brokered exchange among market makers, block positioners, and investors than as something in which the exchange floor and exchange trading systems have a useful role. To see why, we must take a more careful look at international trading.

3.3.4 International Trading

Right now, there is no such thing as an international stock market. Most stocks are traded principally on their home exchange and are held largely by their own nationals.[26] When a person (or institution) wants to buy a foreign stock, he (or it) faces the poor choice between buying on a thin domestic market (if the stock is even traded there) or telling a broker to buy on the stock's home market with little access to price information or ability to monitor the transaction. This is as true for an Englishman or a Japanese as for an American, and it is no wonder that international diversification is more theory than practice.

This situation is about to change under the simultaneous pressure of five developments. First, there has been a massive increase in international capital flows, largely in short-term debt but more recently in equities. For example, U.S. institutional holdings of foreign equities are estimated to have increased from \$1–2 billion to \$10–12 billion over the past decade.[27] Second, American brokerage firms and banks are beginning to compete aggressively in key foreign markets (for U.S. orders for foreign stocks and foreign orders for U.S. stocks).[28] Third, several U.S. exchanges have announced trading linkages with foreign exchanges or U.S. exchanges in another time zone, all with the purpose of expanding international trading on (rather than off) the U.S. exchange.[29] Fourth, the two most important foreign markets are undergoing major structural change (Tokyo with its CATS being extended to First Section trading and London with competitive commission rates and foreign competition bringing about a competing dealer market with automated quotations and someday automated trading). Finally, the technical feasibility of instantaneous automated international trading has been demonstrated and, in conjunction with the first four developments, will encourage international trading and may even lead to an international around-the-clock stock market.

There are several distinct actual or potential international-trading markets involving Americans and our automated trading systems. The most straightforward is the demand among foreigners to buy leading listed U.S. securities during prime U.S. trading hours. This is now done largely by phone or telex through U.S. brokers' foreign offices. The connections are not always instantaneous, and the advantage of an instantaneous locked-in transaction (via satellite through a U.S. broker abroad using an integrated order entry-display-execution system) is considerable. Instinet has announced an agreement with Reuters to do just that.[30]

A closely related market is the (potential) off-hours demand for the same U.S. securities. The importance of this market is increased by the practice of European banks of netting orders for U.S. stocks throughout the European day before sending the net to the United States (Section 2.3.2.1). This netting could be upset if a viable off-hours market for U.S. stocks existed.[31] As we said in Section 3.3.3, the home computer trading demand may be the catalyst that brings together off-hours market maker demand and foreign demand to actualize this market. The stock exchange would have to be a computer because volume would initially be too small to justify opening an exchange floor. The same system used by American brokers' foreign offices to bring orders to the U.S. exchange market during its trading day could make an off-hours market.

OTC stocks comprise another, completely untapped market that has no competition from foreign stock exchanges. It would be a relatively simple matter for a firm such as Instinet to tie its terminals into a satellite transmission system and offer its automated small-order execution service abroad.[32] To provide adequate depth for foreign orders, trading would have to be done during U.S. trading hours (beginning midafternoon, European time). It is a fair bet that European volume would be concentrated at the opening if an opening procedure is organized (Section 3.3.1).

A final market, of considerable potential size, but with greater startup difficulty, is the flow of orders from U.S. residents and institutions for foreign securities. The U.S. exchanges have found it difficult to tap this market for two reasons: (1) relatively few foreign companies are willing to disclose the amount of information in the format required for SEC approval of U.S. exchange listing; and (2) most of the few foreign stocks listed in the United States trade in such thin markets that orders are more likely to be attracted to the home market, despite poor information. A potential solution to the second problem is to make the securities perfectly substitutable (as opposed to having an ADR trade here and a regular share trade abroad). This would make it possible for an investor to buy securities in one market and sell them in another without excessive transaction cost (as can now be done in the CMS-SIMEX and Philadelphia-London futures linkages; see note 29), but it would require an international clearance-settlement arrangement that does not yet exist. It will be interesting to see whether such a settlement system is created first by a multilateral agreement among stock exchanges or by one or more international banks.

The U.S. order flow for foreign securities is a market that can be captured by an automated order entry-display-execution system because it gets around the two difficulties cited: the SEC cannot object to an American using Instinet (say) rather than Nomura Securities' Telex line to send orders to the Tokyo Stock Exchange for a Japanese stock; and the order would be transacted in the liquid home market. Automated display and execution would be made possible by a software linkage (in the Tokyo office of a firm with a seat on the Tokyo Stock Exchange), enabling a broker or investor in Des Moines to bring up the CATS order book in place of the usual market montage on his terminal or PC and to watch his order execute (or if it is a limit order, to "make the market"). Similarly, once London has its automated quotation system (1986), it would be straightforward for a London member firm to act as Designated Market Maker at the best quotes for a U.S.-based automated order entry-display-execution system, just as OTC dealers and regional specialists do now.

It is not clear at this point which model of international equities trading will come to pass: perfectly substitutable securities trading on several stock exchanges around the world, each dominating in its normal time slot, or trading and settlement concentrated in each security's home market, with off-exchange off-hours trading (but not settlement) shifting abroad when the home market is dark.

3.3.5 Automated Block Trading

To date, automation has been a minor (but not trivial) force in block trading, and many think it will stay that way. Telephone block trading (Section 2.3.3) is the dominant mode and may seem to be an effective way to deal with the problem of market power (price pressure).[33] There are reasons to believe that this may change, however.

Most important is the tremendous increase we can expect in the flow of market orders past the internal limit-order book (presently consisting mainly of institutional block orders) on automated order entry-display-execution systems. As we explained (Section 3.3.2), this will increase the probability and expected speed of transactions on the book and will attract smaller limit orders and make it easier for blocks to be dealt.

Once a healthy limit-order book exists, block traders can adapt a technique that they use to advantage in the open calls (*à la criée*) in Paris and elsewhere for use with automated trading systems. This is to put part of the block on the book (anonymously), see if counterpart demand emerges, and then put more on. Such a technique can be used effectively at the opening in a continuous auction exchange if indicated prices or an open book are available. (This is why the specialist gives the crowd some order-book information at the opening.) In the long run, automated trading systems probably offer a richer mixture of the market information and the anonymity necessary for block trading than either the crowd or the telephone.

3.4 CONCLUSION

Automation, particularly in small-order handling, has come rapidly to U.S. stock exchanges, the OTC market, and the various off-exchange markets made by dealers and institutions. So far, its main impact seems to have been on the mechanics, rather than on the basic structure of trading. However, there is reason to believe that in the next few years automated trading will begin to have a powerful effect on the fundamental operation of our market system.

Among the *likely* (though by no means certain) effects are: rising market shares going to the once-nearly-moribund regional exchanges, development of an effective limit-order book for unlisted securities, increased "dealerization" of the listed-equities markets by major brokerage firms, and huge volumes of small public orders passing through automated institutional trading systems on their way to dealers and exchange specialists.

The *possible* (though harder to predict and sometimes mutually inconsistent) effects include: trading in unlisted securities on stock exchanges and private automated trading systems in competition with OTC dealers, fragmentation of the market for listed equities, automated international small-order trading, and radically increased use of automated trading systems by institutions.

There will probably not be *a* stock exchange of the future. The picture that emerges is one of intensive competition among trading systems that are mostly well equipped to survive into the twenty-first century. Indeed, automation's most likely impact is to increase the number of competitors by adding private trading systems to the mix and strengthening some of the regional exchanges rather than to force all trading into a single Big Black Box. It remains to be seen whether fragmentation will be the price for this diversity.

NOTES

1. Since 1973, the Frankfurt Stock Exchange has had the capability of routing orders directly through the banks' computer systems onto the computer at the order clerk's post on the exchange floor, but the system has not been implemented. Both Tel Aviv and Paris have officially studied direct routing of orders from bank computers to an exchange computer, but at this writing neither proposal has been implemented.
2. In France, most investor trading orders are initially given to banks, which pass them on to floor brokers. The direct bank–stock exchange computer link (proposed by the banks) could thus enable the banks to bypass the brokers. Although the banks propose to retain a broker role by entering a broker's identification number along with each order so that the broker can get his commission, the brokers rightly recognize that such a system reduces their potential economic role and that at some future time the political agreement by which they get financial credit for work they do not do may be eliminated.
3. The automated systems in operation at the U.S. exchanges deal with only a portion (small orders) of the order flow coming to the exchange. In addition, in some cases, parts of the order execution–trade reporting process must be initiated manually. Hence these are not all "black box" systems. Note that the precise definition of a "small" order varies from one trading subsystem within an exchange to another. Generally, the small-order trading subsystems deal with *round lots* of under 600 shares or 1000 shares and under. Increasingly, however, "small" orders will come to mean any order for less than block size (10,000 shares).
4. Many of these issues are cross-listed on other Canadian exchanges (e.g., Montreal and Vancouver). Reportedly, CATS has been gaining an increasing proportion of trading volume in these cross-listed issues. Like "small" order, "less actively traded" cannot be quantified precisely, since the initial standards for inclusion in CATS were not defined on volume alone; on a given day, CATS stock may have substantial trading volume.
5. The question could be raised: Why not let the "winning" market maker say how much he would take at his quotation, make a deal for that part of the limit order which he will accept at his quotation, and then let him revise his quotation, giving the next part of the limit order to whichever market maker now has the best quotation? The answer is that each market maker's quotation depends on how much other marker makers on the same side of the market have bought or sold, so it would be necessary to let all market makers revise their quotations after each partial deal, with knowledge of those deals made earlier. If the other market makers could not revisc their quotations, a block order could tick off round lots over several market makers before any could revise their quotations; this would force the market to absorb too much at one time before it could react. This is consistent with the fact that traders in the telephone market try to find a single buyer rather than splitting an order in rapid deals of one or a few lots each to many market makers. If a trader did the latter, the market makers would feel "taken" and the trader would lose his credibility.
6. H. J. Maidenberg, "Automation in Trading," *The New York Times*, December 10, 1984, p. 30.
7. Before R4, a market order might occasionally be executed inside the quotes (i.e., at

a better price). The SEC has expressed concern that this possibility has been traded off for speed of execution. (See Securities Exchange Act Release No. 19858, June 9, 1983.) The NYSE has opposed, on grounds of efficiency, the SEC's suggestion that a stop procedure be added to provide a mechanism for R4 orders to interact with other interests on the exchange floor.

8. The regional exchanges have succeeded in attracting a larger share (now 30%) of under-3000-share-size transactions in NYSE-listed stocks (see "The Big Board's Fight to Stay on Top," *The New York Times*, October 14, 1984, p. F12).
9. The NSTS statistics in this subsection are from Davis (1985).
10. The OTC is third in the world in 1983 dollar volume ($188 billion) after the NYSE ($765 billion) and Tokyo ($235 billion). It is ahead of London ($42 billion), Zurich ($38 billion), West Germany ($34 billion), AMEX ($30 billion), and Paris ($12 billion) *combined*. These figures and some information on CAES and SOES are from Wall (1985).
11. To be allowed to participate in NASDAQ, a dealer must meet minimum capital requirements, maintain firm bid-ask quotes (for at least 100 shares) "not too far away from the market," and report daily trading volume. A NASD rule seeks to keep broker-dealers from executing customer orders at a price more than 5% inferior to the inside quote.
12. See "SEC Expected to Back Major Expansion of OTC Stocks' National Market System," *The Wall Street Journal*, November 16, 1984.
13. Institutional Networks Corp, *Annual Report 1984*, pp. 4, 5.
14. To see how this works, consider a stock on which the inside market is 25 1/2–26 (100 shares both ways). Suppose that Shearson/American Express is the Instinet Designated Market Maker with NASDAQ quotes of 25 1/4–26 1/4. If a market buy order comes in on Instinet, Shearson must sell up to 1000 shares at 26. If it has no inventory or wishes to lay off, it must buy, and may have to pay more than 26 for some shares.
15. Other OTC and "upstairs" market makers include Sherwood Securities, Carl Marks & Co., Sheppards & Chase, Drexel Burnham Lambert, New York and Foreign Securities, and the U.K. firm, Smith Bros.
16. Institutional transaction costs on Instinet range from 3 to 9 cents per share (depending on size) with an upper limit of $2300 per month per terminal, and retail costs are at or below those of discount brokers. Bank employees execute the transactions themselves from a terminal without intermediate telephone contact with a brokerage firm order taker. (See S. McMurray, "Instinet Offers Banks Automated Low-Cost Stock Execution Service," *American Banker*, March 8, 1983.) The Instinet-CBOE relationship was reported in the *Wall Street Journal*, December 11, 1984, p. 50; this article also mentioned an agreement giving CBOE an option (appropriately) to purchase some Instinet shares and warrants and to undertake some joint product-development intiatives.
17. The published Instinet volume is misleading because it comprises only the trades from the internal limit-order book (i.e., it includes only "alternative stock exchange" volume but not "brokerage" volume). If all orders passing through Instinet are included, volumes up to 5,000,000 shares per day have been recorded by mid-1984.

18. A simple programming step would automatically send up to 1000 shares of such an internal limit order to the external market whenever a counterpart quote matches it. Thus, there need be no danger of trade-throughs.
19. Knowing (or having a good estimate of) the transaction price increases the "consumer surplus" of (even atomistic) investors, which makes them more likely to seek to trade stocks or in markets for which the information is available [see Ho-Schwartz-Whitcomb (1985)].
20. Two of us recommended such a move to the NYSE in 1981 [see Ho-Schwartz-Whitcomb (1981)], and a senior AMEX official has mentioned the possibility in print [see Williams (1985)].
21. Note, though, that some dealers will always quote away from the market on the side where they wish to reduce inventory; see Ho-Stoll (1983) or Amihud-Mendelson (1980).
22. Framed in terms of the model of Chapter 8, we are saying that when the smaller limit-order pool faces a proportionately heavier flow of market orders, a limit order placed "at the market" in the smaller pool may actually enjoy a higher probability of transacting and a faster execution time than a similar order in the larger pool.
23. Anderson's Trade*Plus includes on-line quotes, stock execution, portfolio management, and tax-planning menus (see *Securities Week*, July 4, 1983, p. 4). Fidelity's system, "Investor's Express," which takes orders but does not execute automatically, was introduced in mid-1984. Merrill Lynch is also working with IBM (under a joint venture named International Market Net) on a sophisticated multifeatured software program for the IBM PC which will be linked to Instinet when it is completed in late 1985 (*The Wall Street Journal*, April 11, 1984, p. 40, and Institutional Networks Corp, *Annual Report, 1984*, p. 8); this will be used for RRs, but could easily be adapted to home use.
24. See N. Kristof, "World Financial Curbs Eased by Technology and Ideology," *The New York Times*, January 26, 1985, pp. 1, 33.
25. The London Stock Exchange opens at 4:30 A.M. Eastern Standard Time (EST) [1:30 A.M. Pacific Standard Time (PST)] and Tokyo opens at 7 P.M. EST (4 P.M. PST). London closes at a more civilized hour here and Tokyo at a less. (See Table 1 of Chapter 2 for details.)
26. Royal Dutch Shell (London) and Sony (NYSE) are among the exceptions in a world market where about 500 stocks are traded on one or more foreign exchanges but nearly all are traded more heavily at home.
27. See Kristoff, "World Financial Curbs."
28. For example, Merrill Lynch Europe has twice as many employees in Britain as Hoare Govett, the largest British stockbroker; Security Pacific bought into Hoare Govett; and Citibank bought effective control of Vickers da Costa (a British stockbroker with Associate Member status on the Tokyo Stock Exchange and a major trading role in Singapore and Hong Kong) (see *Business Week*, April 23, 1984, p. 67). However, Merrill's offer at $5 million was not enough to make it the first foreign firm to own a seat on the Tokyo Stock Exchange (*The Wall Street Journal*, December 26, 1984).
29. First, the Chicago Mercantile Exchange and the Singapore International Monetary Exchange announced plans to offer substitutable foreign exchange contracts (*The*

Wall Street Journal, September 7, 1984). Next, the AMEX and the Toronto Stock Exchange announced an electronic order-routing system for 36 Canadian stocks listed on both exchanges, expanding the link already in place between Toronto and Boston (*The Wall Street Journal*, December 18, 1984). Then, on the same day, the NYSE and the Pacific Stock Exchange announced that they were seriously considering a merger, and Philadelphia announced negotiations regarding linkages with the Hong Kong Commodity Exchange and the London International Futures Exchange (*The New York Times*, January 13, 1985). An agreement was reached in May 1985 in which Philadelphia and London will form a single market in sterling currency options, with trading in U.S. dollars and clearance through London's International Commodity Clearing House (*The New York Times*, May 27, 1985, p. 34). Geographically most ambitious is a three-continent, four-time zone, 18 1/2 trading hours per day linkage between the Sydney, Vancouver, and Montreal stock exchanges and Amsterdam's European Options Exchange for trading gold and silver options (*The Wall Street Journal*, January 17, 1985). Note that all these linkages involve either futures or options, which are easy to make internationally substitutable, or stocks that are already traded in a single form on North American markets.

30. Under the agreement, Reuters will exclusively market Instinet's electronic quotation and trading system outside North America to Reuters' client network among financial institutions (Institutional Networks Corp., *Annual Report, 1984*, p. 11). Since that announcement, Reuters has offered to buy effective control of Instinet (see "Why the Big Players Want a Piece of Instinet," *Fortune*, August, 19, 1985, p. 145). At this writing, the outcome is unclear.

31. Suppose that the off-hours market opened (or had a batch transaction) at 6 A.M. EST (noon in Zurich). If the net of orders given to European banks up to that time were submitted to the U.S. market instead of being netted against orders arriving at the banks in the afternoon, the total flow going to the United States over the day would be greater.

32. This has already been pilot-tested in the United Kingdom and South Africa (*The Wall Street Journal*, April 11, 1984, p. 40), and will probably be in use (via the Reuters-Instinet tie—see footnote 30) when you read this.

33. Despite the common belief that "dropping a block on the market" causes disadvantageous price pressure, the classic work of Scholes (1972) suggests strongly that it is not the size of the block but rather the information that a block is being offered which causes price pressure (about 1%, on average). This implies that the key to reducing price pressure is maintaining anonymity. Block positioners try to do this by lining up both a buyer and a seller before revealing that they have a client who wishes to sell or to buy. This is often impossible if another broker is already representing the potential buyer or seller.

4

THE IMPACT OF SPECIALIST STABILIZATION*

This chapter develops and tests a model of the effects of thinness[1] on security returns variance[2] in exchanges with and without specialists. Given heterogeneous expectations, nonseparation, and atomistic traders, returns variance is shown to be a decreasing function of the value of shares outstanding (an inverse measure of thinness). We then use the model to consider the impact of specialists on the variance-thinness relationship. To do so, we transform the theoretical relationship into an estimating equation which we apply to data on stocks listed on four exchanges. Two of these, the New York Stock Exchange (NYSE) and the American Stock Exchange (AMEX), are specialist exchanges, while the other two, the First Section of the Tokyo Stock Exchange (TYKO) and the Rio de Janeiro Stock Exchange (RIO), do not have the specialist system. Our results indicate that specialists reduce the variance of thinly held securities.

Our formal model uses a demand formulation to link the advent of idiosyncratic tenders and aggregate demand shifts to variations in security prices, and hence to the generation of returns in a continuous auction market. For this purpose, (1) compound Poisson processes are used to describe the manner in which shifts in the market demand curve to hold a security are generated, and (2) demand elasticity is used to translate idiosyncratic demand shifts into a returns dimension.

The model of the returns generation process is used to obtain the expected value and variance of security returns. This is done first for returns based on bid-ask quotations (which we call quotation returns) and then for returns based on transaction prices (which we call transaction returns). A separate analysis of transaction returns is needed because demand shifts need not trigger transactions, and hence closing transaction prices need not reflect all current information contained in closing quotes.

Our empirical study is aimed at determining whether stock exchange specialists have any measurable impact on the volatility of security prices. Specialists are charged with the responsibility of maintaining a fair and orderly market for the securities assigned to them. In large part, their function implies price stabilization. Prior to our study, however, there was little empirical evidence that specialists do in fact have any impact on price volatility (i.e., returns variance).[3]

Our methodology is to estimate (for samples of stocks on each of NYSE, AMEX, TKYO, and RIO, as well as in pooled regressions) the elasticity of each stock's returns variance with respect to its value of shares outstanding.[4] Our theoretical model suggests that this elasticity will be negative in the absence of specialist intervention. To the extent that the specialist does affect stock price movements, his impact is likely to be proportionately greater for thinner issues. Hence we expect that the cross-sectional returns variance–thinness relationship may be weaker on specialist than on nonspecialist exchanges. Thus comparative analysis of the returns variance–thinness relationship on specialist and nonspecialist exchanges provides evidence on the quantitative significance of specialist price stabilitization efforts.

Section 4.1 discusses the necessary conceptual foundations. It describes the market demand curve to hold a security, and considers two different types of demand shifts, aggregate and idiosyncratic. In Section 4.2, demand elasticity is used to obtain the percentage price change that will result from a market buy or sell order. Section 4.3 then uses compound Poisson processes to complete our model of the generation of quotation returns. The implications of the formulation for the mean and variance of quotation returns and a returns variance–thinness relationship are developed in Section 4.4. In Section 4.5, the model is transformed from quotation to transaction returns. In the process, it is shown that drift in share prices causes transaction returns variance to be systematically larger than quotation returns variance, and that the discrepancy is thinness-related. Section 4.6 discusses the impact of specialists on the variance-thinness relationship, considers other determinants of returns variance, and formulates an estimating equation for variance. The sample selection and results of the empirical study are presented in Section 4.7. Our conclusions are summarized in Section 4.8.

4.1 CONCEPTUAL FOUNDATIONS

4.1.1 The Market Demand to Hold a Security

At any point in time, the market demand for a security is expressed by the set of orders to buy or to sell shares at specified prices. In Figure 1, panel A, we depict the *effective* sell (S^E) and buy (B^E) functions that represent the array of limit orders transmitted to the market. By effective, we mean orders that are

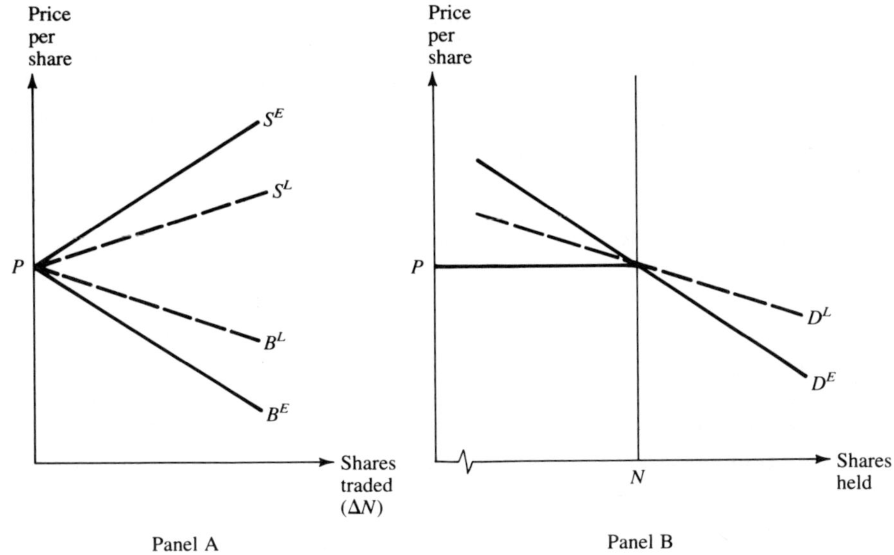

Figure 1 Market demand and supply curves.

actually conveyed to the market (e.g., orders on the limit-order books and discretionary orders held by floor traders), as distinct from the total number that would potentially be transmitted if no transaction costs of placing limit orders or other trading frictions existed.

Sell and buy order functions that express *latent* demand are also shown in panel A by the dashed lines labeled S^L and B^L. The latent sell and buy order functions are more elastic than the corresponding effective functions, since the former depict the limit orders that would result if there were no frictions in the trading process. As Chapters 1 and 5 imply, friction reduces the number of limit orders actually transmitted to the market. The horizontal axis labeled "Shares traded" (ΔN) shows the cumulative (rather than marginal) number of shares to be bought or sold at each price.

Panel A depicts an equilibrium situation in that B^E does not intersect S^E within the positive quadrant, and thus no transaction is triggered by a bid price being greater than an ask price. For reasons of mathematical tractability, we assume a zero bid-ask spread; hence B^E and S^E intersect the vertical axis at the same price P, which we call the market quote.[5]

Panel B of Figure 1 shows the effective and latent demand curves (D^E and D^L, respectively) which are associated with the trade curves depicted in panel A. The "shares to hold" formulation is relevant because investors fundamentally have a demand to hold shares, and their purchases and sales simply have the purpose of, from time to time, adjusting their holdings (rather than changing them at a constant rate over time).[6]

Given N, the number of shares outstanding for a security, the demand-to-hold curves of panel B are obtained from the trade curves of panel A by subtracting from (adding to) N at each price the ΔN given by the sell (buy) functions. Since the trade curves converge on the price axis at P, the demand-to-hold curves pass through the vertical line at N without a discontinuity. Consistent with panel A, the equilibrium price P is given by the intersection of D^E with the vertical line at N.[7]

4.1.2 Reasons for Shifts in Market Demand Curves

Shifts in the market demand curve to hold a security can occur for either of two reasons: aggregate change or idiosyncratic change in demand propensities. An aggregate change is a response to information that is available to all investors. We assume that aggregate demand shifts lead to changes in limit prices which are order preserving in the neighborhood of market equilibrium, so that they do not result in transactions.[8] Hence an aggregate demand shift will produce a new quotation price, but not a new transaction price, for the security.[9]

An idiosyncratic shift of the demand curves occurs when an individual investor receives (or needs) funds, changes his risk-return preferences, or reassesses his evaluation of a security's value. Idiosyncratic demand shifts necessarily are not order preserving. We define an idiosyncratic tender to be a market order that attends such a demand shift; it will necessarily generate a transaction and a new transaction price.

We model the generation of both aggregate shifts and idiosyncratic tenders using mutually independent compound Poisson processes. We assume that aggregate demand shifts are generated by a Poisson process with mean rate γ per unit time. A Bernoulli random variable W indicates the direction of an aggregate demand shift: $W = 1$, with probability p, is an upward shift, which increases the quotation price; $W = -1$, with probability $1 - p$, is a downward shift, which decreases the quotation price. When $p = 0.5$, there is no drift in prices over time, and when $p > 0.5$ ($p < 0.5$), there is upward (downward) drift. Each aggregate demand shift results in a proportional change in the quotation price which is represented by the random variable U.[10] We assume that $E(U)$ and $E(U^2)$ are known finite values.

The generation of idiosyncratic tenders is also modeled as a compound Poisson process. We assume that the frequency with which idiosyncratic tenders reach the market is described by a Poisson process with mean rate λ per unit time. We define a Bernoulli random variable Z such that $Z = 1$ ($Z = -1$), with probability 0.5, indicates that the idiosyncratic tender is a buy (sell) order. Because the probability of $Z = 1$ is 0.5, we do not allow drift in the security's price to result from idiosyncratic tenders. Each tender, whether a buy or a sell, has a dollar value described by the random variable Y. We assume that $E(Y)$ and $E(Y^2)$ are known finite values.

Next consider an arbitrary time interval t of length l units. Let P_t^Q and

P^Q_{t-1} denote the quotation price for a security at the end of periods t and $t - 1$. (We omit the Q superscript on the price variable P when it is clear from the context that the quotation price is meant.) Let P^T_t and P^T_{t-1} denote the most recent transaction price at or before the end of periods t and $t - 1$. If a transaction actually occurs at the end of period t, then $P^Q_t = P^T_t$. The quotation and transaction returns for period t are[11]

$$r^Q_t = \log \frac{P^Q_t}{P^Q_{t-1}} \qquad r^T_t = \log \frac{P^T_t}{P^T_{t-1}} \tag{1}$$

Assume that all periods are of equal length l (for expository purposes, we shall refer to l as a daily trading interval), and that the stochastic processes generating a security's returns are stationary.

4.2 THE IMPACT OF AN IDIOSYNCRATIC TENDER ON A SECURITY'S PRICE

To determine the impact of an idiosyncratic tender on the market price of the security, we first transform its dollar value (Y) into the number of shares tendered, and then determine how much price must change in order to absorb that number of shares. We assume that investors use the security's closing quotation price for the previous trading day in determining how many shares they wish to buy or sell, and that the demand curve is linear in the neighborhood of equilibrium. In Appendix A.2 we show that the impact on the security's quotation price relative of the sth idiosyncratic tender to reach the market during a day is

$$\frac{P_s}{P_{s-1}} = 1 + \frac{Y_s Z_s}{\eta V} \tag{2}$$

where Y_s and Z_s are, respectively, the dollar value and buy-sell indicator associated with the sth idiosyncratic tender, V is the security's market value of outstanding shares at the end of the previous day, and η is the elasticity of the security's market demand to hold curve at its equilibrium point.[12]

4.3 THE GENERATION OF QUOTATION PRICE RETURNS

Assume that the sth demand curve shift was caused by new information. From our definitions of U and W, it follows that the impact on the quotation price relative of an aggregate demand shift is

$$\frac{P_s}{P_{s-1}} = 1 + U_s W_s \tag{3}$$

with U_s and W_s assumed independent for all s.[13]

Equations (2) and (3) generate an expression for the quotation price return over any period t. Since there are $n_I(t)$ idiosyncratic tenders and $n_A(t)$ aggregate demand shifts during period t, it can be shown (see Appendix A.3) that the quotation price return during period t is

$$r_t^Q = \frac{1}{\eta V} \sum_{s=1}^{n_I(t)} Y_s Z_s + \sum_{s=1}^{n_A(t)} U_s W_s \tag{4}$$

4.4 THE MEAN AND VARIANCE OF QUOTATION RETURNS AND THE EFFECT OF THINNESS

4.4.1 Mean and Variance

We now use the quotation returns generation process, given by Eq. (4), to obtain both the expected value and variance of quotation returns for a trading day. Since the summation terms on the right-hand side of Eq. (4) are mutually independent compound Poisson processes, we show in Appendix A.4 that the mean and variance of quotation returns are

$$E(r_T^Q) = \gamma l(2p - 1)E(U) \tag{5}$$

$$\text{Var}(r_t^Q) = \frac{\lambda l E(Y^2)}{\eta^2 V^2} + \gamma l E(U^2) \tag{6}$$

It follows from Eq. (5) that our model of the returns generation process is consistent with efficient capital markets in which the price sequence follows a submartingale [see Fama (1970, p. 386)]. This is because γ and $E(U)$ are parameters of the compound Poisson process modeling intertemporally independent aggregate demand shifts, and we allow for drift in security prices (when $p \neq 0.5$).

Equation (6) shows that quotation returns variance is inversely related to the magnitude of η, the elasticity of the market demand to hold curve at the point of equilibrium. This relationship generates an interesting implication. Referring back to Figure 1, panel B, we see that the elasticity at equilibrium of the latent market demand to hold curve (D^L) is greater than that of the effective demand curve (D^E); this suggests that transaction costs and other trading frictions not only decrease expected (net) returns, but also increase returns variance. Further, returns variance would be greater in a fragmented market because segmenting the stock of limit order impairs their ability to absorb idiosyncratic tenders, and hence causes an inflation of returns variance.

Equation (5) shows that expected quotation returns are independent of the size of the security's market, unless some of the parameters of this equation are functions of V. [See Section 4.4.3 for a discussion of a possible relationship between η, $E(U)$, and V.[14]] The effect of V on variance, however, is not immediately apparent. We examine the variance-V relationship under two alternative assumptions: (1) in Appendix A.5, we consider homogeneous expectations and separation, with the value weight of each security in the portfolio of each investor being equal to the value weight of that security in the aggregate market portfolio; and (2) in Section 4.4.2, we consider heterogeneous expectations and nonseparation, with the number of shareholders for a security (and hence η, the mean arrival rate of idiosyncratic tenders) being proportional to the market value of the security.

4.4.2 Heterogeneous Expectations and Nonseparation

Under heterogeneous expectations and nonseparation, each individual may include or not include any specific asset in his portfolio depending on his own beliefs concerning that asset's potential returns. To model this, we let the arrival rate of idiosyncratic tenders be proportional to the aggregate market value of each security:

$$\eta_i = \mu V_i \tag{7}$$

where μ is the mean arrival rate of random tenders per dollar of market value. Substituting Eq. (7) into (6), we obtain

$$\text{Var}(r_{i,t}^Q) = \frac{\mu l E(Y^2)}{\eta_i^2 V_i} + \eta_i l E(U_i^2) \tag{8}$$

Under heterogeneous expectations and nonseparation, it appears to follow from Eq. (8) that V is a determinant of returns variance; when μ, $E(Y^2)$, η, γ, and $E(U^2)$ are not functions of V, the variance of quotation returns is inversely related to V. To assess more completely the variance-V relationship, we now allow for the possibility that μ, $E(Y^2)$, η, γ, and $E(U^2)$ are functions of V, and conjecture about the signs of the elasticity coefficients for these five relationships. Dropping the i subscript for compactness, differentiating Eq. (8) with respect to V, converting into elasticities, and rearranging, we obtain

$$\varepsilon_{\text{Var}(r_t^Q)\cdot V} = \alpha[\varepsilon_{\mu\cdot V} + \varepsilon_{E(Y^2)\cdot V} - 2\varepsilon_{\eta\cdot V} - 1] + (1-\alpha)[\varepsilon_{\gamma\cdot V} + \varepsilon_{E(U^2)\cdot V}] \tag{9}$$

where

$$\alpha = \left[1 + \frac{\lambda E(U^2)\eta^2 V}{\mu E(Y^2)}\right]^{-1} \qquad 0 < \alpha < 1$$

and for any x, $\varepsilon_{x\cdot V} = (V/x)(dx/dV)$.

If the five elasticities on the right-hand side of Eq. (9) are zero, the sign of the variance-V relationship will be unambiguously negative. However, each of the right-hand-side elasticities might be nonzero.

1. Investors who have greater liquidity needs (and thus on average trade more often) might take positions in less volatile securities. This would cause μ to be negatively related to variance—that is, $\operatorname{sgn}[\varepsilon_{\mu \cdot V}] = -\operatorname{sgn}[\varepsilon_{\operatorname{Var}(r_t^Q) \cdot V}]$. Thus nonzero $\varepsilon_{\mu \cdot V}$ cannot reverse, but rather is a result of, the variance-V relationship.
2. $\varepsilon_{\eta \cdot V}$ might be positive. This is because those securities with larger market values are more intensively analyzed, which could reduce the degree of heterogeneity of investor's expectations for these securities. This would reinforce a negative variance-V relationship.
3. $\varepsilon_{\gamma \cdot V}$ might be positive and $\varepsilon_{E(U^2) \cdot V}$ negative if securities with larger market values represent more diversified corporations and thus are subject to more frequent news events, each of lesser magnitude for the overall corporation. The net effect, $\varepsilon_{\gamma \cdot V} + \varepsilon_{E(U^2) \cdot V}$, would likely be minor.

Significant market power on the part of some traders or market makers can have the following effects:

4. The size of large traders (especially institutions) may lead them to concentrate in large V securities so as to reduce any possible price pressure or signaling effect [see Glosten (1981)]. This can have two effects. First, the dollar value of idiosyncratic tenders [and hence $E(Y^2)$] can be greater for large V securities, making $\varepsilon_{E(Y^2) \cdot V} > 0$. Second, the alleged tendency for institutions to trade more actively than individual investors can make $\varepsilon_{\mu \cdot V} > 0$; this effect could be stronger than the effect described in (1) above, and can conceivably lead to $\varepsilon_{\operatorname{Var}(r_t^Q) \cdot V} > 0$.
5. As discussed in Section 4.6.1 below, on specialist exchanges the impact of specialist intervention is likely to be greater for thinner issues. This could conceivably result in $\varepsilon_{\eta \cdot V} < 0$ and/or $\varepsilon_{E(U^2) \cdot V} > 0$. If this effect is strong, the sign of $\varepsilon_{\operatorname{Var}(r_t^Q) \cdot V}$ may be reversed.

4.4.3 Conclusions Concerning the Effect of Thinness on Variance

We are now able to draw various conclusions concerning a variance-V relationship. Under the special conditions of homogeneous expectations and separation, we show in Appendix A.5 that V is at most a minor determinant of variance. When these conditions are relaxed, however, we conclude that V will, in general, be a major determinant of returns variance. If μ, $E(Y^2)$, η, γ, and $E(\mathrm{U}^2)$ are unrelated to V, the variance-V relationship is seen to be unambiguously negative. Our conjectures concerning the possibility that these variables are related to V lead us to expect that in the absence of substantial market power, quotation returns variance will unambiguously be negatively related to the value of shares outstanding. Whether the sign is also negative for exchanges where participants have substantial market power is an empirical issue which we explore in Sections 4.6 and 4.7.

The analysis developed in this section suggests two additional empirical implications. First, tests of the variance-V relationship may shed light upon the empirical validity of the homogeneous expectations assumption and separation hypothesis. While a finding of no relationship may be inconclusive, observation of a relationship would support the heterogeneous expectations–nonseparation position. The second empirical implication concerns testing for the impact of stock exchange specialists. In Section 4.6.1, we model how specialists may react to idiosyncratic tenders or aggregate demand shifts. We then discuss (in Sections 4.6 and 4.7) the results of a comparative empirical investigation of this relationship for specialist and nonspecialist exchanges (with institutional trading separately accounted for).

4.5 TRANSACTION RETURNS

Sections 4.3 and 4.4 have developed a model for the generation of quotation returns and derived expressions for their mean and variance. Customarily, however, closing quotation prices are not used to compute price ratios over successive trading intervals. Rather, last-transaction prices prior to the end of conventional trading intervals (which for ease of exposition we take to be the same as the behaviorally determined periods of length l) are normally used to compute returns. The difference between last-transaction price and closing quotation price can be substantial, since, as we have suggested, shifts in quotes can occur without necessarily triggering transactions. In this section, we transform our model for quotation returns into a model for transaction returns.

Let x_t denote the length of time between the end of the tth measurement period (e.g., a trading day) and the time of the last transaction prior to the end of day t. Figure 2 illustrates the relevant time measures.[15] Thus, for trading day t, the actual time interval between the two transactions whose prices are used to compute the transaction return is $l + x_{t-1} - x_t$ (rather than l, the length of the trading day). The lengths of time x_t and x_{t-1} are random variables whose joint probability distribution is derived in Appendix A.6.

Now suppose that M fixed measurement intervals of length l are used to make an empirical estimate of the mean and variance of transaction returns. We would get

$$R_T = \frac{1}{M} \sum_{t=1}^{M} r_{t*}^{T} \tag{10}$$

and

$$\hat{\sigma}_T^2 = \frac{1}{M-1} \sum_{t=1}^{M} (r_{t*}^{T} - \hat{R}_T)^2 \tag{11}$$

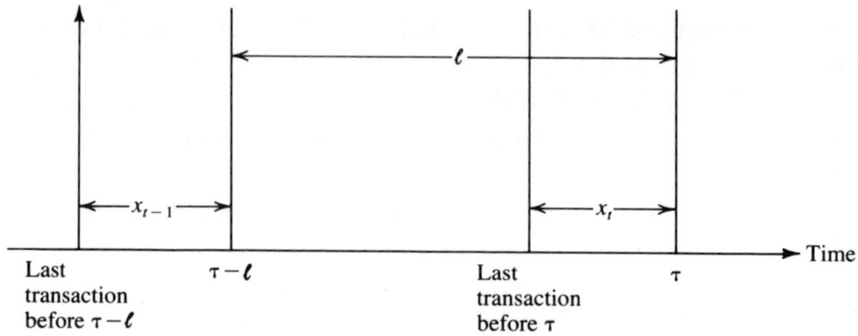

Figure 2 Timing of transactions for periods t and t^*. The time over which period t is measured is $\tau - l$ to τ. The time over which period t^* is measured is $\tau - l - x_{t-1}$ to $\tau - x_t$.

In Eqs. (10) and (11), r_{t*}^T denotes the tth transaction return, and the asterisk (*) indicates that for period t, the transaction return pertains to a time interval of length $l + x_{t-1} - x_t$, rather than to the measurement interval of length l.[16]

In Appendix A.6, we show that the expected values of the estimators of the mean and variance of transaction returns given in Eqs. (10) and (11) are

$$E(\hat{R}_T) = E(r_t^Q) \tag{12}$$

and that

$$E(\hat{\sigma}_T^2) \cong \text{Var}(r_t^Q) + D \tag{13}$$

where

$$D = \frac{2\gamma^2(2p - 1)^2 E^2(U)}{\mu^2 V^2}(1 - e^{-\mu Vl}) \tag{14}$$

Equation (12) shows that the estimator of expected transaction returns is an unbiased estimate of mean quotation returns. In contrast, however, from Eqs. (13) and (14), it is obvious that drift (either upward or downward) in the aggregate demand shift process causes the estimator of transaction returns variance to be greater than the true variance of quotation returns, with D denoting the discrepancy (i.e., the amount by which transaction returns variance is expected to exceed quotation returns variance). Clearly, D is thinness-related. We show in Appendix A.6 that D decreases monotonically as V, the market value of the stock, increases. Hence a negative variance-V relationship should be stronger for transaction returns than for quotation returns.

4.6 THE VARIANCE-THINNESS RELATIONSHIP

The relationship between quotation returns variance and thinness (for which we take the market value of shares outstanding to be an inverse proxy measure) is summarized in Eq. (9) above. Under conditions that we consider to be reasonably realistic—that is, heterogeneous expectations and nonseparation—quotation returns variance is clearly negatively related to market value (unless traders or market makers possess substantial market power). But it is typical to estimate returns variance by use of returns based on transaction prices, rather than quotation prices. Furthermore, our theoretical model has conveniently assumed a zero bid-ask spread, which obviously is unrealistic. However, as discussed in footnote 5 and Section 4.5 above, if a positive bid-ask spread were included in the model and if transaction rather than quotation returns variance were used, then the negative relationship between returns variance and market value exhibited in Eq. (9) would become even stronger. Thus, for convenience, we can use the variables embodied in Eq. (9) as the basis for an empirical study of the returns variance-thinness relationship which is reported in the remainder of this chapter. We shall henceforth use VAR to denote returns variance.

The purpose of the empirical study is twofold. First, it serves as a test of the formal variance-thinness relationship and the underlying theoretical model formulated in Sections 4.1 through 4.5 above. Second, it serves as a test of whether specialists do in fact have an impact on the volatility of security prices.

4.6.1 The Impact of Specialists

In Section 4.4.2, we have noted that if the five elasticities on the right-hand side of Eq. (9) are zero, then $\varepsilon_{\mathrm{VAR}\cdot V}$, the elasticity of returns variance with respect to market value, will be clearly negative. While we discussed several possible influences which could cause the right-hand-side elasticities to be nonzero, we concluded that for nonspecialist exchanges $\varepsilon_{\mathrm{VAR}\cdot V}$ should be negative.

The specialist's impact on Eq. (9) occurs through the terms $\varepsilon_{\eta\cdot V}$ and $\varepsilon_{E(U^2)\cdot V}$. Any trader who enters limit orders in the neighborhood of equilibrium increases $|\eta|$. Several factors may cause the specialist to enter limit orders for his own account which would not be entered in his absence: (1) He faces lower transaction costs than do other traders. (2) He has sole knowledge of the limit-order book, which may bring trading profits (see Chapter 9). (3) The exchanges have elaborate surveillance systems to monitor the performance of their specialists. On the NYSE and AMEX, specialists are judged (and warned, awarded new issues, or even suspended) according to the orderliness of the market that they provide;[17] this induces them to increase the elasticity of the market demand curve and thereby decrease returns variance caused by idiosyncratic tenders.

Also, by maintaining their own limit orders in the face of aggregate demand shifts, specialists can decrease $E(U^2)$. However, specialists' impact on η and $E(U^2)$ will be diminished to the extent that they wish to avoid large inventory changes. Their relative effect may be less for $E(U^2)$ than for η because they may request exchange officials to close the market or absolve them of the continuity responsibility when a major demand shift is perceived.

For three reasons, we believe that in the current U.S. system, any specialist impact on η or $E(U^2)$ would be considerably greater in thinner markets. First, specialists have more market power to absorb excess demand or supply for securities with a smaller value of shares outstanding. Second, the schedules of acceptable maximum price changes (per transaction or per thousand shares traded) which the exchanges use as standards for assessing specialist performance are not directly adjusted for variations in V (although they are adjusted for number of shares traded and price), and the implied constraint on price changes is stricter for low V stocks. Third, the minimum size of specialist transactions (100 shares) is the same for all securities.

Indirect empirical evidence that the impact of specialists is greater in thinner markets is provided by an AMEX report by Forte (1976). That specialists intervene more for thinner issues is suggested by the following: over the three-year period from January 1973 to December 1975, specialist trading profits were negative for thinly traded issues, rose steadily as volume increased, and became positive for heavily traded issues; concurrently, specialist trading profits were negatively related to the specialist's participation percentage (trades for the specialist's own account divided by total trades).

If specialists do intervene more for thinner stocks, we would have $\varepsilon_{\eta \cdot V} < 0$, and possibly $\varepsilon_{E(U^2) \cdot V} > 0$, both of which by Eq. (9) would algebraically increase $\varepsilon_{\text{VAR} \cdot V}$ on specialist versus nonspecialist exchanges. A strong enough specialist impact could even make $\varepsilon_{\text{VAR} \cdot V}$ positive.

A possible contrary hypothesis is suggested by Baumol (1965), who notes, by analogy with macroeconomic policy studies, the possibility that specialists will destabilize prices by misjudging the timing of their intervention. If specialists do intervene more for thinner stocks (as Baumol also believes they will), we should then expect a more negative variance-V elasticity on a specialist exchange.

4.6.2 Other Determinants of Returns Variance

Factors other than the value of shares outstanding also affect returns variance. In large part, these factors reflect the frequency of information arrival, which influences the fundamental determinants of share valuation and the variance of returns.[18] Including these variables in the estimating equation should increase its explanatory power and improve the accuracy of the VAR-V elasticity estimates.

Number of Shares Traded (NST). The NYSE and AMEX define specialist surveillance parameters on NST as well as on P (price per share). On both exchanges, although larger percentage price changes are allowed for lower NST stocks, NYSE and AMEX surveillance officials believe that the parameters force greater specialist intervention for lower NST issues. Thus, to the extent that exchange regulation has such an impact, we would expect the VAR-NST elasticities to be algebraically greater for specialist than for nonspecialist exchanges.

Because empirically there is a strong positive correlation between NST and V, we do not use both in the same regression.

Sales-Asset Variance (SAV). The SAV variable represents instability in the firm's operating performance. A ratio is used to avoid intercorrelation with size variables. SAV should be positively related to VAR, since an increase in SAV implies greater earnings risk. As a proxy for business risk, it embraces many of the explanatory variables that have been shown to be significant in other empirical studies of volatility.

Trading Turnover Ratio (TOR). Differences in trading turnover (the ratio of shares traded to shares held) should reflect differences in the rate of receipt and relative importance of "news" about companies. Since more frequent or more important news causes more frequent or larger aggregate shifts in the demand curve, and hence in price, we should expect VAR to be positively related to TOR, ceteris paribus.[19]

In regressions that do not also include NST, it is possible for the VAR–TOR elasticity to reflect a specialist impact if specialists intervene more for low NST issues, thus raising NST above its natural level for such issues. This is because the strong positive correlation of TOR with NST could cause the elasticity of VAR with respect to TOR to be algebraically greater on specialist exchanges.

Price per Share (P). In part, P may be related to VAR insofar as P may represent a proxy for firm quality and thus may be partially a fundamental determinant.[20] When P serves as a quality proxy, it is expected to be negatively related to VAR.

Price is also expected to bear a negative relationship to VAR because of a price-rounding effect arising from the fact that prices must be quoted as integer multiples of a basic unit (e.g., one-eighth dollar for many U.S. stocks). Rounding causes what otherwise would be a smooth price series to be discrete, and hence increases the variance of returns.[21] The effect is much more pronounced for stocks of lower price, which would suggest a negative VAR-P relationship. In addition, the basic price unit as a percentage of average price differs across exchanges, and may cause interexchange differences in the VAR-P relationship.

A further reason for a negative VAR-P relationship is what we call the commissions as a percentage of price were greater for low- than for high-price shares. Hence, for low-price shares, the potential profit from speculative trading shares. Hence, for low-price shares, the potential profit from speculative trading would be reduced, and the elasticity of the demand for shares would be lower in the neighborhood of market price.

Note that if the surveillance system effectively forces greater specialist intervention for low P issues, then we would also expect to find the VAR-P elasticities to be algebraically greater on specialist than on nonspecialist exchanges.

Relative Size of Institutional Holdings (RINSH). Institutional trading may (algebraically) increase the VAR–V elasticity, and perhaps even make it positive, if institutions tend to be active traders and also focus their interest on higher V securities. However, neither U.S. Securities and Exchange Commission (1971), nor Levine (1974), nor Friend (1979) find any evidence that institutional trading significantly increases volatility, so we have no hypothesis for the sign of the RINSH coefficient. We were not able to obtain data on institutional trading, and used the relative size of institutional holdings instead.

4.6.3 Estimating Equation

We used the following functional form (sometimes replacing V with NST, or using a subset of variables) for the ordinary-least-squares (OLS) regression test:

$$\text{LVAR} = b_0 + b_1\,\text{L}V + b_2\text{LTOR} + b_3\text{L}P + b_4\text{RINSH} + b_5\text{LSAV} + u \qquad (15)$$

where the prefix L indicates that the logarithm of the original variable was used. The functional form of Eq. (15) is reasonable, since it is appropriate to use LVAR rather than VAR as the dependent variable (variance cannot be negative), and we have no reason to impose any particular form of nonconstant elasticity on any independent variable other than RINSH.

The coefficients b_1, b_2, b_3, and b_5 are the (constant) elasticities of VAR with respect to V, TOR, P, and SAV, respectively. The elasticity of VAR with respect to RINSH is b_4RINSH; it rises as RINSH rises, which is reasonable since RINSH is bounded from above by unity.

Pooled regressions including both slope and intercept dummies were also run, using the form

$$\text{LVAR} = \left(b_{01} + \sum_{i=2}^{4} b_{0i}D_i\right) + \left(b_{11} + \sum_{i=2}^{4} b_{1i}D_i\right)\text{L}V + \cdots + u \qquad (16)$$

where D_i is the dummy variable for the ith exchange, b_{j1} is the base (TKYO was arbitrarily chosen) exchange's jth coefficient, and $b_{j1} + b_{ji}D_i$ is the ith exchange's jth coefficient. With intercept and slope dummies on all independent variables for all but one exchange, the coefficients implied by the pooled regressions are identical to those of the corresponding separate exchange regressions, and the t statistics on the dummy coefficients provide a significance test for the deviation of each exchange's coefficients from those of TKYO.

4.7 SAMPLE SELECTION AND TEST RESULTS

Eliminating stocks for which sufficient data were unavailable, we selected 50 stocks for each of TKYO, AMEX, and NYSE, and 28 for RIO by stratified random sampling. Firms were ranked by the market values of shares outstanding as of the end of 1971.[22] They were then divided into deciles, and a random sample was taken from each decile. To avoid any spurious correlation, all independent variables were measured as of December 31, 1971 or for the period ending on that date, while the dependent variable was measured using first quarter 1972 data.

Floating supply (FS) rather than the total number of shares outstanding was used in the empirical definition of V. This is because insiders maintain positions for control as well as for financial return, and because the freedom of insiders to buy and to sell is constrained by governmental regulation.[23]

Table 1 presents the results of the logarithmic regressions of first quarter 1972 returns variance on the explanatory variables previously discussed. All the independent variables in Eq. (15) are included in Reg. Set A. This tests the larger model of the determinants of variance, and also whether specialist intervention in low V stocks algebraically increases the VAR-V elasticity. Reg. Set B more directly tests for a specialist effect by regressing LVAR on LNST and LP. Each regression set consists of four separate exchange regressions and a four-exchange pooled regression with TKYO as the base exchange.

All the separate exchange regressions give F statistics which are significant at the 0.01 level (except for RIO, which is significant at 0.10 in Reg. Set A and at 0.05 in Reg. Set B), and the adjusted $\bar{R}^2$'s are reasonably high (they are predominantly greater than 0.5) for cross-sectional regressions based on noncontemporaneous data. The explanatory power of the regression equation is considerably greater on the two U.S. exchanges because of the greater significance of the LTOR and LP coefficients.

The pooled regressions show that the explanatory power of the equation is increased when the range of the independent variables is extended (the ranges of P and FS in particular differ among exchanges); a four-exchange pooled regression estimate of Reg. Set A yields an $\bar{R}^2$ of 0.675. Pooled regressions (not shown here) on the two U.S. exchanges (using NYSE as the base) show their remarkable structural similarity; the F statistic is 53.46, $\bar{R}^2$ is 0.7888, and neither the intercept nor any of the slope coefficients are significantly different except for LTOR, whose difference is significant at the 0.01 level.

Our findings, by variable, are as follows.

LV. The LV coefficients for the nonspecialist exchanges are uniformly negative and significant, whereas those for the specialist exchanges are positive, though significant at somewhat lower confidence levels. The pooled regression t statistics indicate that the RIO coefficient does not differ significantly from that for TKYO, while those for AMEX and NYSE do differ from TKYO, with significance at the 0.01 level. These results are consistent with our prediction that the VAR-V elasticity is negative on nonspecialist exchanges and may be algebraically increased if specialist intervention reduces returns variance primarily for the thin issues, and/or if institutional trading increases variance primarily for the large V securities. We doubt that institutional trading explains our results

TABLE 1 Four-Exchange Separate and Pooled Regression Results with LVAR as Dependent Variable[a]

Reg. Set	Exchange	Intercept	LV	LNST	LTOR	LP	RINSH	LSAV	$\bar{R}^2$	F
A	TKYO	−4.477	−0.217		0.097	−0.481	−0.053	0.118	0.357	6.45**
		(−3.703)**	(−2.591)*		(1.294)	(−2.890)**	(−0.135)**	(1.301)	0.675(P)	16.96**
	RIO	−5.472	−0.229		−0.380	0.213	0.320	0.020	0.178	2.16
		(−4.910)**	(−1.963)*		(−2.918)**	(1.277)	(0.557)	(0.314)		
		(−0.628)	(0.082)		(−2.944)**	(2.998)**	(0.510)	(−0.962)		
	AMEX	−5.674	0.181		0.299	−0.898	−0.219	0.005	0.678	21.62**
		(−9.015)**	(2.235)*		(3.433)**	(−7.600)**	(−0.417)	(0.111)		
		(−0.987)	(3.295)**		(1.627)	(−2.131)*	(−0.227)	(−1.317)		
	NYSE	−4.480	0.145		0.529	−0.854	1.057	0.093	0.734	28.05**
		(−8.519)**	(1.953)*		(4.079)**	(−5.545)**	(1.008)	(2.267)*		
		(−0.002)	(3.401)**		(2.701)**	(−1.714)*	(0.923)	(−0.298)		
B	TKYO	−7.660		−0.043		−0.646			0.283	10.67**
		(−16.284)**		(−0.789)		(−4.307)**			0.618(P)	27.04**
	RIO	−4.522		−0.301		0.016			0.220	4.81*
		(−6.245)**		(−3.086)**		(0.189)				
		(3.116)**		(−1.930)*		(4.189)**				
	AMEX	−6.237		0.227		−0.738			0.688	54.95**
		(−19.643)**		(3.536)**		(−9.740)**				
		(2.477)**		(2.717)**		(−0.586)				
	NYSE	−6.019		0.203		−0.959			0.572	33.61**
		(−11.015)**		(2.391)**		(−8.095)**				
		(2.526)**		(2.624)**		(−1.902)*				

[a]Beneath each coefficient is its t statistic from the separate regression for that exchange. Beneath that is the t statistic from the four-exchange pooled regression, showing the significance of the deviation of the coefficient from that of the base exchange (TKYO). Pooled regression $\bar{R}^2$ and F statistics are distinguished from the separate regression $\bar{R}^2$ and F statistics by a (P) after the appropriate $\bar{R}^2$.

*Significant at the 0.05 level for the degrees of freedom appropriate to the particular regression. An asterisk by the t statistic from the separate regression indicates that the coefficient is significantly different from 0, while an asterisk by the pooled regression t statistic indicates that the difference between the coefficient and that of the base exchange is significant.

**Significant at the 0.01 level for the degrees of freedom appropriate to the particular regression.

since institutional holdings were small for the AMEX sample and large for the TKYO sample.

LNST. In Reg. Set B, the LNST coefficients are negative for TKYO and RIO, and positive for AMEX and NYSE. The pooled regression t statistics indicate that the LNST coefficients for the two U.S. exchanges are significantly larger at the 0.01 level than those of TKYO (while the RIO coefficients are not). This suggests that the regulatory parameters (which tie permissible price changes to trading volume and share price) do induce specialists to intervene more for low-volume stocks.

LTOR. Except for RIO,[24] the LTOR coefficient is positive for all exchanges in Reg. Set A and significant at the 0.01 level for AMEX and NYSE. The LTOR coefficient is larger for the two specialist exchanges in Reg. Set A, with the NYSE's difference from TKYO significant at the 0.01 level. This corroborates a specialist effect, since, holding P constant, LTOR is positively related to LNST on all four exchanges (see Appendix A.7.2). In Reg. Set A, where LNST is not included, the LTOR coefficient is higher on the two specialist exchanges. As reported in Appendix A.7.2, in Reg. Set D, where LNST replaces LV, there should be no significant differences between the U.S. and TKYO coefficients for LTOR, and there are none.

LP. Except for RIO, the LP coefficients of Reg. Set A for all exchanges are significantly negative, as expected.[25] In Reg. Sets A and B, the LP coefficients for AMEX and NYSE are algebraically smaller than the LP coefficients for TKYO, and the difference is generally significant at the 0.05 level. The LP coefficient in Reg. Set B should reflect the combined effects of (1) thinness and specialist intervention, (2) price as a proxy for quality, (3) price rounding, and (4) decreasing commission rates with increasing P. As discussed in Section 4.6.2, each effect will tend to give a negative LP coefficient in a nonspecialist exchange, while greater specialist intervention in thin stocks would tend to increase algebraically the LP coefficient. Thus finding that the AMEX and NYSE LP coefficients are not larger than the nonspecialist exchange coefficients suggests that the specialist surveillance parameters did not lead specialists to intervene proportionately more for low than for high P stocks.

RINSH. The RINSH coefficient is insignificant for all four exchanges, and has its largest value for the NYSE—an elasticity at the mean value of RINSH of only 0.103. Thus, in accord with the findings of U.S. Securities and Exchange Commission (1971), Levine (1974), and Friend (1979), we have no evidence that institutions are destabilizing. We caution, however, that RINSH may indeed be a poor proxy for institutional trading.

LSAV. The LSAV coefficients are positive, as expected, but only the NYSE coefficient is significant. LSAV could be an imperfect measure of business risk; however, alternative measures, based on earnings volatility, have also been found to be insignificant in our study and by Silber (1975).

4.8 CONCLUSION

In this chapter, we have sought to develop further the economic formulation of the returns generation process. Returns are seen to result from demand shifts which may stem from aggregate change in the informational set available to all investors and/or from idiosyncratic tenders placed by some investors. These underlying stimuli are described by mutually independent compound Poisson processes.

The returns generation model is used to obtain expressions for the expected value and variance of security returns, both for returns based on quotation prices and for returns based on transaction prices. We have also examined the conditions under which returns variance will be a decreasing function of value of shares outstanding, our inverse measure of thinness. Given heterogeneous expectations, nonseparation, and the absence of substantial market power on the part of traders or market makers, we anticipate that thinner issues will be more volatile. This variance-thinness relationship provides a framework for assessing the impact of including designated market makers in a securities market; policy recommendations on this issue are presented in Chapter 9.

Expected quotation and transaction returns are shown to be equal. But we have also demonstrated that drift in the aggregate demand shift process causes the estimator of transaction returns variance to be greater than quotation returns variance, with the discrepancy directly related to thinness. Thus publication of last-transaction prices rather than closing bid-ask prices systematically increases the perception of returns instability, especially for those issues with a smaller value of shares outstanding.

We tested our theoretical model of the returns generation process and examined the impact of specialists on the variance-thinness relationship in an empirical study involving two specialist exchanges (NYSE and AMEX) and two exchanges that do not have specialists (TKYO and RIO). First quarter 1972 daily returns variance was regressed on market value of shares, share price, trading activity, sales variance, and institutional holdings for 178 firms selected by stratified random sampling from the four exchanges. We found that the independent variables we have considered explain a sizable percentage of the across-stock differences in returns variance. The $\bar{R}^2$ are mainly greater than 0.5, and all F statistics are significant, except for the separate regression for RIO in Reg. Set A. For the nonthinness determinants of variance, we generally observe a positive coefficient for the turnover ratio (which proxies the rate of receipt of new information), a negative coefficient for price (which may proxy a stock's quality and can also reflect price rounding and commission effects), an insignificant (but positive) coefficient for our measure of sales variance, and an insignificant coefficient for the percentage of institutional holdings in a security.

The negative returns variance–market value elasticity predicted for nonspecialist exchanges is observed for TKYO and RIO. We expected algebraically larger VAR-N elasticities where specialists exist, and indeed we found them for

AMEX and NYSE. Corroborating evidence stems from the elasticities for NST and TOR. Alternative explanations for these results (based on institutional trading in large V securities or a nonconstant VAR-V elasticity) were examined, and no support was found (see Appendix A.7.3). We conclude that specialist intervention does help to stabilize a market. But both the NYSE surveillance parameters and our regression results suggest that specialists do not stabilize low-priced securities per se. Rather, the dimension of thinness on which specialists operate is shares outstanding or shares traded.

In conclusion, our empirical investigation indicates that specialists do have an impact in reducing the returns variance (and hence the price volatility) of securities, especially for thinner issues. This does not necessarily mean, however, that specialists or other types of designated market makers should be incorporated in security market systems. The various public policy issues involved are complex, and we analyze these in Chapter 9.

NOTES

*This chapter is based on two of our previously published articles. Sections 4.1 through 4.5 draw on material in K. J. Cohen, S. F. Maier, R. A. Schwartz, and D. K. Whitcomb, "The Returns Generation Process, Returns Variance, and the Effect of Thinness in Securities Markets," *Journal of Finance*, Vol. 33, 1978, pp. 149–167. This was our first market microstructure theory paper. It is interesting to note that the friction assumption (cited in Chapter 1 as the key element which distinguishes microstructure theory) is implicit in the analysis in the distinction between effective and latent demand. The representation of friction here is incomplete in that we ignore the bid-ask spread and assume simultaneous response to information. Despite the primitive nature of these assumptions, our results on the variance-thinness relationship and the specialist's impact are reasonable and robust. Sections 4.6 and 4.7 are based on a study funded by a grant from the Nomura Research Institute in which we were joined by Walter L. Ness and Hitoshi Okuda. These empirical results were originally published in K. J. Cohen, S. F. Maier, W. L. Ness, Jr., H. Okuda, R. A. Schwartz, and D. K. Whitcomb, "The Impact of Designated Market Makers on Security Prices: I. Empirical Evidence," *Journal of Banking and Finance*, Vol. 1, 1977, pp. 219–235 (by permission of North-Holland Publishing Company, Amsterdam).

1. Prior to the research reported here, none of the relatively sparse empirical analysis of the effects of thinness reported in the literature was based on an explicit theoretical model. Silber (1975) has examined the effect of thinness-related variables on price volatility for Tel Aviv Stock Exchange securities. In a somewhat different context, the impact of thinness-related variables on bid-ask spreads has been investigated by Demsetz (1968) and Tinic (1972) for the NYSE, Tinic-West (1972, 1974) for the NYSE, OTC, and Toronto Stock Exchange, and Benston-Hagerman (1974) for the OTC.
2. Although we model the effect of thinness on total returns variance rather than on systematic risk (beta), it is obvious from the definition of beta that a reduction in *one*

security's returns standard deviation, ceteris paribus, leads to a proportional reduction in its beta. Alternatively, a proportional reduction in *all* securities' total returns standard deviations (which would leave betas unchanged) leads to an equal proportional reduction in the systematic risk term $[\beta\sigma(r_M)]$ of each investor's portfolio standard deviation.

3. Barnea (1974) asserts that observed deviations from a theoretical ratio of returns variances measured over long and short differencing intervals are evidence of specialist activity. Schwartz-Whitcomb (1976) comment that the deviations reflect serial correlation, which has other causes besides specialist activity, and that some specialist price stabilization efforts will not cause correlation and hence will not affect the time-variance relationship. See also Barnea's (1976) reply.
4. Other possible (inverse) proxies for thinness might be value of shares traded, number of shares traded, number of shareholders, frequency of transactions, density of limit orders, and arrival rate of limit and/or market orders. Some of these are explored in the empirical study reported in Sections 4.6 and 4.7.
5. If our model were to include a positive bid-ask spread, then the resulting model of returns variance would also include components of variance stemming from transaction prices bounding between bid and ask prices and from the size of the bid-ask spread varying. Our model of the bid-ask spread in Chapter 5 (see especially Proposition 5) suggests that generalizing our model to include a positive bid-ask spread would reinforce, rather than reduce, the direction of the variance-thinness relationship derived here.
6. It has become conventional in market microstructure literature to assume a negatively sloping demand to hold curve. We discuss our reasons for this in Appendix A.1.
7. Note that the vertical line at N is not a supply curve; in order to hold constant the definition of what is actually demanded, we treat N as a ceteris paribus variable in the definition of the demand function. This is because a change in N brought about, for instance, by stock dividends/splits or new issues will change per share earnings and dividends, and thus will change price at any quantity.
8. Our assumption differs from that of Copeland's (1976) sequential information arrival model, which assumes that news is revealed to traders one at a time; as traders' demand curves shift seriatim, a sequence of transactions might occur.
9. We could make the weaker assumption that only *some* aggregate demand shifts do not trigger transactions, but assuming that no transactions result from them simplifies our derivation of the bias in the estimator of transaction returns variance in Section 4.5.
10. If P is the quotation price before an aggregate demand shift and if ΔP is the algebraic change in the quotation price resulting from the aggregate demand shift, then $U = |\Delta P/P|$.
11. Throughout this chapter, "log" denotes the natural logarithm. There are both theoretical and empirical reasons for defining a security's returns in logarithmic space, as done in Eq. (1), rather than in arithmetic space. Theoretically, it is easier to chain together returns over adjacent subintervals to create returns over longer intervals when the returns are defined logarithmically. Empirically, logarithmic returns are

more likely than arithmetic returns to be normally distributed (and hence more immediately usable with standard econometric techniques).

12. Note that Eq. (2) is valid regardless of whether the previous quote before the tender was the preceding day's closing quote (P_0), a quote that resulted from an idiosyncratic tender, or a quote that resulted from an aggregate shift in the demand curve.
13. Note that Eq. (3) is valid regardless of whether the previous quotation price before the aggregate demand shift was the preceding day's closing quote (P_0), a quote that resulted from an aggregate demand shift, or a quote that resulted from an idiosyncratic tender.
14. With a returns variance–thinness relationship, expected returns would also be thinness related through a risk-return capital market equilibrium relationship.
15. In measuring time, we ignore the interval between the end of one measurement period and the start of the next measurement period.
16. In practice, the actual length of time, $l + x_{t-1} - x_t$, is not known. Hence an estimator $\hat{R}_T$ of the expected return $E(R_t^T)$ for a measurement interval of length l is subtracted from each return in computing the estimated returns variance. In effect, for $\hat{R}_T$ one simply uses the sample mean of the observed transaction returns.
17. The measures of specialist performance are (a) continuity (the size of transaction-to-transaction price changes, (b) stability of specialist trades (destabilizing trades are defined as buying on a plus or zero-plus tick, or selling on a minus or zero-minus tick), and (c) depth of market (on NYSE, the size of price changes over 1000 shares traded; on AMEX, the number of shares involved in a single transaction, excluding blocks).
18. For a further discussion of the fundamental determinants of returns variance, see Hamada (1969), Beaver-Kettler-Scholes (1970), Pettit-Westerfield (1972), Beaver-Manegold (1975), and Ben-Zion–Shalit (1975).
19. If institutions trade more actively than other investors and if their block trades are destabilizing, those stocks which are institutional favorites may have both high TOR and high variance. This effect will be weakened (though not reversed) if investors who trade more often because of greater liquidity needs tend to hold less volatile securities.
20. Such an effect was shown by Clendenin (1951). Others who have studied the effect of price on volatility include Heins-Allison (1966), Haugen (1970), Klemkosky-Petty (1973), and Blume-Husic (1973).
21. To see this, note that many potential prices which would arise from a continuous distribution must be rounded to conform to the discrete set of allowable prices. While it is equally likely that prices will be rounded toward as away from the mean, the squared deviations resulting from prices rounded away will dominate. Simulations run by Schwartz-Whitcomb (1977b) show that for a \$10 stock of medium returns volatility, rounding increases variance by 15% over perfectly smooth price changes.
22. For RIO, the ranking was based on the value of shares traded in 1971 of the most commonly traded class of shares of each company.
23. The empirical definitions of floating supply and the other variables are given in Appendix A.7, together with some additional regression results and explanations.

24. Contrary to expectations, the LTOR coefficient in the Brazilian regressions showed a significantly negative sign. Market sources in Brazil assert that many shares experienced unusual interbroker trading (Brazilian brokers' own trading is not subject to commissions) in which price was raised steadily, after which shares were unloaded at a profit. This type of market manipulation, which simultaneously increases TOR and reduces VAR, could explain the sign reversal of the LTOR coefficient for the RIO sample.

25. Note that in Reg. Sets A and B, the L*P* coefficient for RIO is insignificantly positive. Possible explanations for the absence of a negative *P* coefficient are: (a) the price rounding effect is must weaker in Brazil than in Japan or the United States, and (b) commission rates do not decrease as rapidly with increasing *P* on RIO as they do on the other three exchanges.

5

THE BID-ASK SPREAD*

As noted in Chapter 1, the literature on the bid-ask spread recognizes that the arrival of random buy and sell tenders is nonsynchronous and, as a result, perceives that a demand exists for immediacy providers who will service buy orders at a somewhat higher price and sell orders at a somewhat lower price. Hence dealers-specialists have been viewed as the suppliers of immediacy, and the bid-ask spread generally has been viewed as the price they impose. As such, spreads have been linked to the existence and magnitude of dealer-specialist costs, and it has been presumed that given a competitive environment, spreads will be greater, the greater the cost to dealers-specialists of providing immediacy.

However, inadequate attention has been given to the fact that, through their limit orders, ordinary traders also supply immediacy to each other and that, by and large, market spreads are not simply a reflection of individual dealer-specialist spreads. In fact, the market spread typically does not even reflect the quotes of any one dealer, but rather is the difference between the lowest ask and the highest bid across all limit orders and dealer quotes.

The market spread is of primary interest because it reflects the price at which immediacy can be *obtained* by ordinary investors trading via market orders. Modeling the size of the market spread is an extremely complex matter, given that markets are composed of numerous limit-order traders (including dealers and the specialist) embedded in a dynamic, interactive environment.

In Section 5.1 we briefly review Demsetz's (1968) seminal article, discuss the problem of modeling the market spread, and consider various implications concerning empirical analysis. Section 5.2 establishes the scenario for our analysis. Section 5.3 focuses on the probability of a limit order executing and shows that, with transaction costs, this probability does not go to unity as the price at which a limit order is placed becomes infinitesimally close to a counterpart market quote. This demonstration underscores an investor's need for an order-placement strategy and provides the foundation for our gravitational pull model. Section 5.4 models the investor's order-placement decision and develops conditions under which he will transmit a limit or, alternatively, a market order to the market, or else do nothing. The analysis is developed in a dynamic programming framework, although we are interested in the descriptive modeling of an investor's decision process rather than in actually generating a normative solution. Section 5.5 demonstrates that implementation of the strategic order-placement decision (which implies the gravitational pull effect) causes a noninfinitesimal bid-ask spread to exist. This section also defines an equilibrium bid-ask spread, discusses conditions under which it will exist, and shows that it is positively related to market thinness. Section 5.6 considers implications for the design of a trading system and summarizes our analysis.

5.1 ISSUES IN MODELING THE BID-ASK SPREAD

5.1.1 The Demsetz Analysis

Demsetz (1968) presents the first formal model of the bid-ask spread as a ". . . markup that is paid for predictable immediacy of exchange in organized markets" (p. 36). Panel A of Figure 1 shows Demsetz's basic diagram. D and S

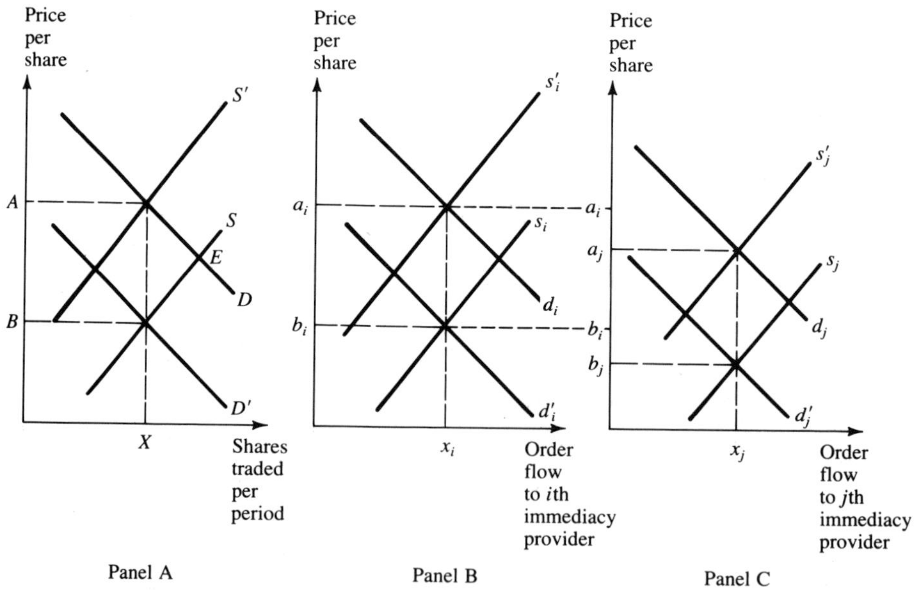

Figure 1 Elaboration of the Demsetz model.

are demand and supply curves that depict the time rate of buy and sell orders as a function of price for investors who transact via market orders so as to achieve immediate, certain execution. At E the two rates are equated. However, buy and sell orders do not generally reach the market at the same moment. Thus Demsetz assumes a separate class of market participants who provide immediacy by standing ready to buy and sell at stated prices.[1] To cover their costs of standing ready, these providers of immediacy must on average sell shares at a higher price than they buy shares. This results in their generating the S' and D' curves (the supply and demand curves that depict the possibilities of transacting with immediacy). The vertical distance between S' and S (and between D and D') is taken by Demsetz to be the gross return per unit to market makers for providing immediacy.

Hence, in the Demsetz model, market equilibrium is given by the intersection of D' with S (and, identically, by the intersection of D with S'). This establishes X as the equilibrium rate at which providers of immediacy will buy (and also sell) shares, A as the ask price at which an investor can obtain immediate purchase, B as the bid price for immediate sale, and A–B as the bid-ask spread. Demsetz takes this spread to be the return per share to providers of immediacy. If there is sufficient competition in the provision of immediacy, the spread, according to Demsetz, will just equal the cost of providing immediacy; one might infer (although Demsetz does not directly state this) that as the cost of providing such services approaches zero, the spread will also approach zero.

Along with this analysis, Demsetz makes a number of insightful points about the specialist function that are not reflected in his formal model. He recognizes that on the NYSE, "the spread is determined by persons acting individually, by specialists, by floor traders, or by outsiders submitting market or limit orders" (p. 39). He states that the specialist is important in that "if there exists no quotation from outsiders that is 'reasonably' narrow, he [the specialist] must offer one of his own to facilitate trading" (p. 38). Further, the specialist faces competition from ". . . (1) rivalry for the specialist's job, (2) competing markets, (3) outsiders who submit limit orders rather than market orders, (4) floor traders who may bypass the specialist by crossing buy and sell orders themselves, and (5) other specialists" (p. 43). Consistent with Stigler (1964), Demsetz also notes that ". . . in equilibrium, the average spread brought about for active securities by competing limit orders will be smaller than for inactive securities. . . . The fundamental force working to reduce the spread is the time rate of transactions" (p. 41).

In the main, these descriptive statements by Demsetz are reasonable, but seem to us to be incompatible with the underlying assumptions of his formal model. In particular, his model implicitly assumes that a separate class of traders (specialists and dealers) are the *sole* providers of immediacy to the market. The greater institutional realism of his discussion raises some interesting questions which, in turn, call for more analysis. Under what conditions will ordinary traders place limit orders? If limit-order traders have heterogeneous trading propensities, will the market spread equal any one individual's spread? If there are enough traders who differ sufficiently in their trading propensities, is it possible for the limit-order book to have entries at virtually every price in the neighborhood of market equilibrium, and hence for the market spread to vanish (or to trivially equal the minimum unit in which prices are quoted, e.g., 1/8 for most NYSE stocks)?

As we noted in Chapter 1, the existing literature has not, by and large, taken account of how the dynamic interaction between market makers affects the individual dealer-specialist quotes and the establishment of the best market quotes. The most common approach in the literature is either to ignore trader interactions, or simply to assume a monopoly dealer. There is not as yet a complete model of the market spread. We now turn to a more detailed discussion of this unsolved problem.

5.1.2 Modeling the Market Spread

Demsetz focused academic attention on the role of market makers in an environment characterized by random, asynchronous order arrival; subsequently, a number of papers have dealt with models of dealer-specialist behavior. These either have modeled a competitive dealer but ignored the interaction of his quotes with other dealers' quotes [e.g., Stoll (1978*a*)], or have assumed a monopoly dealer through whom all trades must be executed [e.g., Garman (1976), Amihud-Mendelson (1980), Ho-Stoll (1981), and Mildenstein-Schleef (1983)]. These various simplifications were required for analytical tractability.

However, most markets contain numerous traders who take account of quotes already established on the market, and who post quotes for a security at various prices. Yet, aside from the work of Ho-Stoll (1980, 1983), no attempt has been made to model the size of the market bid-ask spread (or individual dealer spreads, for that matter) in the dynamic, interactive context that characterizes actual security markets.

True, individuals qua consumers always trade by the equivalent of market orders (i.e., one does not leave an order at the supermarket saying, "If you drop the price to 31 cents, I'll buy a dozen cans of chicken soup"). However, individuals qua investors do sometimes seek to trade by limit orders. Market participants cannot simply be dichotomized into demanders and providers of immediacy. Furthermore, immediacy is a by-product provided freely in any organized asset market when participants, for their own trading purposes, transmit their demand propensities to the market in the form of limit orders. Hence while certain market participants such as dealers and stock exchange specialists do indeed (at a price) provide immediacy to the market, they are not the *only* providers, and the market spread is not simply the price they impose for their services. And since quotes differ across dealers on the OTC and across various limit-order traders (including the specialist) on the exchanges, the market spread (the difference between the lowest ask and the highest bid) will in general be smaller than the spread of any individual trader.

Along with altering one's view of the provision of immediacy, the fact that ordinary investors will transmit limit orders to the market for their own trading purposes highlights the need to model the size of the *market* spread. In our own work in Sections 5.2 through 5.6, we have taken a first step in this direction by demonstrating that a spread will naturally exist in a market comprised of many traders with heterogeneous trading propensities. Also, Ho-Stoll (1983) have addressed the issue of quote determination in a competitive environment that allows for the interaction between many dealers. However, no one has presented a complete model of the size of the market spread.

By and large, the literature has not even clearly differentiated between individual dealer-specialist spreads and the market spread.[2] Because the dealer-specialist has traditionally been viewed as imposing the spread as his price for providing immediacy, one might presume that with a trading system where brokers act as agents but never as principals, if there were no dealer-specialist making the market, there would be no immediacy and there would be no spread. However, once it is recognized that a market spread will naturally exist, it follows that the introduction of a dealer-specialist who (sometimes) sets market quotes will likely make the spread smaller.

Failure to distinguish between individual spreads and the market spread has also been prevalent in various empirical studies. Models that have been developed with reference to individual dealer-specialist spreads have, on a number of occasions, been tested using data on market spreads. These include the empirical studies of spreads on: the NYSE by Demsetz (1968), Tinic (1972), Barnea-Logue (1975), and Branch-Freed (1977);[3] the Toronto Stock Exchange by Tinic-West (1974); and the AMEX by Branch-Freed (1977).

With regard to modeling the market spread, we suggest that a straightforward aggregation from individual spreads is not possible in a system where there is no clear distinction between demanders and suppliers of immediacy, and where traders meet in a dynamic, interactive environment.[4] To see this, consider the following simple aggregation model which ignores the dynamics of the market process. Assume a set of N immediacy providers who all believe that they face identical order-flow schedules (e.g., s_i and d_i in Figure 1, panel B) and identical costs.[5] In this case, all immediacy providers have identical s' and d' curves, the market S' and D' curves would be straightforward aggregates of these, and the market bid and ask quotes (B and A) would be the same as each immediacy provider's own quotes (b_i and a_i). Next consider the case in panel C, where some jth immediacy provider perceives different order-flow schedules, s_j and d_j. Taking account of his (not necessarily different) costs, we have the s_j' and d_j' curves, from which he generates his own quotes b_j and a_j. This suggests that the market spread (at least temporarily) will be $a_j - b_i$.[6]

Now let each of the N immediacy providers have a nonzero personal limit-order spread, S_i. Let S_{ij} be the spread that would describe a pairing of the ith and the jth immediacy providers:

$$S_{ij} = \text{Min}\,(a_i,\ a_j) - \text{Max}\,(b_i,\ b_j)$$

The actual market spread will be given by S_{ij}^{Min}, the smallest element in the set. Because crossing quotes trigger trades, in a no-trade equilibrium we must have $S_{ij} > 0$ for all i, j. But in a noninteractive context, traders set their quotes myopically without reference to the quotes of others, and there is no reason for expecting a lower bound on S_{ij} other than zero. Thus, if it is assumed that the S_{ij} can take on any value in an interval bounded below by zero and that they are selected according to some probability distribution such that

$$\Pr\,(S_{ij} < \epsilon) > 0 \qquad \text{for all } \epsilon > 0 \tag{1}$$

then as the number of immediacy providers, N, increases without bound, the expected value of S_{ij}^{Min} (and hence the expected market spread) goes to zero. For example, if the S_{ij} are uniformly distributed in the interval 0 to S_i^{Max}, then

$$E[S_{ij}^{\text{Min}}] = \frac{S_i^{\text{Max}}}{C_2^N} \tag{2}$$

where C_2^N stands for the number of combinations of N items taken two at a time. As N increases, $E[S_{ij}^{\text{Min}}]$ can be seen to go to zero. Such a proof could be constructed for any probability distribution on S_{ij} that follows Eq. (1), although the rate at which $E[S_{ij}^{\text{Min}}]$ goes to zero as N increases would depend on the probability distribution chosen.

It is thus apparent that given a large number of limit-order traders with heterogeneous trading propensities, the analytical problem gets reversed. Rather than seeking to explain the provision of immediacy by a separate class of people who specialize in providing this service, the objective becomes explaining the existence of the spread itself—that is, explaining why a gap is typically observed in the limit-order book between the array of bid and ask quotations.

Our own analysis of the order-placement strategy of individual traders shows that no trader will place a limit order at a price infinitesimally close to that of a counterpart order already established on the market (see Section 5.5). Hence we must have a strictly positive lower bound on the S_{ij}, Eq. (1) will not be satisfied, and, accordingly, there must be a positive market spread. Our own analysis is limited, however, in that while we have developed an existence proof of the market spread, we have not yet attempted to formulate a complete model of its equilibrium size. Modeling the lower bound on the S_{ij} might be a productive route to follow, although we are not certain.

5.1.3 Implications for Empirical Analysis

Individual dealer-specialist spreads must be distinguished from market spreads. As mentioned above, the literature has focused analytically on the individual spreads, although empirical tests have on a number of occasions used market spreads.

Clear comparisons are difficult to make because of numerous variations of test design, but it appears that, by and large, tests run on market spreads have yielded results that do not differ sharply from those obtained when average dealer spreads are used. Most fortunately, however, for a sample of OTC securities, Hamilton (1978) has presented two sets of regressions that differ only in that one uses his definition of the market spread (see footnote 2) and the other uses the average dealer spread. The overall goodness of Hamilton's regressions, as indicated by the R^2s, is virtually identical for both sets of tests, and the individual independent variables generally have the correct sign and are significant.

Most interestingly, however, when average dealer spreads are used, Hamilton's price and risk variables tend to be more significant, while the number of shareholders shows no clearly systematic difference. On the other hand, the number of dealers per security appears to have a more negative and significant coefficient when regressed on the market spread. These results are expected for the following reasons: for a security, the price and risk variables directly enter the dealer pricing models;[7,8] the number of shareholders (as a long-term proxy for the security's activity variable)[9] enters both the dealer pricing model and our model of the gravitational pull effect (which accounts for the existence of the market spread, as we show in Section 5.5); while the number of dealers would operate primarily through the aggregation process, and thus should have its most direct impact on the market spread.

Along with improving the basic specification of the test design, an explicit model of the market spread should also lead to a more precise empirical definition of some variables. For instance, consider the widely discussed (negative) relationship between spreads and the activity variable. Because on the organized exchanges, the market spread can vary as new orders are placed on the limit-order book or as old orders are withdrawn or executed, it is possible for the book to thin out and for the spread to widen temporarily during periods of unusual trading activity. This could cause an upward bias in cross-sectional estimates of the underlying relationship between spread and market size. Recognition of this suggests a possible solution: use of long-run proxy variables for activity (as did Demsetz and Hamilton) and for a security's market spread (by averaging a "reasonably" large number of intertemporal observations).[10]

An explicit model of the market spread is required for one other reason: the proper interpretation of empirical findings. This is clearly the case in relation to one of the most interesting hypotheses that has pervaded the literature—

that spreads are larger in thinner markets. The general sweep of the empirical findings shows a positive spread-thinness relationship. But this finding is consistent with a number of alternative hypotheses: economies of scale in the dealer-specialist function [Demsetz (1968)], decreasing costs of providing immediacy but not necessarily a natural monopoly [Tinic-West (1974)], the impact of greater competition in the markets for thicker issues and/or market making being less risky for high-volume issues [Smidt (1971)], and industry economies of scale external to the individual dealer-specialist firms [Benston-Hagerman (1974) and Hamilton (1976)].

Into this crowded ring we throw another hat. We contend that the negative impact of market thinness on market spreads might be only weakly related to the cost structure of immediacy providers. Rather, our own analysis will demonstrate that a "natural" market spread would exist in the absence of dealers-specialists, and that this natural spread will itself be negatively related to market activity. Although the behavior of costs on the individual dealer-specialist level could explain the empirical findings (especially when average dealer spreads are used), an unambiguous interpretation along these lines for the market spread is not possible, given the impact of market thinness on the natural spread.

5.2 THE SCENARIO

Consider an investor who maximizes the expected utility of terminal wealth and, for simplicity, let him allocate funds between only two assets: a risk asset and cash (which we take to be the numéraire asset). In the absence of transaction costs, the market would be monitored continuously and appropriate transactions would be made with each change in the market price and the investor's demand propensities. Then, if the price were continuous, there would be no spread and the market price would be determined by a straightforward aggregation of individual demand propensities.

However, a variety of transaction costs influence the investor's trading decisions. The fixed (with respect to number of shares traded) costs of assessing information, monitoring the market, and conveying orders to the market imply that the investor will make trading decisions only periodically. Further, when decisions are made, he will not convey his full set of demand propensities to the market. For one thing, trades that involve sufficiently small portfolio adjustments would not justify the transaction costs incurred.[11] Also, attempts to transmit several limit orders simultaneously would be likely to overload our current system. Furthermore, a continuous auction that does not generate a Walrasian solution cannot readily handle multiple buy-sell orders that, ex ante, are intended to be alternatives.[12]

In light of transaction costs (and also taking account of the timing and magnitude of exogenous cash flows), the investor will establish a discrete set of decision points. In the analysis presented in Section 5.4, we take the frequency of these points as predetermined. Upon reaching a decision point, an investor can do nothing, hit an existing limit order with his own market order, or place his own limit order at a "better" price and run the risk of its not executing. A concurrent strategy issue also exists when the investor finds it prohibitively expensive to convey his entire set of demand propensities to the market; for all intents and purposes, he must select the single best alternative to transmit.

5.3 THE PROBABILITY OF A LIMIT ORDER EXECUTING

In this section, we establish the conditions under which the probability of execution does not approach a limit of unity as the price at which the limit order is placed is taken to be infinitesimally close to the counterpart market quote. Under these conditions, we obtain a probability jump (at the counterpart market quote) that underlies the gravitational pull effect developed in Section 5.5. By showing that the probability jump can be attributed to the existence of transaction costs, we establish the basic linkage between spreads and transaction costs.

Consider the case where an investor contemplates submitting a limit bid at the price P_t^{LB} at time t, and let price be a continuous variable. A similar argument can be constructed for the case of a limit ask. Assume that the limit order will be canceled if it is unfilled by the next decision point at time $t + 1$. Let L be the length of time between decision points t and $t + 1$.

Let P_t^{MA} be the market ask price at time t. Consistent with the random walk version of the efficient market hypothesis, we make the Markov assumption that each subsequent market ask depends only on the preceding market ask. If we also assume that each change in the natural log of the market ask Z_i, is a random variable that is independently and identically distributed over time with mean zero and variance Var (Z_i), then we can model the market-ask-price generation process as a compound Poisson stochastic process:[13]

$$\ln P_t^{MA}(\Delta) = \ln P_t^{MA} + \sum_{i=1}^{N(\Delta)} Z_i \tag{3}$$

where Δ is the time from the last decision point. When Δ equals L, we have $P_t^{MA}(\Delta) = P_{t+1}^{MA}$; when Δ equals $2L$, we have $P_t^{MA}(\Delta) = P_{t+2}^{MA}$; and so on. The number of changes in the market ask that take place in the time interval Δ is $N(\Delta)$. We assume that $N(\Delta)$ follows a Poisson process with arrival rate ν.

The next step is to determine the probability of execution (during a time interval of length L) of a limit bid submitted at a price P_t^{LB}, which is greater than the current market bid (P_t^{MB}) but less than the current market ask (P_t^{MA}). Clearly, as the limit bid price approaches the market ask (from below), the probability of execution increases. One might suppose that this probability approaches unity as the limit bid approaches the market ask; however, this need not be the case. In particular, we have formally proved:[14]

Proposition 1. If P_t^{MA} is generated by the compound Poisson process of Eq. (3), then no matter how closely the limit bid approaches the market ask (from below), the probability of the limit order executing is less than unity in any time interval of finite length.

Since a market order will always execute with probability 1, Proposition 1 gives a probability jump at the market ask.

Transaction costs are crucial to the existence of the probability jump. In the absence of transaction costs, one might expect that, following the work of Merton (1973), the logarithm of the market ask would best be described by a Wiener process with zero drift:

$$d \ln P_t^{\mathrm{MA}}(\Delta) = \sigma \, dZ(\Delta) \tag{4}$$

where σ is the instantaneous variance of the process and $dZ(\Delta)$ is a standardized Wiener process. In this case, the price $P_t^{\mathrm{MA}}(\Delta)$ would experience an infinite number of adjustments in the interval $0 \leq (\Delta) \leq L$. In Appendix B, we restate, formally and prove:

Proposition 2. If $P_t^{\mathrm{MA}}(\Delta)$ is generated by the Wiener process of Eq. (4), then as the limit bid approaches the market ask (from below), the probability of the limit order executing approaches unity for all time intervals of finite length.

Proposition 2 implies that for the Weiner process there will be no probability jump at the market ask.

We next consider whether there is a relationship between the compound Poisson process of Eq. (3) and the Wiener process of Eq. (4). In Appendix B, we restate formally and prove:

Proposition 3. If the random variable Z_i in the compound Poisson process of Eq. (3) has two equally likely possible values, $+\alpha$ and $-\alpha$, and if the arrival rate ν of this compound Poisson process increases without bound while α simultaneously decreases in such a way that $\nu\alpha^2$ is constant, then the compound Poisson process approaches the Wiener process described by Eq. (4) with the variance of the Wiener process, σ^2, equaling $\nu\alpha^2$.

Proposition 3 states that the compound Poisson process can be expected to approach the Wiener process under appropriate assumptions.[15] Thus the probability jump of Proposition 1 would disappear as ν increased and Var (Z_i) decreased. In Appendix B, we restate formally and prove:

Proposition 4. As the arrival rate ν in the compound Poisson process of Eq. (1) increases, the probability of a limit order executing increases for all $P_t^{\mathrm{LB}} < P_t^{\mathrm{MA}}$.

Hence the probability of a limit order executing increases at all $P_t^{LB} < P_t^{MA}$ as the activity proxy ν increases. Stated conversely, the thinner a security (that is, the less frequently investors submit orders to trade in the security), the lower is the probability of execution at each $P_t^{LB} < P_t^{MA}$, and therefore the greater is the probability jump at P_t^{MA}.

The four propositions stated in this section have important implications for the analysis of the impact of transaction costs on bid-ask spreads. Without transaction costs, the market price could be expected to behave as a Wiener process; that is, there would be an infinite number of infinitesimally small price adjustments. Then the investor who was considering placing a limit order could reduce the probability of his order not executing to arbitrarily close to zero by placing his order sufficiently close to the counterpart market quotation.

On the other hand, with transaction costs and a finite number of investors, the market price would generally not behave as a Wiener process. Investors would find continuous adjustments in their portfolios too expensive, and market prices would behave as a stochastic jump process (Proposition 3 shows that this process could generally be expected to approach a Wiener process as the order arrival rate is increased). One such jump process is the compound Poisson, and it also is consistent with an efficient market. Proposition 1 demonstrates that for such a stochastic jump process, a probability jump exists. Proposition 4 shows that the probability jump will be greater for thinner securities. In Section 5.5 we will show that for thinner issues, the larger probability jump leads to larger equilibrium market spreads.

5.4 A MODEL OF INVESTOR ORDER-PLACEMENT STRATEGY

We now consider how an investor will choose between trading via a market order or a limit order, or not seeking to trade at all. The problem is structured as follows. Because of the costs of monitoring the market, let the investor consider rebalancing his portfolio only at preselected points in time, $t = 1, 2, \ldots, T - 1$, where T is the investment horizon.[16] To simplify the analysis, we now consider only the placement of purchase orders for the risk asset (omitting the symmetric case of sell orders without loss of generality).

At any of the $T - 1$ decision points, the investor is faced with three possible courses of action:

(a) Submit a market order to buy shares at the current market ask price of P_t^{MA}.

(b) Submit a limit order to buy shares at a limit bid price of $P_t^{LB} < P_t^{MA}$.

(c) Do nothing.

In modeling the investor's choice among these three alternatives, we make the following assumptions that simplify the analysis without materially affecting the nature of the conclusions. We assume that all orders are for a fixed number of shares ΔN, and that when any market or limit order is executed, it is satisfied fully at the stated price; this avoids the tedium of writing (average) transaction prices and transaction costs as functions of the number of shares exchanged and of defining probabilities of partial execution. We assume that unfilled limit orders are canceled prior to the next decision point; this avoids both the need to include additional state variables (the price and quantity of any limit order outstanding) and the need to analyze additional courses of action (submit a market order and leave the old limit order outstanding, or submit a market order and remove the limit order, etc.). Finally, we assume no lags in the transmission of information and orders; this avoids the complexity of dealing with changes in the current market quotes during the time the investor formulates and implements his decision.

If option (a) is chosen, the market order will be executed, and the investor's holdings at time $t + 1$ become $N_{t+1} = N_t + \Delta N$, for which the investor pays a total cost of $\Delta N\, P_t^{\mathrm{MA}} + C^M$, where C^M is the total cost of transmitting and executing the market order.

If option (b) is chosen, one of two events can take place:

(b1) The limit order is executed. The investor's share holdings then become $N_{t+1} = N_t + \Delta N$, for which the investor pays a total cost of $\Delta N\, P_t^{\mathrm{LB}} + C^{L1} + C^{L2}$, where C^{L1} is the cost of transmitting a limit order to the market and C^{L2} is the cost of executing the order.

(b2) The limit order does not execute and is canceled prior to the next decision point. The investor's share holdings then remain unchanged ($N_{t+1} = N_t$), and his cash is decreased by the cost of transmitting the limit order, C^{L1}.

Option (b) will be chosen over (a) if the gain associated with the possibility of trading at a more favorable price outweighs the loss associated with the probability of not trading at all.

The investor considers four subjective probability distributions in order to make an optimal decision. These are (1) the joint probability distribution of market bid and ask prices at time $t + 1$, conditional upon the quotes at time t; (2) the probability of a limit bid order submitted at time t executing before time $t + 1$; (3) and (4) the joint probability distribution of market bid and ask prices at time $t + 1$, conditional upon the quotes at time t, and further dependent upon whether a limit bid submitted at time t either (3) did or (4) did not execute prior to time $t + 1$. In Appendix B, we discuss in more detail these four subjective probability distributions (only three of which are independent).

A dynamic programming model of the investor's choice among options (a), (b), and (c) is formulated in Appendix B. The investor is assumed to maximize his expected utility of terminal wealth, Max (U_1, U_2, U_3), where U_1 is the expected utility of choosing option (a) (the market-order strategy); U_2 is the expected utility of choosing option (b) (the limit-order strategy); and U_3 is the expected utility of choosing option (c) (the do-nothing strategy). It is convenient to focus on the utility gain, ΔU_1 or ΔU_2, which results from choosing option (a) or (b) rather than option (c): $\Delta U_1 = U_1 - U_3$; $\Delta U_2(P_t^{LB}) = U_2(P_t^{LB}) - U_3$ (note that U_2 and ΔU_2 are functions of the limit bid price). Clearly $\Delta U_2(P_t^{LB} = P_t^{MA}) = \Delta U_1$, since, at this price, the market-order and limit-order strategies are effectively the same.

Let us now consider the conditions under which $U_1 > \text{Max}\ (U_2, U_3)$, in which case the investor will submit a market order, or $U_2 > \text{Max}\ (U_1, U_3)$, in which case the investor will submit a limit order. Suppose that at the current market quotes the do-nothing strategy is dominated (i.e., $\text{Max}\ [U_1, U_2] > U_3$). Given our utility gains [ΔU_1 and $\Delta U_2^{LB}(P_t)$] and the probability function for limit-order execution developed in Section 5.3 above, we know the utility gain from placing a market order and can readily obtain an expected utility gain function for the limit-order strategy. These are depicted in Figure 2; the shape of the function is explained as follows.

1. While the utility of a consummated trade decreases monotonically with P_t^{LB}, the probability of execution increases with P_t^{LB}, with two probability jumps (at the market bid and the market ask). The jump at P_t^{MB} reflects the institutional reality that orders placed at prices less than or equal to P_t^{MB} would not have priority over the current market bid, whereas an order placed at a price above P_t^{MB} would be at the top of the limit-order book. The jump at P_t^{MA} follows from Proposition 1.
2. Since the probability of execution is constant to the right of P_t^{MA}, the expected utility gain has a peak at P_t^{MA}, corresponding to the utility gain of transacting via a market order.

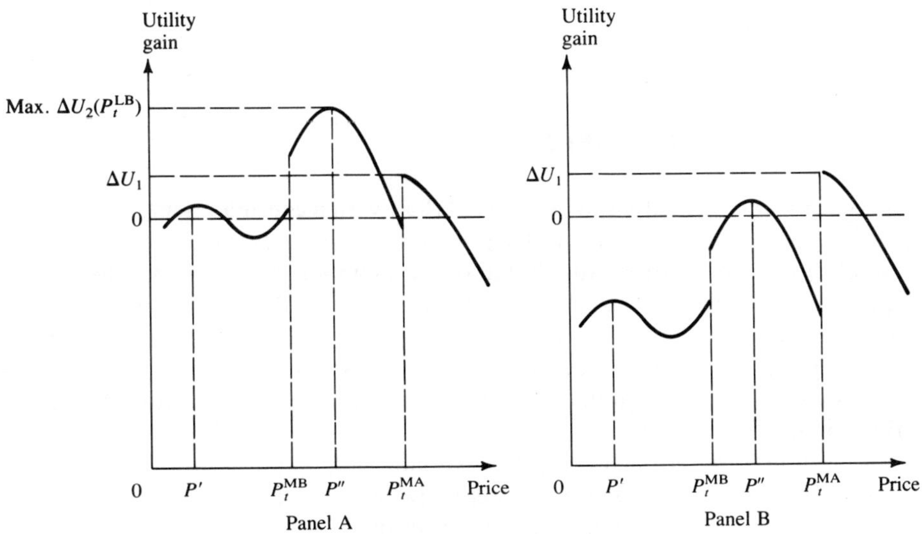

Figure 2 Illustrative utility gain functions.

3. The probability of execution increases between P_t^{MB} and P_t^{MA}, with the greatest relative increase just to the right of P_t^{MB}. We expect this large probability increase in this neighborhood because the strategy considerations of other investors might lead them to place limit orders just to the right of P_t^{MB} in order to capture the largest price advantage. Hence the second peak in the expected utility gain function will occur at some point P'', between P_t^{MB} and P_t^{MA}.
4. The probability of execution decreases rapidly in a neighborhood just to the left of P_t^{MB} because of existing limit orders on the book. However, since there would be a clustering of limit orders near P_t^{MB}, we would expect the probability of execution to decrease more slowly as the limit price, P_t^{LB}, moves further from P_t^{MB}. Hence we might find a third peak in the expected utility gain function to occur at some point P' to the left of P_t^{MB}.

Which of the three peaks in $\Delta U_2(P_t)$ will dominate depends on the particular form of the probability function for limit-order execution as well as the utility function. In the particular diagram presented in Figure 2, panel A, $\Delta U_2(P_t^{LB})$ has positive values (hence a do-nothing strategy is dominated), has values greater than ΔU_1 (hence the market-order strategy is dominated), and gives a global maximum at P''. Assuming only one limit order per investor, the optimal strategy is to place a limit bid at P''. The setting of such a bid quotation can be considered a Stigler (1961) type of search activity.[17]

Clearly the limit-order strategy need not always be superior; in selecting this strategy, the investor also accepts the chance that the order may fail to execute, in which case the investor would be worse off than had he done nothing since he would have also lost the cost of placing the order. If the probability of failing to execute is high enough and $\Delta U_1 > 0$, the investor will prefer the market order strategy as illustrated in Figure 2, panel B.[18]

5.5 THE MARKET SPREAD

It is clear from the analysis in Section 5.4 that, with a continuous auction market, each investor's order-placement decision is made with reference to prices already established in the market—the bid and ask quotations which define the market spread. In turn, each investor's order may affect the market spread, possibly causing subsequent traders to react. Hence the market spread is the product of a dynamic interactive process. In this section, we show that a nonzero market spread must exist, define the equilibrium market spread, and relate a security's equilibrium spread to its thinness.

The limit-order book comprises the limit orders transmitted to the market by many traders, and the spread is essentially a gap in the limit-order book. Therefore, having established that individual investors will sometimes seek to trade via limit orders, we must show why a noninfinitesimal gap in the array of such orders exists between the market quotes. We do so by considering the impact that the jump in the probability of a limit order executing (Section 5.3) has on the investor's optimal order-placement strategy (Section 5.4).

Due to continuity of the utility function, and because of the discontinuous drop in the probability of execution that occurs at the market ask as we move to lower prices, we must have a discontinuous drop in $\Delta U_2(P_t^{\text{LB}})$ as we move past the market ask to lower prices. Then because of continuity of the probability function until we get to the market bid (at which point another discontinuous drop occurs), it necessarily follows that $\Delta U_2(P_t^{\text{MA}})$ cannot exceed ΔU_1 within a nonzero neighborhood to the left of P_t^{MA}. Hence no limit bid will be placed infinitesimally close to the market ask, and therefore we must have a nonzero bid-ask spread.

Intuitively viewed, consider an investor who is thinking about whether or not to place a limit bid at some price below the market ask. As the potential limit price rises toward the market ask, it becomes relatively more attractive to transact at the market ask with certainty. At some point, the investor will prefer buying at a discretely higher, unitary probability of execution. In other words, certainty of execution at the market ask creates a kind of gravitational pull which causes investors to jump their price once their potential limit bid gets close enough to the market ask. This clears out limit bids when they get too close to the market ask, thereby leaving a nonzero spread.

We next consider the issue of an equilibrium market spread.

Definition. In a dynamic trading process, we define the *equilibrium market spread* as the bid-ask spread at which, for the next instant of time, the probability of the spread increasing is equal to the probability of the spread decreasing.[19]

This definition does not imply that if away from equilibrium the spread will necessarily move toward it on the next order, but only that it is more likely to do so than not.

We assume that a unique equilibrium exists. To examine the reasonableness of this assumption, first consider an arbitrarily small spread. Because the probability of a limit order being placed has a discrete jump at P_t^{MA}, we have already argued that there will be no limit orders placed in some nonzero neighborhood below P_t^{MA} by *all* investors seeking to buy the security. (The generalization from a single investor to all investors takes place simply by choosing the smallest neighborhood found among all investors.) Therefore, for a sufficiently small bid-ask spread, the unconditional probability of the spread increasing must exceed the unconditional probability of the spread decreasing as analyzed from the standpoint of the buyer. A similar argument holds for the seller.

Now consider what occurs when the spread widens. The larger the spread is, the greater the potential utility gain from an optimally priced limit order, while the utility gain from a market order will remain unchanged or fall. The gain in utility occurs because the shares can be bought (or sold) at a lower (or higher) price via limit order than by market order.[20] With the rise in utility $U_2(P_t^{\mathrm{LB}})$, investors will begin to shift their preferences from market orders to limit orders. As more and more investors shift to limit orders, the probability of the spread increasing falls, while the probability of it decreasing rises.

One of two situations must occur. Either the spread would tend to reach a point at which the two probabilities would be equal, in which case it would be the equilibrium market spread, or the limit-order book would be empty on one or both sides.[21] Since when the order book is empty market orders cannot transact, we would be at a point where the probability of a limit order is greater than that of a market order. Although such a point might be achieved without the equilibrium market spread ever being attained, we believe that it would be atypical.[22]

Our definition of the equilibrium market spread provides a direct link between the market spread and thinness. Recall that Proposition 4 showed that the probability of a limit order executing decreases, for all values of P_t^{LD}, as a security's order arrival rate decreases. Thus, ceteris paribus, thin issues have a lower probability of limit orders executing than do thick issues. This lower probability in turn decreases the proportion of investors choosing limit orders over market orders at any given size of the spread; this implies that, for a thinner issue, a wider spread would be required for the forces that increase and decrease the spread to be in equilibrium. Hence we have:

Proposition 5. Thinner securities will, ceteris paribus, have larger equilibrium market spreads.

5.6 CONCLUSION

Our proof of the existence of market spreads treats prices as continuous and allows for heterogeneous trading propensities. The proof is not dependent on traders' demand for immediacy or on market makers' cost of providing immediacy.

The literature on bid-ask spreads does not appear to have recognized that aggregation from individual to market spreads is a considerably more complex process than the standard aggregation from individual to market demand and supply functions. Neither has it been established that ordinary investors may sometimes seek to trade via limit orders, at other times via market orders, and hence that these investors will at times supply and at other times demand immediacy. In addressing these issues and the order-placement strategies that they imply, we have sought to establish the links between transaction costs, market thinness, and market spreads.

We have first established that, with transaction costs, the probability of a limit order executing does not rise to unity as the price at which the order is placed gets infinitesimally close to a counterpart market quote. We have shown next that the resulting investor trading strategies generate what we have referred to as a gravitational pull effect. Essentially, in the neighborhood of the current market bid and ask quotations, what might otherwise have been limit orders are instead submitted as market orders (at slightly less desirable prices) so as to achieve certainty of execution. These market orders trigger trades which clear limit orders off the book, widening the market spread. The gravitational pull effect explains why market spreads may be substantial even in markets composed of many limit-order traders. Finally, we have defined an equilibrium market spread (where the forces that tend to widen and to narrow the spread are in balance) and have shown it to be positively related to a security's thinness (measured inversely by the order arrival rate).

Our formulation has several implications for systems design. A primary objective should be to expand the extent and frequency with which investors interact with the market by minimizing various transaction costs. Decreasing variable transaction costs will decrease individual spreads and generate a greater order flow; decreasing the costs of monitoring and communicating with the market will also increase the frequency with which investors rebalance their portfolios; and consolidating the currently fragmented system (by, e.g., instituting a consolidated limit-order book) will reduce search costs and further shrink spreads by increasing the effective thickness of the market. These costs are all a function of market structure and hence should be amenable to reduction by appropriate system design. However, a major cost of interacting with the market is the cost of decision making, and this might not be subject to significant reduction by exchange organization. For this reason, it is possible that, especially for thinner issues, spreads will remain sizable in a restructured national market system.

NOTES

*The principal source of the material in Section 5.1 is K. J. Cohen, S. F. Maier, R. A. Schwartz, and D. K. Whitcomb, "Market Makers and the Market Spread: A Review of Recent Literature," *Journal of Financial and Quantitative Analysis*, Vol. 14, 1979, pp. 813–835. Sections 5.2 through 5.6 are a slightly modified version of K. J. Cohen, S. F. Maier, R. A. Schwartz, and D. K. Whitcomb, "Transaction Costs, Order Placement Strategy, and Existence of the Bid-Ask Spread," *Journal of Political Economy*, Vol. 89, 1981, pp. 287–305 (© 1981 by the University of Chicago).

1. Demsetz recognizes several different types of market participants as providers of immediacy: specialists, dealers, floor traders, and limit-order traders.
2. Hamilton (1976, 1978) is one of the few academicians to distinguish clearly between the two. In his empirical investigation, he has considered both average dealer spreads and, for the OTC, the market spread which he measures as ". . . the difference between the mean of the three highest bid prices and the mean of the three lowest ask prices" (1978, p. 495). Although vis-à-vis the inside spread, the definition overstates the size of the market spread, Hamilton's empirical observations led him to conclude that on the OTC, average dealer spreads are much larger than are market spreads [see Hamilton (1978, pp. 495 and 501)]. In their OTC study, Benston-Hagerman (1974) also use a measure of the market spread. Garbade-Silber (1976) as well recognize that the cost of

liquidity services is not simply related to the size of average dealer spreads when quotes are not identical across dealers. Stoll (1978b) also distinguishes between average dealer spreads and the inside quotation (his tests correctly use the former).

3. In addition, Hamilton (1978) refers to the spreads obtained from the NYSE as specialist spreads. Although data on these spreads are generally obtained initially from the specialists by floor reporters, these spreads need not reflect the specialists' own quotes (the quotes can come from floor traders or from the limit-order book).
4. In our model in Sections 5.2 through 5.5, an equilibrium spread cannot be determined by the solution of a simultaneous system of equations because the model assumes that investors make their trading decisions *after* they first observe the market quotes. It is this sequencing over time that generates the need for a dynamic analysis. For a similar reason, our model does not apply directly to the initial formulation of spreads at the start of any trading session on a continuous auction exchange.
5. We here assume for convenience that each immediacy provider receives an equal share of the order flow; accordingly, the scale of the quantity axis in panel B is $(1/N)$th that of panel A, where N is the number of immediacy providers.
6. It is clear that in this situation immediacy provider j will be a net seller of shares, and immediacy provider i will be a net buyer. While this type of unbalanced situation cannot persist forever, we do commonly observe that during particular periods specific immediacy providers are active on only one side of the market. Furthermore, since the true order schedules shift randomly over time, there is no reason in this model to expect all immediacy providers to converge over time to a common perception of their order-flow schedules. [Garbade-Silber (1976, p. 728) make a similar point.]
7. Price enters through the inventory variable, since inventories are measured in dollar amounts.
8. Stoll (1978b) also finds risk to have a significant effect, and he too uses dealer spreads. Demsetz, and Tinic-West, on the other hand, do not find risk to be significant in their studies of the market spread.
9. Demsetz (1968) and Benston-Hagerman (1974) also used the number of shareholders to proxy long-run average volume.
10. Note that in light of this expanded data requirement, and given the difficulty of getting reliable data on spreads, a procedure for inferring spreads from transactions data developed by Smidt (1979) would be particularly important.
11. It can readily be demonstrated that variable as well as fixed transaction costs make sufficiently small portfolio adjustments prohibitively expensive.
12. That is, if any array of buy and sell orders from one investor is executed sequentially, the desired quantities at each price should be dependent on the exact sequence of purchase and sales followed.
13. For expositional simplicity we assume that the stochastic processes have no drift (that is, their expected value is zero). It should be noted that even though $\ln P_t^{\text{MA}}$ is assumed to have no drift, the price series itself, P_t^{MA}, may have drift. For example, when $\ln (P_{t+1}^{\text{MA}}/P_t^{\text{MA}})$ is normal, with mean zero and standard deviation σ, then $P_{t+1}^{\text{MA}}/P_t^{\text{MA}}$ is log normal with mean $\exp[\sigma^2/2]$.

    There will be a realization of the random variable Z_i at each point of time when any one of the following events occurs to affect the specific limit order which sets the market ask: (a) it is withdrawn; (b) it executes against a crossing buy order; or (c) it remains on the book but is no longer the market ask since a lower limit sell has been submitted [events (a) and (b) necessarily result in a change in the market ask when price is continuous and utility functions are heterogeneous, which implies a zero probability of having two or more orders at a specific price]. Only event (b) is associated with transactions; hence the number of Z_i which materialize during any interval will usually exceed the number of transactions in that interval.

14. See Appendix B for a formal restatement and proof of this proposition.
15. The particular distribution chosen for Z_i in Proposition 3 is not critical. Other appropriately chosen discrete or continuous distributions can also be shown in the limit to go to the Wiener process.
16. Note that the rebalancing points need not be the same for all investors, so that trades can occur at any time when the market is open even if specific traders are not continually in the market.
17. By the placement of such a limit order, a seller or buyer announces his propensity to trade with the hope of getting the attention of a counterpart market participant who would also be willing to trade.
18. There are two other versions of Figure 2. One would be analogous to panel A, but with the global maximum at P' (below the market bid). The second version would be where the zero point on the utility gain axis is higher than both max $\Delta U_2(P_t^{LB})$ and ΔU_1; in this case, the investor would do nothing.
19. Note that the probability is not conditioned on the current status of individual investors, recent prices, or other market conditions.

    Note that we use the term "equilibrium market spread" to refer to one particular point in the probability distribution of the market spread, rather than to refer to a statistic for the central tendency of the entire distribution. We do not adopt a central tendency definition (such as expected value, mode, or median) of the equilibrium spread because it does not provide a ready link between the market forces that generate the spread and thinness. For empirical research, the average market spread is likely to be a reasonable proxy for our definition of the equilibrium market spread.
20. We assume that the spread does not impart any information to the investor on the direction of future price movements.
21. No other possibility exists. So long as the probability of the spread increasing is greater than the probability of it decreasing, the spread will on expectation grow—limited only by the collapse of the limit-order book on one side or the other.
22. With regard to the assumption of uniqueness, investors might have utility functions that could lead to more than one equilibrium market spread. Consider the case where an investor views a very wide spread as signaling the advent of new information that may cause a price adjustment of unknown direction. The investor sensing greater risk might now choose a do-nothing strategy over placing either a limit or market order. This could support a very wide market equilibrium spread. Of course, investors would eventually conclude that the new information was not forthcoming, and trading would resume at its former frequency with the old equilibrium spread reestablished.

6

SERIAL CORRELATION AND THE INTERVALLING-EFFECT BIAS IN BETA*

Over the years, the literature has reported a number of diverse and seemingly anomolous empirical phenomena concerning returns calculated from closing transaction prices. The most notable are these:

1. Despite only weak serial correlation in individual securities' returns,[1] market index returns display significant positive serial correlation. The effect is greatest for short differencing (i.e., returns measurement) intervals and for indexes giving the most weight to thin (low market value) securities.[2]
2. OLS beta estimates are quite sensitive to changes in the differencing interval; thin security betas rise and very thick security betas fall as the differencing interval is lengthened.[3]

Two elements of commonality among the phenomena, an intervalling effect and a thinness relationship, are evident, and a third, nonzero cross-serial covariance, is implicit.[4]

In this chapter, we provide a unified microstructure explanation of these diverse empirical phenomena. We show how friction in the trading process leads to a pattern of price-adjustment delays that may be fairly long lived. These delays in turn result in serial correlation in observed (i.e., calculated from recorded transactions) security and index returns and bias in ordinary-least-squares-estimated (OLSE) beta. The model predicts the sign, thinness relationship, and intervalling effect that we observe empirically for index serial correlation and OLSE beta. It also leads to three alternative adjustment procedures for producing unbiased estimates of beta. Our results are consistent with the efficient market hypothesis because we get countervailing sign effects for individual-security serial correlation, and because observed transaction prices may not reflect prices at which one can actually buy and sell the security. That is, traders may not be able to develop profitable trading rules based on observed serial correlation patterns.

The first inkling that there might be a microstructure explanation for any of these phenomena is the suggestion by Fisher (1966) that nonsynchronous trading (a tendency of some securities to have their last transaction earlier in the day than others or to miss a day altogether) may cause index serial correlation. This was made a bit more explicit by Schwartz-Whitcomb (1977a). The first formal model of the bias in OLSE beta (plus an adjusted estimate) was given by Scholes-Williams (1977). Independently, we were developing a model of index serial correlation (CMSW 1979b) also based on nonsynchronous trading.

This early literature (and much of the considerable beta-bias literature that followed) shares two limitations. First, while we were all probably beginning to recognize the elements of commonality among the empirical phenomena, our formal models dealt with only one phenomenon at a time (and sometimes ignored the thinness dimension). Second, all the early work assumed that the sole cause of the phenomenon modeled is nonsynchronous trading; in other words, that if only there were a transaction at 4 P.M. every day, the observed closing price would be the true price. This assumption leads to several testable implications (all of which we believe are false): 1. Since the stocks in a "blue chip" index such as the Dow Jones Industrial Average (DJIA) all trade many times a day, that index's serial correlation of daily returns must be slight and must disappear rapidly as you lengthen the differencing interval. 2. If you were to identify transaction times, measure a security's returns over the actual intervals between trades, and regress them against the returns on a high synchronous (e.g., blue chip) index over the same intervals, the OLS beta would have negligible bias. 3. If you were to measure returns based on *quotation* rather than *transaction* prices, you could entirely eliminate the anomolous phenomena.

Section 6.1 analyzes those frictions in the trading process that cause price-adjustment delays. The result is a frictions equation, which shows how, for a security, a sequence of observed returns (based on recorded transaction prices) is related to an underlying sequence of true returns (i.e., those returns which would be observed in a frictionless world). Section 6.2 develops the relationship between thinness and the magnitude of price-adjustment delays. Section 6.3 takes the basic step in developing all our results by restating the cross-serial covariance between two securities using the frictions equation. Section 6.4 then models serial correlation in a market index and compares the magnitude of correlation in equally weighted versus value-weighted indexes. Section 6.5 uses the basic cross-serial covariance model to explore the relationship between true beta and observed OLSE beta. While this relationship yields an adjustment for OLSE beta, it suffers from some of the same defeats that plague previous adjustment methods, discussed in Section 6.6. Consequently, Section 6.7 models the intervalling effect and presents an asymptotic beta estimator (and a method of inferring the asymptote from limited data). Section 6.8 is a summary and conclusion.

6.1 THE IMPACT OF FRICTION ON OBSERVED RETURNS

Much of the microstructure literature assumes or concludes that transaction prices differ from what they would be in a frictionless environment.[5] As we show in Chapter 5, friction results in a bid-ask spread (which will figure in our frictions equation below and, briefly, in our model of serial correlation). Friction also results in at least three types of price-adjustment delay:

1. *Transaction price adjustments lag quotation price adjustments.* Quotes can be updated without an accompanying transaction, and the last transaction generally occurs at a random point in time before the end of the trading day. Hence closing transaction prices typically reflect out-of-date information. This is the price-adjustment delay cited by Scholes-Williams (1977) and CMSW (1979b).

2. *Specialists-dealers impede quotation price adjustments.* Specialist intervention to make an orderly market by satisfying exchange continuity requirements directly impedes the adjustment of prices to a new equilibrium level. In addition, the models of Amihud-Mendelson (1980) and Ho-Stoll (1981) show that the quotes of any specialist-dealer will depend on his inventory position. Thus if a specialist-dealer develops an unbalanced inventory position by, for example, being a net buyer, he will subsequently set his quotes to redress the imbalance by being, on expectation, a net seller. Hence if the specialist-dealer accumulates inventory while handling the trades generated by news in one period, he will work off the imbalance in subsequent periods. As a result, price adjustments attributable to the initial period's news will continue until the specialist-dealer's inventory is rebalanced.

3. *Quotation price adjustment lags for individuals traders.* Given transaction costs, it is optimal for an investor to accumulate "news bits" for periodic review rather than continuously to assess the import of each news bit as it arrives, as demonstrated by Goldman-Sosin (1979). Further, when assessments are made, we have shown in Chapter 5 that with transaction costs, an investor may find a do-nothing strategy to be optimal even if a trade would have been sought in a frictionless environment.

Since an accumulation of news is required before a trade is sought, new orders transmitted to the market reflect in part the impact of old information. In addition, since continuous monitoring of the market is prohibitively expensive, limit orders left with specialists-dealers can go "stale" without being withdrawn. Thus even if an investor were to submit his order immediately upon the receipt of information, if it hits a stale limit order, the transaction occurs at a price that reflects out-of-date information. Finally, large traders might feel that their orders would have an unduly large impact on price. For this reason, large traders sometimes breaks up their orders for execution over time.

Some of the price-adjustment delays might be relatively brief: those caused by transaction price changes lagging behind quotation price changes; by specialists seeking to make an orderly market; by stale limit orders being left on the book; and by some traders breaking up their large orders. But other delays might be quite protracted: those caused by specialists-dealers attempting to redress their inventory imbalances; and by individuals seeking to trade only when information, decision, and transaction costs are sufficiently compensated for.

The impact of any price-adjustment delay will clearly diminish as the differencing interval is increased. Since delays are finite, this suggests that the reported empirical anomalies will be less apparent in longer differencing interval data, as indeed they are. This is modeled formally in Section 6.7.

In the model of the effect of friction that follows, we define *returns* as the natural logarithms of price relatives adjusted for dividends and splits. In a frictionless world, a series of true returns $r_{j,t}$ would be generated for security j in successive discrete time periods t. With friction in the trading process, however, we can only obtain a series of observed returns $r^o_{j,t}$. Although Proposition 1 in this chapter can be proved regardless of the process by which true returns are generated, for the remaining propositions it is convenient to assume the following:

A1. The true return for security j in period t is generated by the market model[6]

$$r_{j,t} = \alpha_j + \beta_j r_{M,t} + e_{j,t} \tag{1}$$

We model the relationship between observed and true returns as

$$r^o_{j,t} = \sum_{l=0}^{N} (\gamma_{j,t-l,l} r_{j,t-l} + \theta_{j,t-l,l}) \tag{2}$$

where we further assume:

A2. $\gamma_{j,t,l}$ and $\gamma_{k,\tau,m}$ are independent for all $j \neq k$, t, τ, l, and m.
A3. $\theta_{j,t,l}$ and $\theta_{k,\tau,m}$ are independent for all $j \neq k$, t, τ, l, and m.
A4. $\gamma_{j,t,l}$ are independent of $r_{M,\tau}$ and $e_{k,\tau}$ for all j, k, t, τ, and l.
A5. $\theta_{j,t,l}$ are independent of $r_{M,\tau}$ and $e_{k,\tau}$ for all j, k, t, τ, and l.
A6. $\gamma_{j,t,l}$ and $\theta_{k,\tau,m}$ are independent for all $j \neq k$, t, τ, l, and m.
A7. $E(\gamma_{j,t,l}) = E(\gamma_{j,\tau,l}) = E(\gamma_{j,l})$ for all j, t, τ, and l.
A8. $E(\Sigma_{l=0}^{N} \gamma_{j,l}) = 1$ for all j.

The random variables $\gamma_{j,t-l,l}$ in Eq. (2) relate the observed return generated in one period to the true returns generated in that period and in N prior periods. Alternatively stated, the $\gamma_{j,t,0}, \gamma_{j,t,1}, \ldots, \gamma_{j,t,N}$ comprise a delay distribution that shows how the true return generated in period t impacts on the returns actually observed during period t and the next N periods [Eq. (2) implies that the true return generated at period $t - N$ will have no remaining impact on returns observed after period t]. Moreover, assumption A8 above indicates that on average each real return $r_{j,t}$ will be fully reflected in the future observed returns.

The random variables $\theta_{j,t-l,l}$ in Eq. (2) reflect the "bouncing" of transaction prices between the bid and the ask quotations. We arbitrarily let the bid define the base-level price and view each transaction at the ask as a momentary jump in the process. Hence, $\theta_{j,t,0}$ is positive (equal to the percentage spread) if the last transaction in period t is at the ask and 0 if it is at the bid.[7]

6.2 THE RELATIONSHIP BETWEEN PRICE-ADJUSTMENT DELAYS AND MARKET SIZE

We expect security analysis to be both more frequent and more intensive for larger issues. The reason is because any news bit that would have a given percentage price impact would have a greater total monetary impact for securities of larger total market value.

When security analysis is undertaken more frequently, orders to trade will clearly reflect more up-to-date information. Effectively, each news bit will remain in "inventory" for a shorter time before it is acted upon.

The connection between the intensity of the analysis and the magnitude of price-adjustment delays is less obvious. To the extent that security analysis generates useful information, more intensive analysis ought to increase the homogeneity of investor expectations; and we suggest that with expectations being more nearly homogeneous, price-adjustment delays will be shorter. The reason is twofold: (1) any trader who (ex post) would agree with the market assessment of security values would be less apt to seek a trade after he eventually does reassess his portfolio holding in a security, and (2) any given trade will have a smaller impact on security price the more elastic the market's demand for the security. This is consistent with the argument we present in Chapter 4 that the demand curve to hold a security is less elastic the more heterogeneous are expectations, and that the less elastic the demand curve, the greater will be the price impact of a buy or sell order of any given size.

Another link between price-adjustment delays and market size is provided by the fact that the bid-ask spread for a security is negatively related to its trading activity, as discussed in Chapter 5. Hence larger issues should have smaller spreads, and thus trades should occur more frequently in response to informational change since a new order is more apt to trigger a trade when the spread is small. This would keep transaction prices more up-to-date for the larger issues.

It is unlikely for NYSE securities, however, that trading delays of this type would account for the correlation structure that appears to be present in the data.

We conclude that the expected magnitude of its price-adjustment delays should be inversely related to the market value of shares outstanding of a security. On average, we expect smaller (i.e., thinner) issues to have larger price-adjustment delays. Thus in empirical research, such as reported in Chapter 7, we use market value as an (inverse) proxy for thinness, and on average we expect a stock of relatively low market value to have greater price-adjustment delays than a stock of relatively high market value.

6.3 SERIAL CORRELATION AND SERIAL CROSS-CORRELATION IN SECURITY RETURNS

In this section we state propositions indicating that there may be nonzero serial correlation in a security's observed returns and positive serial cross-correlation between two securities' observed returns even though true returns have zero serial correlation and zero serial cross-correlation. While these propositions are consistent with empirical findings, they are of use mainly as stepping stones to the results on market index returns in the next section.

The basic step in developing all our results in this section and the next is to write the serial covariance between the observed return of security j and the observed return n periods earlier of security k using Eq. (2), which defines observed returns in terms of the price-adjustment delays (γ) and spreads (θ):

$$
\begin{aligned}
\operatorname{Cov}(r^o_{j,t}, r^o_{k,t-n}) = {} & \operatorname{Cov}\left(\sum_{l=0}^{N} \gamma_{j,t-l,l} r_{j,t-l};\quad \sum_{l=0}^{N} \gamma_{k,t-n-l,l} r_{k,t-n-l}\right) \\
& + \operatorname{Cov}\left(\sum_{l=0}^{N} \theta_{j,t-l,l};\quad \sum_{l=0}^{N} \theta_{k,t-n-l,l}\right) \\
& + \operatorname{Cov}\left(\sum_{l=0}^{N} \gamma_{j,t-l,l} r_{j,t-l};\quad \sum_{l=0}^{N} \theta_{k,t-n-l,l}\right) \\
& + \operatorname{Cov}\left(\sum_{l=0}^{N} \theta_{j,t-l,l};\quad \sum_{l=0}^{N} \gamma_{k,t-n-l,l} r_{k,t-n-l}\right)
\end{aligned} \tag{3}
$$

Now if $j = k$, this is the autocovariance, and our assumptions do *not* enable us to eliminate any of the four terms in the messy expression above. However, we can simplify the first, third, and fourth terms somewhat (see Appendix C) so as to express the autocovariance of a security's observed returns in terms of the variance of its true returns and terms involving price-adjustment delays and spreads. Thus we get:

Proposition 1. Even with zero serial correlation in the true returns series for a security, its observed returns will generally exhibit nonzero serial correlation if price-adjustment delays and/or bid-ask spreads exist.

$$\begin{aligned}\text{Cov}\,(r^o_{j,t}, r^o_{j,t-n}) = &\left[\text{Var}\,(r_{j,t}) \sum_{l=0}^{N-n} E(\gamma_{j,l}\gamma_{j,l}\gamma_{j,l+n})\right.\\ &\left. + E^2(r_{j,t}) \sum_{l=0}^{N} \sum_{m=0}^{N} \text{Cov}\,(\gamma_{j,t-l,l};\quad \gamma_{j,t-n-m,m})\right]\\ &+ \left[\text{Cov}\left(\sum_{l=0}^{N} \theta_{j,t-l,1};\quad \sum_{l=0}^{N} \theta_{j,t-n-l,l}\right)\right]\\ &+ \left[E(r_{j,t}) \sum_{l=0}^{N} \sum_{m=0}^{N} \text{Cov}\,(\gamma_{j,t-l,l};\quad \theta_{j,t-n-m,m})\right]\\ &+ \left[E(r_{j,t}) \sum_{l=0}^{N} \sum_{m=0}^{N} \text{Cov}\,(\gamma_{j,t-n-l,l};\quad \theta_{j,t-m,m})\right] \qquad (4)\end{aligned}$$

The first term in brackets represents the impact of price-adjustment delays. If there were no price-adjustment delays ($\gamma_{j,t,0} = 1$, $\gamma_{j,t,l} = 0$ for all $l \geq 1$, j, and t), then the first term would be zero (and the third and fourth terms would also be zero).

Similarly, the second term represents the impact of the bid-ask spread. If there were no returns variability attributable to the bid-ask spread ($\theta_{j,t,l} = 0$ for all j, t, and l), these terms would be zero (and the third and fourth terms would also be zero).

Proposition 1 and the definition of θ show that the θ_j's cause returns to be negatively serially correlated as transactions bounce randomly between the bid and ask prices. The sign of serial correlation introduced by the γ_j's, however, depends on their specific structure, and the microstructure literature contains speculations that support both positive and negative covariance of the γ's.[8] Thus while Proposition 1 predicts nonzero serial correlation, the sign and relationship to a security's thinness are indeterminate. The empirical evidence appears to suggest a positive relationship between serial correlation and market size, with thinner issues exhibiting predominantly negative serial correlation, and the thicker issues exhibiting predominantly positive serial correlation. This is not surprising since the positive relationship between thinness and expected spreads we demonstrated in Chapter 5 probably holds for the second moment of the spread as well.

To model the serial cross-correlation between the observed returns of two securities, we again use Eq. (3). However, now by A5 and A6, $\theta_{j,t,l}$ is independent of $r_{k,\tau}$ and $\gamma_{k,\tau,l}$ for all $j \neq k$. Thus all terms but the first drop out (and stay out for the rest of the chapter). We require the following regularity condition on the price-adjustment delay variables:[9]

$$E(\gamma_{j,l}) \geq 0 \qquad \text{for all } j \text{ and } l$$

Now, using the market model assumption A1 and the three independence assumptions A3, A5, and A6, Eq. (3) can be rewritten in terms of the securities' "betas," their expected price-adjustment delays, and market variance (see Appendix C). Thus we have:

Proposition 2. The serial cross-correlation in the observed returns of securities j and k is nonzero and has the sign of $\beta_j \beta_k$.

$$\text{Cov}\,(r^o_{j,t}, r^o_{k,t-n}) = \beta_j \beta_k \text{ Var}\,(r_{M,t}) \sum_{l=0}^{N-n} E(\gamma_{j,l}) E(\gamma_{k,l+n}) \tag{5}$$

Since $E(\gamma_{j,l})$ and $E(\gamma_{k,l+n})$ are assumed nonnegative by the regularity condition, the sign of $\beta_j \beta_k$ must determine the sign of the serial cross-correlation of order n.

6.4 SERIAL CORRELATION IN MARKET INDEX RETURNS

We are now ready to apply the results of Section 6.3 to serial correlation in market index returns. After looking at serial correlation in *any* index, we will compare the levels of serial correlation in equally weighted versus value-weighted indexes.

We define the observed market index return as

$$r^o_{M,t} = \sum_k x_k r^o_{k,t}$$

where x_k are constant weights for each security in the index and are the same weights used to determine true $r_{M,t}$ in Eq. (1). We then have

$$\text{Cov}\,(r^o_{M,t}, r^o_{M,t-n}) = \sum_j \sum_k x_j x_k \text{ Cov}\,(r^o_{j,t}, r^o_{k,t-n}) \tag{6}$$

Substituting from Proposition 2, ignoring those terms where $j = k$, and using the regularity condition yields[10]

$$\text{Cov}\,(r^o_{M,t}, r^o_{M,t-n}) = \text{Var}\,(r_{M,t}) \sum_j \sum_k x_j x_k \beta_j \beta_k \sum_{l=0}^{N-n} E(\gamma_{j,l}) E(\gamma_{k,l+n}) \tag{7}$$

from which the next proposition then follows:

Proposition 3. A market index constructed from observed returns for a large number of securities with mostly positive betas will have positive serial correlation of returns.

Proposition 3 explains the empirical observation that index returns are positively autocorrelated. Index serial correlation is shown to be a function of the serial correlation of its component securities as well as the serial cross-correlations between these securities' returns. For a diversified index made up of a large number of positive beta securities, positive serial cross-correlations will dominate the individual securities' serial correlations, thereby inducing positive serial correlation in the index regardless of the signs of the individual-security serial correlations.[11]

To develop the next result, we define a security k to be thin relative to other securities i if it obeys the following condition:

$$E(\gamma_{k,l}) > E(\gamma_{i,l}) \qquad \text{for } l \geq 1$$

This definition says that thin securities will experience "strictly greater expected price-adjustment delay" than other securities.[12] By this definition, the term $\Sigma_{l=0}^{N-n} E(\gamma_{j,l})E(\gamma_{k,l+n})$ will be greater for a thin security k than for thicker securities i. Assuming no systematic difference in β_k for such securities and recognizing that x_k will be larger in an equally weighted index, we have:

Proposition 4. A value-weighted market index constructed from observed returns will have smaller serial correlation than a similarly constructed equally weighted market index.

In other words, since an equally weighted index gives more weight to thinner issues, and since these issues display stronger serial cross-correlation among themselves (due to greater price-adjustment delays), an equally weighted index will exhibit greater positive serial correlation than a similarly constructed value-weighted market index.

6.5 RELATIONSHIP BETWEEN OBSERVED BETA AND TRUE BETA

In this section, we use the model of price-adjustment delay to explore the relationship between true beta and observed beta. The result (Proposition 6) serves several purposes. It can be rearranged to yield a consistent estimator of true beta (Corollary 1) that generalizes the Scholes-Williams estimator and corrects a minor error in Dimson's. It also provides a framework within which to examine the asymptotic effect on observed beta of increasing the differencing interval; this will be used in Section 6.7 to develop two alternative adjustment procedures for OLS beta.

We start from a step in the proof of Proposition 2 (see Appendix C) that enables us to relate the covariance of two securities' true returns to the observed covariances and serial cross-covariances of their returns over the entire delay structure.[13] The relationship can be stated as follows:

Proposition 5. The contemporaneous covariance between the observed returns of securities j and k equals the contemporaneous covariance between their true returns minus the sum of the serial cross-covariances of their observed returns for all leads and lags up to N periods. For all $j \neq k$ we have

$$\text{Cov}(r^o_{j,t}, r^o_{k,t}) = \text{Cov}(r_{j,t}, r_{k,t}) - \sum_{n=1}^{N} \text{Cov}(r^o_{j,t}, r^o_{k,t-n}) - \sum_{n=1}^{N} \text{Cov}(r^o_{j,t-n}, r^o_{k,t}) \tag{8}$$

To turn Proposition 5 into an expression for observed and true betas, we first sum Eq. (8) over all securities using the weights $\{x_k\}$ to get symmetrical expressions for Cov $(r^o_{j,t}, r^o_{M,t})$ and Var $(r^o_{M,t})$.[14] Then substituting these expressions into the definition of observed beta

$$\beta^o_j = \frac{\text{Cov}(r^o_{j,t}, r^o_{M,t})}{\text{Var}(r^o_{M,t})}$$

invoking the stationarity assumption (A1), and rearranging (see Appendix C), we get:

Proposition 6. The observed beta of security j is a function of the true beta of j, the observed intertemporal market beta, and the observed lead and lag betas of security j up to N periods:

$$\beta^o_j = \beta_j\left(1 + 2\sum_{n=1}^{N} \beta^o_{M+n}\right) - \sum_{n=1}^{N} (\beta^o_{j+n} + \beta^o_{j-n}) \tag{9}$$

where we further define

$$\beta^o_{M+n} = \frac{\text{Cov}(r^o_{M,t+n}, r^o_{M,t})}{\text{Var}(r^o_{M,t})}$$ observed intertemporal market beta (index serial correlation)

$$\beta^o_{j+n} = \frac{\text{Cov}(r^o_{j,t+n}, r^o_{M,t})}{\text{Var}(r^o{}_{M,t})}$$ observed security lead beta

$$\beta^o_{j-n} = \frac{\text{Cov}(r^o_{j,t-n}, r^o_{M,t})}{\text{Var}(r^o_{M,t})}$$ observed security lag beta

$$\beta_j = \frac{\text{Cov}(r_{j,t}, r_{M,t})}{\text{Var}(r_{M,t})}$$ true security beta

Proposition 6 can easily be solved for β_j and used with OLS estimators of the various observed betas to obtain a consistent estimator of true beta:

Corollary 1. A consistent estimator of true beta can be found by the formula

$$\hat{\beta}_j = \frac{b^o_j + \sum_{n=1}^{N} b^o_{j+n} + \sum_{n=1}^{N} b^o_{j-n}}{1 + 2\sum_{n=1}^{N} b^o_{M+n}} \tag{10}$$

where b_j^o, b_{j+n}^o, b_{j-n}^o, and b_{M+n}^o are OLS regression estimators of β_j^o, β_{j+n}^o, β_{j-n}^o, and β_{M+n}^o, respectively.

It is clear from Corollary 1 that b_j^o, the OLS regression estimate of systematic risk, will generally be a biased estimator of true β_j. Whether Corollary 1 yields the best possible estimator of beta in practice depends in part on whether we can identify N, the maximum length of price-adjustment delays, and in part on the other alternatives available. In the next section, we examine the alternatives reported in the literature by others.

6.6 COMMENT ON TRADE-TO-TRADE AND SCHOLES-WILLIAMS/DIMSON BETAS

Two alternative approaches to avoiding or adjusting for the bias in beta have appeared in the literature. The first is trade-to-trade betas. Schwert (1977), Franks-Broyles-Hecht (1977), and Marsh (1979) directly matched measurement times with trading times to avoid the distortion introduced by transaction prices lagging quotation prices. One difficulty with this approach is that the exact time of each trade must be known and an index must be available that is updated nearly continuously and in which each security trades nearly continuously. More important, this correction does not compensate for the other (lengthier) sources of price-adjustment delay (our numbers 2 and 3 in Section 6.1). For this reason, we would predict that trade-to-trade betas, even with good data, would still exhibit bias.[15]

The second approach, Scholes-Williams (1977) and Dimson (1979), involves regressing individual security returns on synchronous and nonsynchronous market index returns.[16] The Scholes-Williams consistent estimator of β_j can be expressed as a special case of our Corollary 1. Their estimator is

$$\hat{\beta}_j = \frac{b_j^o + b_{j+1}^o + b_{j-1}^o}{1 + 2b_{M+1}^o} \tag{11}$$

which is identical to our estimator given in Eq. (10) when $N = 1$. Their estimator does not contain higher-order lead and lag betas because of their fundamental assumption that a transaction occurs in each measurement period and their implicit assumption that only nonsynchronous trading causes price-adjustment delay. Hence any information lost due to an interval of nontrading at the end of one period will be observed in the immediately following period when the next trade is assumed to occur. Thus their assumptions lead to a special form of our frictions equation:

$$r_{j,t}^o = \gamma_{j,t,0}\, r_{j,t} + \gamma_{j,t-1,1}\, r_{j,t-1}$$

which in turn could hold only if $N = 1$ in our formulation, which by our Eq. (10) then yields Eq. (11) above.[17] Ignoring higher-order lead and lag betas can lead to an inconsistent beta estimator which still contains intervalling-effect bias (see Section 7.3.2).

The consistent estimator of beta derived by Dimson (1979) and given in his equation (12) (p. 204 of his article) is (in our notation)

$$\hat{\beta}_j = b_j^o + \sum_{n=1}^{N} b_{j+n}^o + \sum_{n=1}^{N} b_{j-n}^o$$

Unfortunately, Dimson's estimator is incorrect.[18] Dimson also suggests that the coefficients b_{j-n}^o, b_{j+n}^o all be estimated simultaneously using multiple regression as opposed to being estimated independently as suggested by Scholes-Williams. Such an approach would not yield estimators consistent with our definitions of β_j^o, β_{j+n}^o, and β_{j-n}^o.

Dimson brings up the important issue of the correct selection of the value for the parameter N. The appropriate selection of this parameter represents a direct conflict between model and statistical accuracy. On the one hand, the greater the number of lead and lag terms that are estimated, the better potentially is the model's representation of reality. On the other hand, the more such terms are included in Eq. (10), the greater is the potential noise introduced in the estimation process. In other words, as N increases, the model becomes both more realistic and less biased, but the statistical efficiency of the estimator declines.[19] For this reason, our generalization/correction of the Scholes-Williams/Dimson procedure may not be the best way to adjust beta for price-adjustment delay bias.

6.7 INTERVALLING EFFECT AND AN ASYMPTOTIC ESTIMATOR OF BETA

In order to develop an alternative means of adjusting beta, let us consider what happens when we increase the differencing interval over which returns are measured. Let $\hat{\beta}_j(L)$ be the estimator defined by Eq. (10), where the OLS estimators $b_j(L)$, $b_{j+n}^o(L)$, $b_{j-n}^o(L)$, and $b_{M+n}^o(L)$ are computed using nonoverlapping consecutive measurement periods of length L. Since $E[\gamma_{j,n}(L)]$ is the sum of short-period expected price-adjustment delays, it can be shown (see Appendix C) that A8 implies that $E[\gamma_{j,n}(L)]$ goes to 1 or 0 as L goes to infinity for $n = 0$ or $n \geq 1$, respectively. Hence it follows that all the lead-lag betas go to zero as L goes to infinity. Since $\hat{\beta}_j(L)$ is a consistent estimator of β_j, we have:

Proposition 7. The asymptotic estimator defined by

$$\beta_j^* = \lim_{L \to \infty} b_j^o(L)$$

is a consistent estimator of the true beta β_j, where $b_j^o(L)$ is the observed OLS regression beta based on nonoverlapping periods of length L.

Proposition 7 provides an alternative method by which a consistent estimator of true beta (β_j) can be calculated. To implement the asymptotic estimator of Proposition 7 (since taking L to the limit is not practical), one can regress observations of $b_j^o(L)$ for different L on an appropriate function of L, obtaining β_j^* as the asymptote.

We turn next to the distribution across securities of the bias in β_j^o and to those characteristics of a security that determine the bias. This will lead to another adjustment procedure whereby we can use a single $b_j^o(L)$ plus a security's market value to infer asymptotic beta.

First, let us consider whether the price-adjustment delay biases must be distributed around 1. We know that the weighted average of the *true* betas of the securities used to compute r_M must be 1, but is this also true for the *observed* betas? This would seem to follow from the definition of β_j^o as an OLS estimator, but it can be proved rigorously (see Appendix C) by summing Eq. (9) over all securities weighted by their participation in the market index and applying the stationarity assumption and the property $\Sigma_j x_j \beta_j = 1$.[20] Thus we have:

Proposition 8. The observed systematic risk β_j^o satisfies

$$\sum_j x_j \beta_j^o = 1 \qquad \text{if } \sum_j x_j \beta_j = 1$$

Proposition 8 states that whatever bias is introduced into the measurement of β_j will be positive for some securities and negative for others, with the weighted average over all securities equal to zero.

To discriminate between securities having positive and negative biases, we rearrange Eq. (9) and rewrite observed serial covariances in terms of true contemporaneous covariances and expected price-adjustment delays (see Appendix C) to obtain:

Proposition 9. Whether observed beta overestimates or underestimates true beta depends on the variance-covariance structure and the expected price-adjustment delay structure; specifically, for any security j whose true beta is positive, $\beta_j^o \gtreqless \beta_j$ as

$$\frac{1}{\beta_j} \sum_k x_k \operatorname{Cov}(r_{j,t}, r_{k,t}) \sum_{n=1}^{N} E(\gamma_{k,n}) + \sum_{l=1}^{N} E(\gamma_{j,l})[E(\gamma_{k,0}) - E(\gamma_{k,l})]$$

$$\gtreqless 2 \operatorname{Var}(r_{M,t}^o) \sum_{n=1}^{N} \beta_{M+n}^o$$

Proposition 9 gives somewhat intricate general conditions under which observed beta over- or underestimates true beta, but the key determinant is the structure of security j's expected price-adjustment delays *relative* to that of other securities. To simplify these conditions and arrive at a comparison of the relative magnitude of beta bias between two securities, we must restrict the question considerably. We do this in the next proposition (see Appendix C for proof) by considering two securities, i and j, that are identical but for the fact that j is thinner than i (has greater price-adjustment delay[21]).

Proposition 10. If the price-adjustment delay variables are such that $E(\gamma_{k,t,0}) \geq E(\gamma_{k,t,1}) \geq \cdots \geq E(\gamma_{k,t,N})$ for all securities k with at least one inequality holding strictly for each security, and if security j has cumulatively greater expected price-adjustment delay than security i and is otherwise identical ($x_j = x_i$, $\beta_j = \beta_i$, and securities i and j have the same covariances with all other securities), and if securities i and j have positive covariances with all other securities, then

$$\beta_j^o < \beta_i^o$$

Put differently, Proposition 10 states that under the given reasonable conditions for the price-adjustment delay variables, the observed beta will underestimate a positive true beta to a greater extent, ceteris paribus, the greater the expected price-adjustment delay of the security.

Propositions 9 and 10 together identify securities with positive betas and relatively lengthy price-adjustment delays as being those securities for which beta will be underestimated by the usual OLS estimators. Conversely, securities with positive betas and relatively short price-adjustment delays are likely to have their betas overestimated by the usual OLS technique. These propositions are the key to our second new approach to estimating β_j. The approach is to estimate cross-sectionally for a sample of securities the difference between β_j^* and $\beta_j(L)$ as a function of a measurable surrogate for the price-adjustment delay characteristics of the security. Possible (inverse) proxies for price-adjustment delay are the security's value of shares traded or its value of shares outstanding. A bias correction factor can then be computed which, together with an OLS regression determined $b_j^o(L)$, can give an estimate of β_j^* and therefore of β_j for securities not in the cross-sectional sample. An empirical implementation of this approach is presented in Chapter 7.

6.8 CONCLUSION

In this chapter we have demonstrated that even if capital markets are efficient in the sense that they generate true returns that have zero serial correlation and zero serial cross-correlation, then due to friction in the trading process which results is positive bid-ask spreads and price-adjustment delays, when we base our measurements on observed returns, we will find that:

1. Individual security returns are serially correlated.
2. A market index composed of a large number of securities will have positive serial correlation.

3. A value-weighted market index will have smaller serial correlation than a similarly composed equally weighted market index.
4. OLS beta estimates will be biased, with the absolute bias
   a. going to zero as the differencing interval increases without bound;
   b. greater for otherwise-identical securities with greater expected price-adjustment delays.

Because precise measures of beta are needed for a variety of purposes, a considerable body of literature has sought to develop adjustment procedures for what is commonly called nonsynchronous trading (although we believe this to be only one aspect of price-adjustment delay). Our Corollary 1 develops from first principles and generalizes to N price adjustment leads and lags the Scholes-Williams/Dimson adjustment procedure. This method may not lead to good estimators, however, because it is impossible to specify N precisely. Use of too large an N leads to an inefficient estimator, while use of too small an N causes incomplete adjustment.

Our analysis suggests two additional approaches to adjusting for the intervalling-effect bias: (1) an asymptotic beta estimate, and (2) an inferred asymptotic estimator based on a security's market value and its observed beta. These approaches yield consistent estimators of beta even in the presence of long-lived price-adjustment delays and do not require that N be specified. The asymptotic estimator doubtless yields the more precise estimates of the two and would be best where a long calendar span of data and sufficient computing time are available. The inferred asymptotic estimator has the compensating advantage of requiring only a limited number of short-period return observations, making it desirable for use where beta is nonstationary. Both are implemented in Chapter 7, which also reports the results of comparative tests of all the alternative beta adjustment methods.

NOTES

*This chapter brings together and recasts three of our papers along with unpublished material. Our earliest model of serial correlation in market indexes, K. J. Cohen, S. F. Maier, R. A. Schwartz, and D. K. Whitcomb, "On the Existence of Serial Correlation in an Efficient Securities Market," *TIMS Studies in the Management Sciences*, Vol. 11, 1979, pp. 151–168, presents a much more limited model of price-adjustment delays than the present chapter. Our article, K. J. Cohen, G. A. Hawawini, S. F. Maier, R. A. Schwartz, and D. K. Whitcomb, "Implications of Microstructure Theory for Empirical Research on Stock Price Behavior," *Journal of Finance*, Vol. 35, 1980, pp. 249–257, states (without proof) several of the propositions presented here (and others we omit here). Our article, K. J. Cohen, G. A. Hawawini, S. F. Maier, R. A. Schwartz, and D. K. Whitcomb, "Friction in the Trading Process and the Estimation of Systematic Risk," *Journal of Financial Economics*, Vol. 12, 1983, pp., 263–278, states and proves several other propositions presented here. In unifying this body of work, we have substantially modified a number of proofs and added several others.

1. Fama (1970) reports weakly positive serial correlation in the daily returns of blue chip stocks, and generally insignificant serial correlation in returns measured over longer differencing intervals. Hawawini (1977) reports predominantly negative daily autocorrelation of thinner-issue returns.
2. Fisher (1966) documented the observation of positive index serial correlation, and showed that it implies that the prices of different securities do not adjust simultaneously to common information. The observation of index autocorrelation without individual issue autocorrelation has come to be called the Fisher effect. (There is a different and earlier Fisher effect, named after Irving Fisher, prominent in the literature: nominal interest rates change approximately one-for-one with changes in expected inflation.) Scholes-Williams (1977) and Dimson (1979) report that index serial correlation is greater for more broadly based indexes and Ibbotson-Sinquefield (1982) report high and significant serial correlation in the annual returns of a small firm index.
3. See Altman-Jacquillat-Levasseur (1974), Pogue-Solnik (1974), Schwartz-Whitcomb (1974), Scholes-Williams (1977), Schwert (1977), Dimson (1979), Marsh (1979), Ng (1981), Saniga-McInish-Gouldey (1981), CMSW (1983), McInish-Wood (1985a), Fung-Schwartz-Whitcomb (1985), and others.
4. Schwartz-Whitcomb (1977a) report two other seemingly anomolous phenomena which are clearly results of the basic phenomena: (a) autocorrelation of market model residuals is weakly positive for daily data, but it becomes predominantly negative as the differencing interval increases; (b) market model R^2 coefficients increase as the differencing interval is lengthened. See also Francis (1975), Hawawini-Vora (1980), and McInish-Wood (1985b).
5. Besides the references that support the specific price-adjustment delays we list in the text below, Oldfield-Rogalski-Jarrow (1977) present empirical evidence suggesting that transaction arrivals can best be described by a (sporadic) jump process instead of a continuous-time diffusion process, Goldman-Beja (1979) model the dynamic behavior of prices based on a distinction between actual prices and frictionless equilibrium price, and Ho-Schwartz-Whitcomb (1985) prove that with friction, transaction prices are not generally Pareto-efficient equilibrium prices.
6. We make the usual assumptions about the process generating $r_{j,t}$, that is: (a) $r_{M,t}$ and $r_{M,\tau}$ are independent and identically distributed for all $t \neq \tau$; (b) $e_{j,t}$ and $e_{j,\tau}$ are independent and identically distributed for all $t \neq \tau$ and $E(e_{j,t}) = 0$ for all j and t; (c) $e_{j,t}$ and $e_{k,\tau}$ are independent for all $j \neq k$ and all t and τ, including $t = \tau$ where the dependence introduced from defining $r_{M,t}$ as a weighted sum of all the $r_{j,t}$ is ignored because of the large number of securities in $r_{M,t}$; and (d) $r_{M,t}$ and $e_{j,\tau}$ are independent for all j, t, and τ.
7. The specification of $\theta_{j,t,l}$ for l other than 0 is relegated to Appendix C because it requires quite a bit of explanation. As we shall see, all terms involving θ fall out after Proposition 1 (i.e., the spread does not figure in serial cross-correlation and therefore in index serial correlation or beta bias).
8. Goldman-Beja (1979) demonstrate that "nonclairvoyant" specialists who attempt to absorb a fraction of all excess demand will introduce negative serial correlation into observed returns (when there is nonzero drift in true returns and if they do not overcompensate). Schwartz-Whitcomb (1976) argue that negative serial correlation might also result from specialist intervention to satisfy a depth requirement that on

the NYSE delimits the size of permissible price changes. Alternatively, positive serial correlation would result from specialist intervention to provide price continuity, from specialist-dealer inventory rebalancing, and from the breaking up of large orders. In addition, delays in updating limit orders on the book can lead to positive serial correlation as those traders who respond quickly enough to new information have an opportunity to hit orders that have not yet been revised (and in so doing, to generate a trade at an intermediate price).

9. It should be noted that the regularity condition does not preclude a positive or negative serial correlation pattern in the $\gamma_{j,t,l}$. Such a pattern could introduce positive or negative serial correlation into the observed returns. This regularity condition was satisfied by the models used in Scholes-Williams (1977), Dimson (1979), and CMSW (1979b).

10. The reason for ignoring terms where $j = k$ is that when $j = k$ the independence conditions needed to derive Proposition 2 do not hold. In this case, Cov $(r^o_{j,t}, r^o_{j,t-p})$ is given by Proposition 1 and the sign is indeterminate, so we could not determine the sign of index serial covariance. The effect of ignoring those terms where $j = k$ vanishes in the limit as the number of securities approaches infinity, so long as no security's weight is large (for the same reason that portfolio variance goes to average covariance—because the terms where $j \neq k$ increasingly dominate the terms where $j = k$).

11. Intuitively, if a market index formed from observed returns is serially correlated, the market model residuals [the $e_{j,t}$ in Eq. (1)] should be also. This is demonstrated rigorously in Appendix C.

12. This assumption was satisfied in CMSW (1979b), where price-adjustment delays were due solely to transaction price adjustments lagging quotation price adjustments and the process generating these was Poisson.

13. The proof of Proposition 5 does not require that the price-adjustment delay variables $\gamma_{j,t,l}$ and $\gamma_{j,t,m}$ be independent. As we shall see in Section 6.6, recognition of this is the key to obtaining the appropriate form for Dimson's model, and to relaxing the requirement of Scholes-Williams that a transaction be observed in each measurement period used in the estimation process.

    Shanken (1985) uses our Eq. (8) in Proposition 5 to investigate the covariance and factor structures of common stock returns. Shanken's empirical evidence indicates that the usual estimator of the covariance matrix of daily returns provides a distorted view of the covariance/factor structure. His alternative estimator, based on our Proposition 5, reveals roughly twice as much covariation in individual common stock returns. When his alternative estimator is used, the number of factors identified also appears to increase.

14. See Appendix C for the exact expression. Note that once again we ignore terms where $j = k$, and again the effect of this omission vanishes in the limit as the number of securities comprising the market becomes indefinitely large.

15. Empirical evidence supporting this prediction is presented by Ord-McInish-Wood (1984). Their method and results will be discussed in more detail in Chapter 7.

16. This method was anticipated to some extent by Pogue-Solnik (1974) and Ibbotson (1975). Additional contributions were made by Schwert (1977) and Theobald (1983). This adjustment method is beginning to be used in event studies wherever a systematic bias in beta due to firm size might cause anomolous results; see, for example,

Reinganum (1981). Theobald (1983) approaches the problem from a somewhat different analytical framework, but produces an estimator identical to that of Scholes-Williams (1977). One difference is that Theobald makes a correction to the Scholes-Williams estimator for the fact that the number of observations would be less for lead and lag betas than for simultaneous betas. For most applications this would be of no practical significance.

17. Scholes-Williams also assume that the process generating the delay structure in observed betas is both independent and identically distributed over time. This assumption makes it impossible to extend their basic result to the case where securities do not trade at least once in each period. Even with securities that trade relatively frequently, a day can arise where no trade occurs; Scholes-Williams had to discard such observations in their empirical work. As pointed out by Dimson (1979), this in turn leads to a loss of information which can increase the size of the confidence interval around the Scholes-Williams beta estimator. Our assumption in Eq. (2) is only that the delay variables *across* securities are stationary and independent. There can, however, be complex dependency patterns over time for a given security.
18. The error in Dimson's analysis appears to be in the derivation of his equation (11) [Dimson (1979, p. 203)]. Dimson attempts to equate the appropriate terms in his equation (9) with those in his equation (10) to derive equation (11). The basic problem is that all terms that are dependent upon M_{t+k} are not equivalenced. This is because $\hat{\beta}_{i+k}$ is itself dependent upon M_{t+k}; therefore, equation (11) omitted at least one term. In addition, the equivalence used to derive equation (11) requires only that all terms associated with M_t in equation (9) must equal all terms associated with M_t in equation (10), not that each subterm be equal. Thus the corrected form of Dimson's estimator is our Eq. (3).
19. Further discussion of the work of Scholes-Williams and Dimson can be found in Fung (1981) and in Fowler-Rorke (1983).
20. See Fama (1976, pp. 60–61) for a proof of this property.
21. Technically, Proposition 10 can be proved with a weaker thinness definition than we used in proving Proposition 4: a security j has "cumulatively greater expected price-adjustment delay" than security i if

$$\sum_{l=m}^{N} E(\gamma_{j,t,l}) > \sum_{l=m}^{N} E(\gamma_{i,t,l}) \qquad \text{for all delay periods } m = 1, \ldots, N$$

7

A PROCEDURE FOR ESTIMATING BETA FROM DAILY DATA*

In Chapter 6 we presented a model of the intervalling-effect bias in OLS estimates of beta. We now develop and test operational procedures for adjusting estimated betas for the intervalling-effect bias. Why bother? Since Proposition 7 in Chapter 6 shows that OLSE betas get closer and closer to becoming consistent estimators of true beta as the differencing interval increases, why not just use monthly interval returns and stop worrying about the intervalling-effect bias?

The reason for wanting to be able to use daily data is that beta estimates are known to be nonstationary.[1] There is good theoretical reason for beta to change when there is a change in the firm's financial risk or business risk (e.g., resulting from a major merger). Another example would be AT&T's agreement with the federal government to divest its operating companies and to establish regional entities. Instead of waiting for enough months to pass to make a reasonable estimate from monthly data, following the issue of these new stocks we would be tempted to use, say, the first six months of daily returns. However, we will present empirical evidence in this chapter that most daily-interval OLSE betas would be severely biased.

Even if we stick to monthly data, some OLSE betas will still be considerably biased. Propositions 9 and 10 of Chapter 6 imply that the betas of very thin firms and a few very thick firms contain the most bias, and we might expect this bias not to decay to insignificance until intervals longer than a month are used. In cross-sectional efficient market hypothesis studies, this persistant bias is likely to cause a spurious association of firm size (or an empirical proxy such as price-earnings ratio) with abnormal returns.[2] This makes an effective intervalling-effect adjustment procedure valuable.

The model in Chapter 6 implies two adjustment procedures which we implement empirically here.[3] Our first procedure for obtaining unbiased beta estimates involves computing an asymptotic estimator of beta. This is the limit that the OLS estimator will approach as the differencing interval is increased without bound. Our second procedure involves estimating the extent to which the difference between a security's asymptotic beta and its OLSE beta for any specific differencing interval is related to the value of that security's outstanding shares (which we take as an inverse proxy measure of the security's expected price-adjustment delay). The advantage of the second procedure is that we can infer a security's asymptotic beta, knowing only the beta obtained for some short differencing interval and the market value of the shares outstanding. This is desirable when, due to nonstationarity, reasonable estimates of asymptotic beta cannot be made by means of the more direct route (which requires the use of longer-period data).

The chapter is organized as follows. In Section 7.1, we develop the methodology for our empirical tests. Section 7.2 presents our empirical results on U.S. data. Section 7.3 summarizes the findings of Fung-Schwartz-Whitcomb (1985) on French data and of McInish-Wood (1985a) and Ord-McInish-Wood (1984) on U.S. data; these include direct comparisons of the Scholes-Williams (1977) adjustment procedures with ours. Concluding remarks are contained in Section 7.4.

7.1 TEST METHODOLOGY

7.1.1 The Sample and the Price Data

The sample consists of 50 NYSE common stocks selected by stratified random sampling according to the following procedure. The population of common stocks that remained listed on the NYSE throughout the four-year period from January 1, 1970 to December 31, 1973 was ranked according to the market value of their shares outstanding as of the last trading day of 1971, the midpoint of our sample period,[4] and stratified by value into deciles. A random sample of five common stocks was obtained from each decile, producing a stratified random sample of 50 common stocks. Firms whose shares have not been publicly held since 1965 were excluded from the sample and replaced by randomly selected alternates belonging to the same decile. For the four-year period considered, each of the 50 firms had 1010 daily price observations. The Standard & Poor's Composite 500 Stock Index was used as the market index. The returns of firm j and the index over differencing intervals of length L days are measured by taking the natural logarithm of price relatives, adjusted for cash and stock dividends.

7.1.2 Estimation of the Intervalling Effect on Beta Coefficients

A two-pass regression analysis is undertaken to estimate the intervalling effect on each security's beta coefficient.

1. A first pass based on the market model is used to estimate the beta coefficient of each of the 50 securities in the sample for 14 different lengths of the differencing interval L according to

$$r_{jLT} = {}_1a_{jL} + {}_1b_{jL}r_{MLT} + {}_1e_{jLT} \tag{1}$$

where

$$j = 1, \ldots, 50$$
$$L = 1, \ldots, 6, 8, 10, 12, 14, 15, 16, 18, 20$$
$$T = 1, \ldots, 960/L$$

The lower prescript 1 on the right-hand side of Eq. (1) indicates that these are pass 1 coefficients and residuals. Note that we use only 960 of our 1010 daily returns because 960 is a common multiple for the largest number of the chosen values of L (12 of the 14).

2. A second pass is used to estimate the intervalling effect on the beta coefficient of each of the 50 securities in the sample. The 14 estimated beta coefficients for each security obtained from the first pass are regressed against the inverse of the length of the 14 corresponding differencing intervals raised to the positive power n according to

$${}_1\hat{b}_{jL} = {}_2a_j + {}_2b_jL^{-n} + {}_2e_{jL} \tag{2}$$

where

$$j = 1, \ldots, 50$$
$$L = 1, \ldots, 6, 8, 10, 12, 14, 15, 16, 18, 20$$
$$n > 0$$

The lower prescript 2 on the right-hand side of Eq. (2) indicates that these are pass 2 coefficients and residuals.

The justification for Eq. (2) comes from Chapter 6. It is argued there that the strength of the delayed price-adjustment bias will be reduced as the length of the differencing interval increases. Moreover, Proposition 7 states that in the limit, as the length of the differencing interval increases without bound, the OLS estimator of beta (based on observed returns) will approach an asymptote that is a consistent estimator of true beta. Clearly, data limitations (as well as the underlying stationarity assumption) prevent one from literally estimating OLSE betas based on arbitrarily large differencing intervals. Hence a functional form

[Eq. (2)] was chosen for which (a) the dependent variable (OLSE beta for a differencing interval of length L) approaches an asymptote (the intercept term) as the independent variable L increases without bound, and (b) the difference between the dependent variable and its asymptote monotonically decreases as L increases. Since these desired properties are consistent with the independent variable $(1/L)$ being raised to any positive power, this element of generality was incorporated into Eq. (2).

In order to use linear regression analysis to estimate the coefficients in Eq. (2), the value of the positive power n must be specified in advance. Since the theory does not indicate what the value of n should be, we determine it experimentally. As we report in Section 7.2.2 (see especially footnote 8), we run regressions for various values of n and the value that, on average, produces the best linear fit between ${}_2\hat{b}_{jL}$ and L^{-n} is selected (this turns out to be $n = 0.8$).[5]

In the absence of an intervalling effect on the estimated betas, ${}_2\hat{b}_j$ should be insignificantly different from zero regardless of the value of the positive power n. Securities whose beta coefficients rise (fall) as the differencing interval is lengthened will have negative (positive) estimated slopes ${}_2\hat{b}_j$. Furthermore, the larger the *absolute value* of the estimated coefficient ${}_2\hat{b}_j$ for any given security, the stronger is the intervalling effect on that security's beta coefficient. In other words, the estimated coefficient ${}_2\hat{b}_j$ can be used as a quantitative proxy variable to measure the intervalling effect on a security's beta.

7.1.3 The Estimated Asymptotic Beta Coefficient

Since $\lim_{L\to\infty} E({}_1\hat{b}_{jL}) = E({}_2\hat{a}_j)$, the estimated asymptotic beta coefficient (our first adjustment procedure) is given by the intercept of Eq. (2), ${}_2\hat{a}_j$.[6]

7.1.4 Estimation of the Intervalling Effect–Thinness Relationship

A third pass is carried out by regressing the estimated coefficient ${}_2\hat{b}_j$ (the proxy for the intervalling effect) of the 50 securities against the logarithm of the market value of their shares outstanding (the inverse proxy for a security's relative price-adjustment delay). The regression equation is

$$ {}_2\hat{b}_j = {}_3a + {}_3b \ln V_j + {}_3e_j \tag{3} $$

where $j = 1, \ldots, 50$, V_j represents the market value of shares outstanding at midpoint of sample period, and 3 is the prescript for the regression pass.

The justification for Eq. (3) stems from Propositions 7 through 10 of Chapter 6. By these results and the hypothesized inverse relationship between a security's market value and its expected price-adjustment delay, we predict that the bias will be negative for thin stocks, and that it will increase algebraically to become positive for very thick stocks. Hence we expect ${}_3\hat{b} > 0$. The exact functional form for the third-pass regressions is not theoretically determinate, and we report in Section 7.2.4 our experiments with an alternative functional form and other proxy measures for thinness.

7.1.5 Using the Intervalling Effect–Thinness Relationship to Infer Asymptotic Betas

Suppose that one wishes to calculate an approximate asymptotic value for the beta coefficient without having to replicate the full intervalling-effect study involving the first and second passes (e.g., for a stock where too short a calendar period of data is available). This can be done for a single first-pass regression for any value of L for stock k and from knowledge of the third-pass intervalling effect–thinness relationship embodied in Eq. (3). We shall use the term *inferred asymptotic beta*, denoted by b_k^*, for this estimate of stock k's beta.

It should be noted that the first- and second-pass regressions, based on Eqs. (1) and (2), are run on a stock-by-stock basis. Thus the empirical results reported in Section 7.2 really constitute 50 separate and independent tests of the first- and second-pass regressions. However, the third-pass regression, based on Eq. (3), is a cross-sectional regression that uses data on all stocks in our sample. This procedure could have two drawbacks. First, estimating the coefficients of Eq. (3) from the cross section of all 50 stocks and using these coefficients to obtain inferred asymptotic betas could bias the results. This is because data pertaining to stock k would have been used in the cross-sectional third-pass regressions, whose coefficients, in turn, were used to obtain the calculated asymptotic beta for stock k. Second, since only one cross-sectional sample would have been used to estimate the third-pass regression, there would be no way of knowing how robust the results would be for different samples of stocks.

Fortunately, there is a way of overcoming both these drawbacks which makes efficient use of all our available data and produces almost unbiased [see Lachenbruch (1967)] results. This involves transforming the original sample of stocks into a sequence of hold-out samples, each of which is obtained by deleting one stock from the cross section used to estimate the third-pass regression. This approach to obtaining hold-out samples is analogous to an approach used by Lachenbruch (1967) and Lachenbruch-Mickey (1968) for discriminant analysis and by Allen (1974) and Allen-Cady (1982) for regression analysis. We use 50 different third-pass regressions, each based on a different set of stocks.

Specifically, for each stock k, we run the regression

$$ {}_2\hat{b}_j = {}_3a_k + {}_3b_k \ln V_j + {}_3e_j \tag{4} $$

which is based on Eq. (3) but includes only the 49 observations $j = 1, \ldots, k-1, k+1, \ldots, 50$. By using the estimated coefficients from Eq. (2), equating the error term to zero, and rearranging, we have

$$ {}_2\hat{a}_k = {}_1\hat{b}_{kL} - {}_2\hat{b}_k L^{-n} \tag{5} $$

Since the regression coefficients ${}_3\hat{a}_k$ and ${}_3\hat{b}_k$ estimated from Eq. (4) were not obtained by use of any data pertaining to stock k, it is legitimate to use these coefficients and Eq. (4) to infer a value for ${}_2\hat{b}_k$ as follows:

$$ {}_2\hat{b}_k = {}_3\hat{a}_k + {}_3\hat{b}_k \ln V_k \tag{6}$$

Substituting Eq. (6) into Eq. (5), we obtain the inferred asymptotic beta for stock k:

$$ b_k^* = {}_1\hat{b}_{kL} - ({}_3\hat{a}_k + {}_3\hat{b}_k \ln V_k)L^{-n} \tag{7}$$

7.2 EMPIRICAL RESULTS

7.2.1 Regression Results for the First Pass

Results for the first-pass regressions based on Eq. (1) are summarized in Table 1. The average value of the estimated betas tends to fall as the length of the differencing interval[7] is shortened (first row). However, this is not the case for all securities in the sample, as will be seen in Section 7.2.2. There is a slight increase in the average standard error of the estimated betas as L increases (second row) and the average t statistic falls as L rises (third row), since the number of observations diminishes. The fourth and fifth rows give the across-firms minimum and maximum estimated beta coefficients, respectively. The average R-square deteriorates as L is shortened (sixth row), a result explained by Schwartz-Whitcomb (1977b) and Hawawini (1980). The seventh and eighth rows give the minimum and maximum values for R-square, respectively. All intercepts ${}_1\hat{a}_j$ in Eq. (1) are insignificantly different from zero at the 0.05 level of significance.

7.2.2 Regression Results for the Second Pass

Results for the second-pass regressions based on Eq. (2) and using the positive power $n = 0.8$ are presented in Table 2.[8] Note that for the majority of securities, the estimated slope ${}_2\hat{b}_j$ is negative; thus estimated betas tend to rise as L increases. Some securities yield estimated slopes ${}_2\hat{b}_j$ insignificantly different from zero. The security with the largest market value in the sample, number 50 (Eastman Kodak), has a significantly positive beta-L relationship. This conforms to the theoretical model; by our sample selection procedure, we would expect few of our stocks to be thicker than the weighted average of S&P's 500 stocks.

The estimated asymptotic betas are given by the estimated intercepts ${}_2\hat{a}_j$ in Eq. (2) and are reported in the first column of Table 2. Note their high t statistics compared to L-day betas (see Table 1, third row).

TABLE 1 Summary Statistics for First-Pass Regressions

$$\hat{r}_{jL} = {}_1\hat{a}_{jL} + {}_1\hat{b}_{jL}\, r_{ML}$$

L (Days)	1	2	3	4	5	10	15	20	$({}_2\hat{a}_j)$[a]	(b_j^*)[b]
Avg $({}_1\hat{b}_{jL})$[c]	0.963	1.047	1.036	1.072	1.140	1.262	1.307	1.381	1.334	1.396
$\sigma({}_1\hat{b}_{jL})$	0.462	0.471	0.466	0.472	0.486	0.525	0.564	0.624	0.571	0.566
Avg $t({}_1\hat{b}_{jL})$[d]	10.478	9.380	7.901	7.662	7.537	6.439	5.535	5.531	22.057	—
Min $({}_1\hat{b}_{jL})$[e]	0.279	0.245	0.270	0.239	0.327	0.374	0.334	0.253	0.348	0.542
Max $({}_1\hat{b}_{jL})$[f]	2.144	2.202	2.184	2.229	2.403	2.844	2.887	2.970	2.929	2.780
Avg (R^2)	0.1095	0.1644	0.1756	0.2023	0.2361	0.3048	0.3283	0.4045	—	—
Min (R^2)	0.0204	0.0456	0.0557	0.0655	0.0767	0.0955	0.0700	0.1714	—	—
Max (R^2)	0.3916	0.4861	0.4978	0.5171	0.5081	0.5248	0.5963	0.6973	—	—

[a] Estimated asymptotic betas [see Eq. (2)]. Included for convenience; see Table 2.

[b] Inferred daily asymptotic beta [see Eq. (9)]. Included for convenience; see Table 5.

[c] All averages are for 50 securities.

[d] All ${}_1\hat{a}_{jL}$ are insignificantly different from zero at the 0.05 significance level.

[e] All Min $({}_1\hat{b}_{jL})$ belong to the same company (Union Electric).

[f] All Max $({}_1\hat{b}_{jL})$ belong to the same company (Monogram Industries).

TABLE 2 Summary Statistics for Second-Pass Regressions[a]

$${}_1\hat{b}_{jL} = {}_2\hat{a}_j + {}_2\hat{b}_j(L)^{-0.8}$$

Firm[b]	${}_2\hat{a}_j$	$t({}_2\hat{a}_j)$	${}_2\hat{b}_j$	$\lvert t({}_2\hat{b}_j)\rvert$	R-Square	Durbin-Watson Statistics	b_j^{*c}
1	0.967	17.859	−0.936	4.306	0.6071	1.906	1.379
2	0.889	18.047	−0.897	4.033	0.5754	2.011	1.293
3	1.035	20.909	−0.738	5.477	0.7104	1.531	1.230
4	0.689	23.613	−0.839	4.725	0.5793	1.917	0.705
5	2.314	18.872	−1.150	3.438	0.4962	2.061	2.255
6	1.457	42.393	−0.659	3.021	0.4320	2.205	1.961
7	1.501	34.562	−0.612	5.166	0.6898	1.462	1.770
8	2.541	26.464	−1.296	4.949	0.6712	1.760	2.363
9	2.362	32.389	−0.869	4.369	0.6140	1.680	2.393
10	1.152	20.476	−0.380	2.481	0.3392	2.276	1.561
11	0.973	17.446	−0.313*	1.401	0.1406	1.729	1.473
12	1.360	25.206	−0.483	3.200	0.4605	1.804	1.606
13	1.928	29.917	−0.706	4.013	0.5731	1.723	2.060
14	1.306	11.294	−0.759	2.408	0.3257	1.619	1.387
15	2.929	30.422	−0.405	4.007	0.5723	2.056	2.780
16	1.003	24.463	−0.476*	1.583	0.1727	1.763	1.485
17	1.766	21.825	−0.486	2.122	0.2729	2.402	1.982
18	2.345	37.531	−0.384	5.187	0.6916	2.018	2.255
19	1.170	18.811	−0.617	3.635	0.5240	2.024	1.201
20	0.885	15.888	−0.520	3.420	0.4937	1.796	0.964
21	1.567	16.181	−0.367	2.904	0.4127	1.893	1.566
22	1.659	18.118	−0.789	4.763	0.6541	1.858	1.232
23	1.897	12.457	−0.454*	1.094	0.0907	2.845	2.015
24	1.236	11.697	−0.268	2.785	0.3927	1.755	1.214
25	2.257	23.970	−0.429*	1.834	0.2189	1.458	2.234
26	1.226	22.726	−0.621	4.221	0.5975	1.850	1.212
27	1.004	13.221	−0.858	3.767	0.5419	1.578	0.979
28	1.160	22.005	−0.685	4.762	0.6504	2.586	0.963
29	0.764	21.239	−0.414	4.217	0.5972	1.857	0.793
30	0.810	21.491	−0.079*	0.769	0.0469	1.981	1.160
31	1.543	13.149	−0.191*	0.597	0.0288	1.969	1.743
32	0.554	21.437	−0.289	4.099	0.5833	1.733	0.715
33	2.068	15.233	−0.276*	1.667	0.1881	1.997	2.102
34	1.673	21.274	−0.391*	1.826	0.2173	1.418	1.672
35	1.367	18.575	−0.714	3.854	0.5532	1.615	1.119
36	1.899	25.005	−0.105*	0.506	0.0209	2.183	2.214
37	0.597	18.847	−0.312	3.623	0.5225	1.623	0.634
38	0.596	14.683	−0.087*	0.786	0.0489	2.162	0.802
39	0.968	11.991	−0.041*	0.187	0.0029	2.106	1.068
40	0.348	15.106	−0.117*	1.858	0.2235	2.374	0.512
41	0.971	19.293	−0.350	2.551	0.3517	1.597	0.974
42	1.168	26.981	−0.286	4.963	0.6724	2.293	0.810
43	1.008	27.651	−0.010	2.112	0.2710	2.194	1.021

(continued)

TABLE 2 (*continued*)

Firm[b]	${}_2\hat{a}_j$	$t({}_2\hat{a}_j)$	${}_2\hat{b}_j$	$\|t({}_2\hat{b}_j)\|$	R-Square	Durbin-Watson Statistics	b_j^{*c}
44	1.050	25.719	0.050*	0.458	0.0166	2.226	1.272
45	1.247	34.759	−0.125	4.350	0.6120	2.405	1.024
46	0.850	18.604	−0.131	2.513	0.3448	2.455	0.592
47	0.925	19.892	−0.206*	1.864	0.2246	1.862	0.639
48	1.359	29.639	0.053*	1.223	0.1108	1.659	1.133
49	0.827	22.829	0.122*	0.224	0.0042	2.089	0.696
50	0.827	30.905	0.432	5.453	0.7124	2.045	0.896

[a] Asterisks indicate coefficients *not* significantly different from zero at the 0.05 significance level.

[b] In Tables 2 and 5, the firms are ranked in increasing order of market value of shares outstanding at the end of 1971 (hence 1 is the smallest and 50 is the largest firm in the sample).

[c] b_j^* data included for convenience; see Table 5.

7.2.3 Comparison of *L*-Day Betas and Asymptotic Betas

Table 3 contains the cross-correlation matrix for estimated and asymptotic betas. The high values of the cross-correlation coefficients indicate that a security which exhibits high estimated beta for a given length L of the differencing interval tends to retain this characteristic when L is changed or in the limit when L is taken to infinity. Not unexpectedly, we usually observe slightly higher correlations for adjacent lengths of the differencing interval L than for nonadjacent values of L. Asymptotic betas are highly correlated with L-day estimated betas, with somewhat higher correlations for large L.

In Table 4, mean-square "errors" are given for estimated L-day betas compared to their respective estimated asymptotic betas.[9] The MSE tends to decrease as the length of the differencing interval increases.

Tables 3 and 4 indicate that for our sample, the intervalling-effect bias in

TABLE 3 **Cross-Correlation Matrix for Estimated Betas**

	${}_1\hat{b}_{j,1}$	${}_1\hat{b}_{j,2}$	${}_1\hat{b}_{j,3}$	${}_1\hat{b}_{j,4}$	${}_1\hat{b}_{j,5}$	${}_1\hat{b}_{j,10}$	${}_1\hat{b}_{j,15}$	${}_1\hat{b}_{j,20}$	${}_2\hat{a}_j$	b_j^*
${}_1\hat{b}_{j,1}$	1.000									
${}_1\hat{b}_{j,2}$	0.987	1.000								
${}_1\hat{b}_{j,3}$	0.977	0.975	1.000							
${}_1\hat{b}_{j,4}$	0.948	0.974	0.953	1.000						
${}_1\hat{b}_{j,5}$	0.937	0.959	0.948	0.978	1.000					
${}_1\hat{b}_{j,10}$	0.891	0.921	0.906	0.963	0.952	1.000				
${}_1\hat{b}_{j,15}$	0.857	0.864	0.882	0.881	0.888	0.891	1.000			
${}_1\hat{b}_{j,20}$	0.848	0.869	0.876	0.907	0.902	0.955	0.891	1.000		
${}_2\hat{a}_j$	0.882	0.901	0.908	0.934	0.931	0.962	0.962	0.966	1.000	
b_j^*	0.867	0.891	0.870	0.896	0.876	0.897	0.878	0.886	0.920	1.000

TABLE 4 Mean Square Errors for Estimated Betas[a]

	${}_1\hat{b}_{j,1}$	${}_1\hat{b}_{j,2}$	${}_1\hat{b}_{j,3}$	${}_1\hat{b}_{j,4}$	${}_1\hat{b}_{j,5}$	${}_1\hat{b}_{j,10}$	${}_1\hat{b}_{j,15}$	${}_1\hat{b}_{j,20}$	${}_2\hat{a}_j$	b_j^*
${}_2\hat{a}_j$	0.210	0.144	0.147	0.112	0.083	0.031	0.030	0.032	0.000	0.055
b_j^*	0.266	0.187	0.206	0.168	0.139	0.079	0.084	0.084	0.055	0.000

[a] Mean square errors are computed according to the equation in footnote 9 and analogous equations.

beta is substantial for differencing intervals up to 10 days. This, in turn, suggests that price-adjustment delays are nontrivial.[10]

7.2.4 Regression Results for the Third Pass

The estimated intervalling-effect coefficients, ${}_2\hat{b}_j$ were regressed on the logarithm of the market value of shares outstanding for the cross-sectional sample of all 50 securities as specified in Eq. (3). All 50 securities were used (as opposed to the Lachenbruch holdout sample procedure reported in Section 7.2.5 below) so as to provide a single estimate for our entire sample; the estimated coefficients could be used to infer asymptotic betas in a different sample of securities. The resulting equation is[11]

$$\begin{aligned} {}_2\hat{b}_j &= -2.637 + 0.181 \ln V_j \qquad R^2 = 0.6608 \\ & \quad (-11.462) \quad (9.670) \qquad\quad \text{DWS} = 2.091 \end{aligned} \tag{8}$$

where it should be recalled that V_j is measured in thousands of dollars. Equation (8) is the estimated intervalling effect–thinness relationship. The slope has the predicted positive sign, and both the estimated intercept and slope are significantly different from zero as indicated by the t statistics given in parentheses. The single variable $\ln V_j$ explains approximately two-thirds of the variation in the dependent variable ${}_2\hat{b}_j$. All told, these results are quite striking for a third-pass regression based on cross-sectional data.

7.2.5 Calculation of the Inferred Asymptotic Betas and Comparisons with *L*-day Betas and Estimated Asymptotic Betas

Applying the procedure discussed in Section 7.1.5, the inferred asymptotic beta of security k for $L = 1$ is given by

$$\hat{b}_k^* = {}_1\hat{b}_{k1} - ({}_3\hat{a}_k + {}_3\hat{b}_k \ln V_k) \tag{9}$$

using Eq. (7) for $L = 1$. The inferred asymptotic betas are reported in the last column of Table 5. Also reported in Table 5 are the estimated coefficients ${}_3\hat{a}_k$ and ${}_3\hat{b}_k$ from the third-pass regressions excluding k, based on Eq. (4).

TABLE 5 Summary Statistics for Third-Pass Regressions

$_2\hat{b}_k = {_3\hat{a}_k} + {_3\hat{b}_k} \ln V_j;\ j = 1, \ldots, k-1, k+1, \ldots, 50$

k[a]	$_3\hat{a}_k$	$t(_3\hat{a}_k)$	$_3\hat{b}_k$	$t(_3\hat{b}_k)$	R-Square	b_k^{*}[b]
1	−2.6316	−10.901	0.18077	9.2324	0.64458	1.379
2	−2.6153	−11.005	0.17955	9.3084	0.64832	1.293
3	−2.6505	−11.169	0.1822	9.4577	0.65555	1.230
4	−2.6226	−11.069	0.18011	9.3632	0.65100	0.705
5	−2.5490	−11.211	0.17462	9.4590	0.65561	2.255
6	−2.6605	−11.271	0.18293	9.5443	0.65965	1.961
7	−2.6693	−11.347	0.18359	9.6108	0.66276	1.770
8	−2.5181	−11.640	0.17238	9.8121	0.67197	2.363
9	−2.6088	−11.103	0.17910	9.3856	0.65208	2.393
10	−2.6931	−11.761	0.18526	9.9582	0.67845	1.561
11	−2.6943	−11.878	0.18529	10.0530	0.68255	1.473
12	−2.6648	−11.453	0.18317	9.6872	0.66629	1.606
13	−2.6287	−11.213	0.18060	9.4791	0.65657	2.060
14	−2.6198	−11.208	0.17996	9.4730	0.65628	1.387
15	−2.6682	−11.550	0.18337	9.7650	0.66984	2.780
16	−2.6467	−11.366	0.18183	9.6016	0.66233	1.485
17	−2.6403	−11.336	0.18138	9.5728	0.66099	1.982
18	−2.6478	−11.426	0.18183	9.6445	0.66432	2.255
19	−2.6294	−11.313	0.18072	9.5575	0.66027	1.201
20	−2.6366	−11.319	0.18115	9.5584	0.66031	0.964
21	−2.6469	−11.430	0.18176	9.6463	0.66410	1.566
22	−2.6189	−11.514	0.18020	9.7354	0.66849	1.232
23	−2.6383	−11.340	0.18124	9.5722	0.66096	2.015
24	−2.6482	−11.523	0.18174	9.7167	0.66764	1.214
25	−2.6383	−11.346	0.18123	9.5749	0.66109	2.234
26	−2.6307	−11.397	0.18096	9.6294	0.66363	1.212
27	−2.6274	−11.886	0.18112	10.0620	0.68296	0.979
28	−2.6315	−11.520	0.18117	9.7401	0.66871	0.963
29	−2.6365	−11.342	0.18117	9.5692	0.66082	0.793
30	−2.6370	−11.658	0.18065	9.8057	0.67168	1.160
31	−2.6350	−11.445	0.18071	9.6347	0.66387	1.743
32	−2.6354	−11.356	0.18092	9.5689	0.66081	0.715
33	−2.6350	−11.359	0.18088	9.5702	0.66087	2.102
34	−2.6405	−11.367	0.18161	9.5911	0.66184	1.672
35	−2.6578	−11.955	0.18358	10.9550	0.68584	1.119
36	−2.6250	−11.383	0.17989	9.5674	0.66074	2.214
37	−2.6381	−11.333	0.18132	9.5534	0.66008	0.634
38	−2.6224	−11.330	0.17971	9.5195	0.65848	0.802
39	−2.6181	−11.353	0.17930	9.5316	0.65905	1.068
40	−2.6254	−11.290	0.18004	9.4907	0.65712	0.512
41	−2.6558	−11.438	0.18300	9.6575	0.66492	0.974
42	−2.6512	−11.369	0.18254	9.5896	0.66178	0.810
43	−2.6150	−11.241	0.17912	9.4318	0.65431	1.021
44	−2.6069	−11.237	0.17838	9.4166	0.65358	1.272
45	−2.6346	−11.233	0.18097	9.4494	0.65515	1.024
46	−2.6656	−11.283	0.18374	9.5116	0.65811	0.592

TABLE 5 *(continued)*

k[a]	${}_3\hat{a}_k$	$t({}_3\hat{a}_k)$	${}_3\hat{b}_k$	$t({}_3\hat{b}_k)$	R-Square	b_k^*[b]
47	−2.7215	−11.618	0.18863	9.8382	0.67313	0.639
48	−2.6513	−11.032	0.18245	9.2727	0.64657	1.133
49	−2.6426	−10.924	0.18168	9.1695	0.64144	0.696
50	−2.6001	−10.290	0.17802	9.5778	0.61022	0.896
All firms	−2.6366	−11.462	0.18115	9.6703	0.66081	

[a] See footnote b of Table 2.

[b] The b_k^* were computed from Eq. (9).

Inferred asymptotic betas based on daily betas are good estimators of estimated asymptotic betas with a mean square error (MSE) of 0.055, as shown in Table 4. They are highly correlated with estimated asymptotic betas (0.920 in Table 3) as well as with estimated L-day betas, as shown in Table 3. The holdout sample procedure that we applied makes efficient use of all available data and produces almost unbiased results. Our results presented in Table 5 indicate that the coefficients of the third-pass regression are reasonably stable over different (albeit overlapping rather than independent) samples of NYSE stocks during the period 1970–1973. We do not know, however, if they would be similarly stable over a different universe of stocks and/or different calendar periods.

7.3 CORROBORATIVE TESTS AND COMPARISON OF ALTERNATIVE BETA ADJUSTMENT PROCEDURES

The model we have presented in Chapters 6 and 7 has been tested and compared to other adjustment procedures. We look at two studies: one, using Paris Bourse data, by Fung-Schwartz-Whitcomb (1985), and the other, using NYSE daily and trade-to-trade data, by McInish-Wood (1985a) and Ord-McInish-Wood (1984).

7.3.1 Tests on Paris Bourse Data

Unlike the continuous auction of the NYSE, the Paris Bourse is a periodic call market, where most trading orders are batched for one transaction a day.[12] By the logic of Chapter 6, this may dampen the intervalling effect due to asynchronous closing transactions on continuous markets. On the other hand, traders not present on the floor of the Bourse are unable to obtain any indication of probable clearing prices prior to the call. Hence there may be a tendency for blocks to be "worked" more slowly in Paris and for the correction of random demand imbalances to occur more slowly. The result would be slower convergence to an asymptotic beta.

Because of these structural differences, Fung-Schwartz-Whitcomb (1985) sought to verify the predictions of Chapter 6's intervalling-effect model and to compare our adjustment procedures with that of Scholes-Williams (1977) using Paris data. The sample consists of prices from January 3, 1977 to April 3, 1980 for 52 major Paris stocks for which market-value-of-shares-outstanding data for December 31, 1979 were available and for which no probable errors in price were observed.[13] The index used is the Compagnie des Agents de Change value-weighted index. The test design for estimating the intervalling effect and adjusting beta is identical to that described in Section 7.1 except that a broader set of second-pass functional forms is tested, the log function instead of the power function is chosen,[14] and a Box-Cox test of the validity of the choice is presented.[15]

Table 6 summarizes the second-pass results for the Paris sample and should be compared with the NYSE results in Table 2. Because a value-weighted index was used in both studies, only a few stocks (generally with very large market values) have significantly positive second-pass slope coefficients. In both samples, the lowest-value stocks tend to have the largest negative second-pass slope coefficients. The French asymptotic beta estimates average 0.971, substantially smaller than the U.S. average (1.334). This appears to be because there is a negative association between asymptotic beta and firm size in the U.S. sample, and because the U.S. stocks are thinner relative to their index than is the case with the French sample.

The Paris third-pass results, when all 52 stocks are included in the regression, are

$$\begin{aligned} {}_2\hat{b}_j &= -3.442 + 0.1615 \ln V_j \qquad && R^2 = 0.173 \\ &\quad (-3.604) \quad (3.230) && \text{DWS} = 1.4059 \end{aligned} \tag{10}$$

TABLE 6 Paris Bourse Sample: Summary Statistics for Second-Pass Regressions, OLS Betas versus Log [(1 + (1/Interval L)]

Firm Size		Averages, Across Firms in Each Size Group						
Rank[a]	Millions of Dollars	${}_2\hat{a}_j$	Average Inferred Beta[b]	${}_2\hat{b}_j$	No. 0	No. Sig.[c]	R^2	Durbin-Watson
1-10	0.5496	1.014	0.997	−0.7163	9	9	0.294	1.7257
11-20	1.0170	0.010	1.022	−0.3603	8	5	0.123	2.1797
21-30	1.7936	0.900	0.918	−0.2156	7	6	0.160	1.9980
31-40	3.2904	1.000	0.999	−0.2987	10	6	0.144	1.9047
41-50	6.3974	1.100	1.077	−0.3718	10	7	0.214	1.5308
51-52	15.9593	0.408	0.507	0.4604	0	0	0.170	1.4566

[a] Firms are ranked in increasing order of their value of shares outstanding on December 31, 1979.

[b] Inferred betas are averaged across 32 return intervals and across firms.

[c] Significant at 0.05 (one tail, d.f. = 30). ${}_2\hat{b}_j$ is significantly positive for firms 51 and 52. All ${}_2\hat{a}_j$ are significantly positive.

Source: Table 2 of Fung-Schwartz-Whitcomb (1985).

Equation (10) confirms, on the Paris sample, the prediction in Chapter 6 that the intervalling effect is positively related to the value of shares outstanding (the inverse proxy for price-adjustment delay).[16]

However, the Paris results, while statistically significant, are substantially weaker than the comparable NYSE results (the row labeled "All firms" in Table 5). The most likely explanation is that V, unadjusted for insider holdings, is a poorer proxy for delayed price adjustment in France. We also observe that because the Paris sample is less heterogeneous with respect to V than the NYSE sample and more stocks are close to the index average V, there are a greater number of insignificant second-pass betas. When these are excluded, the sample is reduced to 29 and $t({}_3\hat{b})$ rises to 4.1 and R^2 to 0.39 while the regression coefficients are practically unchanged.[17]

The Paris Bourse data sample is used to calculate three alternative sets of adjusted betas: estimated adjusted betas (second-pass intercept), inferred asymptotic betas [Eq. (7)], and Scholes-Williams (1977) adjusted betas (hereafter, S&W beta). By the model of Chapter 6, the estimated asymptotic betas should reflect the most complete adjustment, but they make the largest data and data-processing demands. Thus the estimated asymptotic betas are used as a standard of comparison for the other two "practical" adjustment procedures.

Table 7 reports the MSEs against estimated asymptotic betas for (unadjusted) OLSE betas, inferred asymptotic betas, and S&W betas at different measurement intervals. Surprisingly, the S&W betas have greater MSEs at every interval than even the OLSE betas, while the inferred asymptotic betas have relatively low MSEs. It is also surprising that, despite the relatively weak French third-pass results, the French inferred asymptotic betas have lower MSEs than their U.S. counterparts at every differencing interval. As we suggested in Chapter 6, the reason the S&W betas are in such disagreement with the estimated asymptotic betas is that with short-interval returns their one-interval lag does not comprehend the full delayed price-adjustment effect.

To determine whether intervalling-effect bias remains in the S&W betas, the French second- and third-pass regressions were replicated with S&W betas substituted for OLSE betas in the second pass. The null hypothesis that the sec-

TABLE 7 Paris Bourse Sample: Mean Square Errors of Various Beta Estimates versus Asymptotic Betas, Selected Return Intervals

Interval	OLS Betas	Inferred Betas	S&W Betas
1	0.0835	0.0379	0.1429
5	0.0383	0.0314	0.0877
10	0.0206	0.0215	0.0741
20	0.0283	0.0242	0.1082
32	0.0316	0.0322	0.1670

Source: Table 3 of Fung-Schwartz-Whitcomb (1985).

ond-pass slope coefficients $[{}_2\hat{b}_j(\text{S\&W})]$ are randomly distributed around zero, largely insignificant, and independent of ln V_j was tested by the third-pass regression:

$$
{}_2\hat{b}_j(\text{S\&W}) = \underset{(-4.116)}{6.072} + \underset{(3.750)}{0.2893} \ln V_j \qquad R^2 = 0.220 \qquad \text{DWS} = 1.995 \tag{11}
$$

The results are very similar to the third-pass results of Eq. (10). Indeed, the fit is somewhat better and the ln V_j coefficient more highly significant when S&W betas instead of OLSE betas are used to estimate ${}_2\hat{b}_j$. Hence, for the French sample, the S&W adjustment procedure does not appear to reduce the intervalling effect or to weaken its relationship to firm size.

7.3.2 Tests on Daily and Trade-to-Trade Data

Two working papers by McInish-Wood (1985a) and Ord-McInish-Wood (1984) provide perhaps the most comprehensive test to date of the various beta adjustment procedures suggested by others. The key element of their test design is to construct five portfolios using a linear-programming (LP) model that maximizes interportfolio differences in average time between trades (their thinness measure) but holds constant across portfolios variables that are known to be determinants of beta. Thus each portfolio should have a beta of 1 (when an equally weighted index of the stocks in the sample is used). Using daily returns and a unique data set consisting of six months of trade-to-trade returns, they estimate betas by OLSE and by the Scholes-Williams, Dimson, Fowler-Rorke-Jog, trade-to-trade, and CHMSW inferred asymptotic beta techniques. Their main results are:

1. OLSE betas, whether calculated from daily or trade-to-trade returns, are less than 1 for thin portfolios (measured by mean time from last trade to market close) and greater than 1 for thick portfolios.
2. When the differencing interval was increased by increments from a few minutes to 30 days, OLSE beta estimates converged to 1 for each of the five portfolios, with the thin-portfolio betas converging from below and the thick-portfolio betas from above.
3. The Scholes-Williams, Dimson, and Fowler-Rorke-Jog (1984) adjustment procedures, when applied to daily data, reduce the spread of beta estimates by only about 20 to 30%, leaving thin-portfolio betas less than 1 and thick-portfolio betas greater than 1.
4. The trade-to-trade beta procedure [of Schwert (1977), Franks-Broyles-Hecht (1977), and Marsh (1979)—see Section 6.6] also leaves thin-portfolio betas less than 1 and thick-portfolio betas greater than 1. Depending on whether a synchronous or nonsynchronous index is used, the procedure imparts downward or upward bias to beta estimates.

5. The CHMSW inferred asymptotic beta procedure appeared to be as ineffective as the other procedures in reducing the spread of beta estimates across the five portfolios.[18] However, it should be noted that the test is inadvertently biased against our procedure, since each portfolio is constrained to nearly the same average V.[19] Thus remaining differences in price-adjustment delay across portfolios are due to differences in average time between trades, which we do not use in our estimating equation. Whether an unbiased test of our procedures (including estimated asymptotic beta) could be made using a modification of the McInish-Wood procedure is not yet clear.

7.4 CONCLUSION

In this chapter we have presented tests of our model of the impact of various price-adjustment delays on the measurement of beta. Our model assumes that true returns are generated by an underlying unbiased process, and it implies that a security's delayed price-adjustment bias (the extent to which the beta calculated using observed transaction price data differs from the beta for the true underlying returns generation process) will tend to vanish as the differencing interval is lengthened. Our formulation also suggests that, for a given differencing interval, true beta will be underestimated for securities with relatively long price-adjustment delays (i.e., for securities with small market values), while for securities with relatively shorter price-adjustment delays than those of the average security in the market index, beta will be overestimated.

Our empirical tests have generated results that conform well to our theoretical expectations. Our test design consists of three regression passes. In the first pass, betas are estimated for 14 different values of the differencing interval L for each of 50 NYSE common stocks. The second-pass regressions relate beta to L for each security. The second-pass slope coefficient measures the strength of the intervalling effect and the intercept is an estimate of the asymptotic value of beta that is approached as L is increased without bound. Then, the third pass is a cross-sectional test that estimates the intervalling effect–thinness relationship by regressing the slope of the second-pass regressions on the value of shares outstanding for the stocks in the sample. The significance of the third-pass test strongly confirms the presence of a delayed price adjustment, and shows that market value is a major determinant of its magnitude and direction.

The analysis also suggests two new approaches to eliminating the delayed price-adjustment bias, and hence to obtaining more meaningful beta estimaters from very short-period (e.g., daily) returns data. The first, which is based on the second-pass regressions, is to estimate the asymptotic value of beta that is approached as L is increased without bound. The adjustment appears to be substantial: a cross-sectional regression shows that the proportional difference between unadjusted one-day beta estimates and estimated asymptotic betas is significantly related to the logarithm of value of shares outstanding. The other approach, based on the third-pass regression, uses the intervalling effect–thinness relationship to "correct" a stock's short-period beta by taking account of that stock's value of shares outstanding.

The close association we have observed between the inferred asymptotic betas obtained through the latter approach, using a Lachenbruch holdout sample procedure and the estimated asymptotic betas obtained by the former, gives us additional confidence that both correction methods improve the quality of beta estimates obtained from short-period data. The comparative value of the second approach, which is based on the intervalling effect–thinness relationship, is that just one time-series regression, based on short-period data, need be run for a security. That is, with this method, the only additional information beyond the cross-sectional intervalling effect–thinness relationship needed to adjust the estimated short-period beta is the aggregate market value of that security.

A study by Fung-Schwartz-Whitcomb (1985) confirms that a significant intervalling effect, positively related to value of shares outstanding, also exists for Paris Bourse data. This study shows that the Scholes-Williams adjustment procedure does not eliminate the intervalling effect in beta, but that our inferred asymptotic beta adjustment appears to do so. Studies by McInish-Wood (1985a) and Ord-McInish Wood (1984) further corroborate (1) our predictions concerning the bias in beta caused by the intervalling effect, (2) the asymptotic reduction in beta bias as the length of the differencing interval is increased, and (3) the failure of several other adjustment procedures to eliminate completely the intervalling effect in beta. However, their test design makes it impossible to perform an unbiased test of our adjustment procedures.

Our empirical results clearly suggest that meaningful beta estimates can be obtained from daily returns data. The next step toward implementing the adjustment procedure would be to test the stationarity (intertemporally and cross-sectionally) of the third-pass coefficients. Furthermore, it would be interesting to rerun many of the efficient market hypothesis tests that have produced anomalies to see if the abnormal returns are reduced by proper beta adjustment.[20]

NOTES

*The principal source of the material in this chapter is K. J. Cohen, G. A. Hawawini, S. F. Maier, R. A. Schwartz, and D. K. Whitcomb, "Estimating and Adjusting the Intervalling-Effect Bias in Beta," *Management Science*, Vol. 29, 1983, pp. 135–148. Additional material, specifically identified, comes from W. K. H. Fung, R. A. Schwartz, and D. K. Whitcomb, "Testing Alternative Adjustment Procedures for the Intervalling-Effect Bias in Beta Estimates Using Paris Bourse Data," *Journal of Banking and Finance*, Vol. 9, 1985, pp. 443–460 (by permission of North-Holland Publishing Company, Amsterdam).

1. Sunder (1980) gives evidence on the nonstationarity of beta, as well as extensive references to other literature. Fisher-Kamin (1985) develop and implement a method, based on the Kalman filter technique, for estimating nonstationary betas where a

sufficient data set exists and where firms are not of such extreme sizes as to introduce meaningful intervalling-effect bias into monthly beta estimates.

2. The findings of Basu (1977), Banz (1981), and Keim (1983) established, respectively, that firms with low P/E ratios earn excess returns, that small market value accounts for the P/E effect, and that half of the annual small firm effect could be accounted for by January trading. Reinganum (1981) and Roll (1981) consider bias in beta estimates as an explanation. See the discussion in footnote 20 for additional relevant considerations.
3. A third procedure is suggested by Corollary 1 to Proposition 6. The corollary gives a consistent estimator that generalizes the Scholes-Williams (1977) estimator and corrects Dimson's (1979). We do not implement that estimator here, primarily because of the efficiency loss due to measurement error when reasonable values of N are used.
4. Market value of shares outstanding is measured at the midpoint of the four-year sample period in order to obtain values close to their actual average over the four years.
5. Fung-Schwartz-Whitcomb (1985) also test the log function, $f(L) = \ln(1 + L^{-n})$, as well as the power function, on their French data set. They find that the log function with $n = 1$ gives a better and more nearly linear fit than the power or exponential function. Ng (1981), on the other hand, finds that the power function with $n = 0.8$ gives the best fit on U.K. data.
6. Fung-Schwartz-Whitcomb (1985) establish formal conditions under which ${}_2\hat{a}_j$ is a consistent estimator of true β_j.
7. For compactness, results for the other values of L were omitted from the tables. These omissions do not affect the interpretation of the results.
8. Regressions were run with values of $n = 0.1, 0.2, 0.4, 0.5, 0.6, 0.7, 0.8, 0.9, 1.0, 1.2,$ and 2.0. As n dropped, the average value of R-square improved and that of the Durbin-Watson Statistic (meaningful as a linearity test since the data are arrayed in increasing order of L) increased from a value smaller than 2 to a value larger than 2. The best average value of the Durbin-Watson Statistic (i.e., closest to 2) was found at $n = 0.8$, the power that was selected. A two-variable regression was also run with L^{-1} and L^{-2} as independent variables. The goodness of fit was poorer than that of a single-variable regression with L^{-1} as the independent variable.
9. The mean-square-error coefficient is computed as follows:

$$\text{MSE}\,({}_1\hat{b}_{jL}) = \frac{\sum_{j=1}^{50} ({}_1\hat{b}_{jL} - {}_2\hat{a}_j)^2}{50}$$

10. Note that the impact on beta of any price-adjustment delay will be longer than the length of the delay itself when the observations are temporally contiguous. The effect, however, decays rapidly with increases in the differencing interval once the interval exceeds the length of the maximum price-adjustment delay.
11. Regressing ${}_2\hat{b}_j$ on V_j rather than on $\ln V_j$ produced an estimated equation with significant coefficients and the predicted sign but with a smaller R-square (0.3150). Other proxies for thinness, such as the number of shares traded and the logarithm of number of shares traded, were alternatively used as independent variables. The results were similar, but not quite as strong.
12. In the forward market at the Bourse, bilateral continuous trading following the call occurs, but most transactions occur at the call. See Chapter 2 for a more detailed

discussion of the differences in trading structures between call and continuous markets.

13. The definition of "probable errors" and the procedure for handling days on which individual stock or index data are unavailable are discussed in Fung-Schwartz-Whitcomb (1985). An interesting data anomaly is the fact that the major stocks trade on both cash and forward markets and cash and forward prices are randomly interspersed in the time series. This introduces a (certeris paribus) tendency toward negative serial correlation and reduces the positive index serial correlation predicted in Chapter 6.
14. The power function, $f(L) = L^{-0.8}$, which we found to fit best on NYSE data, evidenced a nonlinear second-pass fit on Paris data. When the absolute magnitude of n was lowered, the fit became better and more nearly linear, which suggests a slower rate of convergence toward an asymptote for the French betas. However, the generally best value of n resulted in an excessive rate of change of beta for large L and gave intercepts which corresponded poorly with visually estimated asymptotes. The log function, $f(L) = \ln(1 + L^{-1})$, gives appropriate convergence behavior at both small and large values of L, and was adopted.
15. In this application, the Box-Cox methodology is used to test the linearity of the log function; linearity cannot be rejected in two-thirds of the 52 fitted equations. Alternatively, the methodology could be used to select the "best" functional form in each equation, but if the best form was not the same in every case, the third pass (which uses a second-pass intercept as the dependent variable) could not be run legitimately. The test design and results are reported in an appendix to Fung-Schwartz-Whitcomb (1985).
16. The Lachenbruch holdout sample results, like the U.S. results, are very similar to the full third-pass regression; only in a few cases does excluding a stock alter the coefficients by as much as 10 to 15%.
17. In addition, sampling fluctuations in first-pass beta due to the fact that the interval lengths are mostly not integer divisions of the calendar span (unlike the NYSE sample) results in random error in the second-pass slope coefficients and weakens the third-pass fit.
18. CHMSW betas for all five portfolios exceed 1, due perhaps to a scalar difference in measurement of V_j between us and McInish-Wood (who use our coefficients).
19. Literally, average share price and book value are constrained to be equal across portfolios, but V does not vary much [except for the most frequently trading portfolio; see McInish-Wood (1985a, Table 1a)].
20. Frankly, we doubt that the entire small firm effect can be eliminated by proper adjustment of beta. The difference we would expect between OLSE and adjusted betas is just not large enough to account for the magnitude of realized excess returns reported in the main studies. We suspect that another piece of the explanation lies in the fact (see Chapter 5) that bid-ask spreads are greater for small firms. Because of this, returns based on last-transaction prices overstate the returns that could actually be earned on an immediate execution strategy more for small than for large firms [see Stoll-Whaley (1983)]. It should be noted, however, that in related work, French-Roll (1985) find that adjusting for the bid-ask spread accounts for only 3% of the observed deviation of variance-time ratios from those implied by serial independence

of returns. Another part of the explanation must lie in whatever causes the "January effect," since that accounts for half of the small firm effect [see Keim (1983)]. Whether there are additional "microstructure" explanations for the small firm and other size-related anomalies, such as the January effect, we do not yet know. There may also be microstructure explanations for the anomalous results found by comparing Fama-MacBeth's (1973) and Tinic-West's (1984) cross-sectional "tests" of the CAPM (or, if you prefer, estimates of the two-factor model).

8

THE CONSOLIDATION/ FRAGMENTATION DEBATE

8.1 BACKGROUND[1]

One of the most fundamental design features of a market system is the extent to which orders are consolidated in the trading process. There are two major dimensions to the consolidation of orders: (1) the spatial consolidation of orders in a single trading arena, and (2) the temporal consolidation that is realized by batching orders over time for simultaneous execution at a single price. In this chapter, we consider the spatial consolidation of orders. A comparative analysis of call market versus continuous market trading is beyond the scope of the current book, and is left for future analysis. However, some of the issues involved should be recognized as being closely related to those which we deal with here.

Spatial consolidation is not an all-or-nothing feature of a trading system. For simplicity, one might think in terms of two polar extremes, with a continuum of intermediate possibilities. At one extreme, a highly fragmented system can be pictured as a set of separate market centers which may be partially united by the profit-motivated behavior of arbitrageurs, but by no formal intermarket linkage system. At the other extreme, a highly consolidated system can be pictured as a single limit-order book where all orders must be entered, and where strict price priority and secondary trading priority rules are maintained.

The current U.S. exchange markets lie between these two extremes. Orders brought to an exchange are consolidated to the extent that they are placed on the specialist's limit-order book; however, orders are also held by floor traders and worked in the crowd at the specialist's post. Most orders for NYSE- and AMEX-listed securities are transmitted to these two national exchanges, but orders for cross-listed securities also go to the regional exchanges (the Boston, Cincinnati, Mid-West, Pacific, and Philadelphia exchanges). The national and regional exchanges are linked by the Intermarket Trading System (ITS—see Chapter 2), but this linkage, which mainly facilitates the preservation of price priority rules (best-priced orders trade first), does not achieve a full consolidation of the order flow in the sense of a consolidated limit-order book (CLOB). In addition, the current market structure is fragmented in that third-market firms trade exchange-listed stocks OTC, because the recent relaxation of off-board trading restrictions has led to in-house trading in some stocks by some member firms, and because block trades negotiated in the upstairs market are executed on the trading floor simply as put-throughs.

In the past decade, there has been much debate concerning the spatial consolidation of orders in a trading system. This debate has largely focused on off-board trading restrictions for member firms (NYSE Rule 390 and AMEX Rule 5) and on the institution of appropriate intermarket linkages (such as the Consolidated Transactions Tape, the Consolidated Quotations System, and the ITS). We review the recent history in Section 8.1.1 below. First, however, it is helpful to put forth the issues that should be addressed in order to define appropriately the effects of fragmentation. These issues, which we discuss in Section 8.2, include:

1. The maintenance of price priority
2. The maintenance of secondary priority rules
3. The consolidation of information concerning the order flow
4. The public-goods nature of various services provided by a securities exchange
5. Interdealer competition
6. Intermarket competition
7. The desirability of servicing the disparate needs of different traders
8. Fairness

We consider each of these eight issues in light of the actual trading system that exists for listed securities and the various proposals for altering it, rather than in terms of the polar opposites of complete consolidation and complete fragmentation. Thus we spend considerable time assessing the probable effects of increased dealer activity by brokerage firms if off-board trading restrictions are relaxed, but we do not attempt to resurrect a discussion of the CLOB proposals.[2]

8.1.1 Recent History

Market professionals, academicians, and even regulators share a fundamental belief in competition and in the efficiency of a free-market system. Much of the recent change in the underlying structure of the securities markets has therefore been designed to strengthen competition within the system. This was clearly the case with the Congressionally mandated removal, in 1975, of fixed minimum brokerage commissions.

In the 1975 Securities Acts Amendments, Congress established the dual objectives of increasing competition in the securities markets and of achieving a national market system (NMS). Congress adopted, as two of its criteria for an NMS, the preservation of auction trading principles and a reduction in market fragmentation. More to the point, Congress set forth five goals for an NMS to achieve: (1) the economically efficient execution of transactions; (2) fair competition among brokers, dealers, and markets; (3) broad availability of information with respect to quotations and transactions; (4) the practicability of executing investors' orders in the best market; and (5) an opportunity for investors' orders to meet without the participation of a dealer. Beyond this, Congress did not specifically define what the NMS would be; rather, it left the task of implementing the objectives of an NMS largely to the SEC.[3]

Because the U.S. securities markets have been dominated by a single trading arena, the NYSE, much of the SEC's efforts to promote competition over the past 10 years have been directed at loosening the grip that the NYSE has on securities trading. One NYSE rule in particular has been of paramount concern: Rule 390, the off-board trading restriction which, with minor exceptions, forces member firms to execute principal orders for listed securities on the exchange floor.[4] The SEC has argued that such trading restrictions are anticompetitive and unnecessary; therefore, since the mid-1960s, the SEC has taken various steps to eliminate them.

In June 1977, the SEC announced that by the end of the year it would mandate the removal of Rule 390. In response, a loud cry of alarm was sounded throughout the industry. Accordingly, the SEC backed off and Rule 390 was allowed, for the time being, to stand.

Then the SEC instituted Rule 19c-3: effective July 18, 1980, exchange members were free to make off-board markets for issues that were listed on an exchange for the first time after April 26, 1979. As of mid-1984, approximately 600 listed securities were subject to Rule 19c-3 [see Williams (1985)]. The expectation of many [including us; see CMSW (1982)] was that the introduction and eventual extension of this rule would lead to the gradual demise of the organized securities exchanges; thus far, this has not occurred.

The day before SEC Rule 19c-3 became effective, the *Wall Street Journal* (July 17, 1980, p. 3) reported that Merrill Lynch and Morgan Stanley both announced plans to trade stocks in-house. The article also stated: "Most major broker-dealers say they will begin trading listed stocks if competitive pressures make such a move advisable." But by mid-1983, virtually all of the large firms, including Merrill Lynch, Morgan Stanley, Paine Webber, and Goldman Sachs, ceased their market-making activities in 19c-3 stocks. According to SEC Release 20074 (1983, p. 6), the stated reasons for these broker-dealers withdrawing from market making "were varied, and included the need to redeploy scarce personnel during the current active securities markets, frustration and inefficiencies in the current operation of the ITS/CAES linkage and dissatisfaction with trading in the current Rule 19c-3 environment." There was speculation in the news media (*The Wall Street Journal*, March 22, 1983, p. 7) that the brokerage houses were coerced by exchange specialists to cease trading in 19c-3 stocks. Whatever the reasons, the SEC's attempt to promote competition among market makers did not succeed. And so, the debate has continued.

Following the introduction of the 19c-3 experiment, there has also been a continuing debate concerning an "order exposure" rule.[5] A number of different order exposure rules for 19c-3 stocks have in fact been proposed [see, e.g., Securities and Exchange Commission (1982)]. We will not argue here the merits or defects of any of the specific proposals, but merely reiterate that while order exposure is essential to prevent some of the negative effects of market fragmentation, it is not immediately obvious that a rule is needed to bring it about. In any event, no one specific rule has yet been adopted.

Rule 19c-3 allowed off-board trading on an experimental basis for recently listed securities only, in an attempt to resolve the disagreement concerning whether this would on balance be helpful or harmful to the quality of the securities markets. Following the introduction of this experiment, the SEC has provided some data and analysis in their two monitoring reports on Rule 19c-3 [see Securities and Exchange Commission (1981, 1983)]. Unfortunately, the SEC's conclusions are not definitive. The SEC's 1981 report states (p. 4):

> In summary, the adoption of the Rule does not appear to have had an adverse effect on market quality. In addition, it appears that the primary markets have not had significant difficulty in competing with OTC market makers for order flow. However, since the adoption of the Rule, there has not been substantial OTC trading in most Rule 19c-3 Common Stocks. Accordingly, it is not possible at this time to reach any conclusions regarding the effects on the markets of an active OTC market in Rule 19c-3 Common Stocks.

In commenting on the SEC's 1981 report, the New York Stock Exchange (1982b, letter of transmittal) states that there are "serious flaws" in this SEC report which make it "of limited utility in evaluating the validity of the Rule 19c-3 experiment" since it "did not deal with a number of very important adverse impacts of Rule 19c-3 that are inherent and inevitable, and bear directly on the Report's major topics (i.e., market quality, market-making competition and execution quality)." The NYSE further stated that "the most important conclusions expressed or implied in the Monitoring Report, and the interpretations thereof, were based on questionable methodologies and/or data." The SEC's (1983) report on Rule 19c-3 merely presents additional data, without attempting to interpret its significance with respect to the impact of this rule on market quality.

The 19c-3 experiment, therefore, has not as yet generated conclusive results. While the withdrawal of the large brokerage firms from off-board market making might seem to imply the inherent unprofitability of these operations, there is no way of knowing what the results might have been if Merrill Lynch, Bache, and the others had been allowed to make 19c-3 markets for the big stocks, such as IBM and DuPont, or if a better linkage than ITS had been available (see Chapter 3). Thus, in a sense, the SEC has been sent back to the drawing board.

Those opposed to off-board trading have continued to argue that the market fragmentation which such trading involves, especially in the absence of perfect intermarket linkages and an enforceable order exposure rule, constitutes a per se violation of some of the principles in the Securities Acts Amendments of 1975, which mandated the establishment of an NMS. For example, the New York Stock Exchange (1982c, pp. 2–3) states:

> In the Securities Acts Amendments of 1975 and its legislative history, particularly in Section 11A of the Act, Congress spelled out its objectives for a national market system for listed securities. In broadest terms, Section 11A seeks the elimination of market fragmentation through linkages, so that there may be maximum access to all markets by all participants and maximum interaction and competition among orders under auction/agency principles. . . . In the absence of an effective order exposure rule, Rule 19c-3, by its very nature, contravenes the foregoing objectives.

Academicians have also remained divided on the issue. For example, the studies of Tinic-West (1972, 1974) suggest the value of interdealer competition. Hamilton (1979) concluded that the beneficial competitive effects of fragmentation outweigh the harmful effects. On the other hand, we have previously concluded [see CMSW (1982)] that fragmentation has a detrimental effect on market quality. Mendelson (1984) also concluded that market fragmentation is undesirable, since it results in a lower expected trading volume, in a larger price variance faced by individual traders, and in lower expected overall gains from trading. The Cohen-Conroy (1985) empirical analysis of the effects of Rule 19c-3 found that those stocks which attracted exchange member market makers had lower percentage spreads (which resulted from increased competition in market making), but that this came at the expense of higher returns variance (which resulted from increased fragmentation of the order flow). Our own analysis has continued to lead us to favor consolidation, although it is not clear that an order exposure *rule* is needed, and it may be possible for consolidation to be achieved without regulatory intervention.

8.1.2 Intermarket Linkages and Recent Developments in the OTC Markets

The SEC's 19c-3 experiment clearly placed the principal regulatory body for the securities industry in a position of actively promoting multiple trading arenas for the same security. Other efforts to promote competition among markets have led to the Consolidated Quotation System (CQS), the Intermarket

Trading System (ITS), and the Cincinnati Stock Exchange's National Securities Trading System (NSTS).[6] These communication linkages among different marketplaces appear to have been only moderately successful, at best, and they have not as yet diminished the importance of the NYSE as a dominant trading arena.

A more resounding success has been the recent development of the OTC markets. Primarily through improvements in its NASDAQ system, the OTC markets have become a very competitive force in the industry. In fact, the OTC market appears strong enough to have caused the AMEX, in recent years, to lose substantial market share: between 1979 and 1983 the number of companies listed on the AMEX has declined by 12%, while the number listed on NASDAQ has increased by 53%. Interestingly, the NYSE has been hurt only slightly (the number of companies listed on the NYSE declined by 1% between 1979 and 1983).[7]

The competition between the exchanges and the OTC market is not primarily competition for the order flow itself. Rather, it is competition for corporate listings. That is, it is the corporations themselves that have increasingly chosen the NASDAQ OTC market over an exchange listing. The reasons for this are varied. Some companies cite the reporting requirements of the exchanges; others note the additional fees imposed by the exchanges. But, most important for our purposes here, some companies might simply be responding to the quality of the market that they feel they can obtain by having multiple dealers active in their securities as opposed to a single specialist.

A multiple-dealer system without perfect intermarket linkages must, to some extent, be a fragmented system. Therefore, observing that the OTC's recent success has largely been attributed to improvements in NASDAQ, which is an intermarket linkage system, might suggest that good intermarket linkages are all that are needed to overcome the problems that might attend market fragmentation. However, we believe that there is more to the story; this will be evident in our discussion in Sections 8.2 and 8.3.

As Amihud-Ho-Schwartz (1985, Chap. 1) note, the difference between the OTC markets and the exchange markets involves more than a multiple dealer market versus a consolidated market with a single specialist. Various rules and principles differ between the two alternative market systems. For instance, OTC market makers have far greater freedom to choose the stocks they wish to trade; OTC dealers are not constrained by an elaborate system of trading rules and market surveillance; OTC market makers are allowed to have direct contact with their customers; OTC market makers deal in both primary and secondary issues; the public order flow is a far greater source of liquidity in the exchange markets; the consolidation of the public order flow on the exchange markets provides an informational advantage which the OTC dealers do not have; and so on.

In our analysis here, we restrict our attention to the exchange markets. The question that we address is the desirability of consolidating the order flow within that system. Our conclusions do not directly address the desirability of the exchange system itself versus its chief competitor, the OTC system.

8.1.3 Two Markets

To clarify the arguments involved in the consolidation/fragmentation debate as it pertains to the stock exchanges, it is useful to distinguish between two different markets: the market for marketability (i.e., trading) services, and the market for the shares that are traded. That is, following the distinction made by Bloch-Schwartz (1978a, 1978b), we recognize that the securities markets in fact involve an amalgamation of two distinct markets and hence that two different types of prices are established: a transaction (or execution) fee, and the underlying price of the securities themselves. However, the provision of trading services necessarily accompanies the exchange of securities. Thus there is a conflict which is fundamental to the organization of the market: competition for the provision of trading services can adversely affect the quality of competition for pricing the securities that are traded. As a result, a trade-off exists between tighter pricing of shares and more competitive pricing of trading services.

For example, a national market system that resulted in the consolidation of all orders for a particular security would maximize the extent to which public orders provide liquidity and immediacy of execution, and would help to ensure that trades are executed at reasonable prices.[8] This would satisfy three of the five goals that Congress set forth for an NMS (broad availability of quotes and transactions information, the practicability of executing orders in the best market, and the opportunity for investors to meet without the participation of a dealer). However, consolidation in a single marketplace might reduce competition in the market for marketability services. Thus such a unified marketplace might seemingly conflict with the other two goals that Congress set forth (the economically efficient execution of transactions and fair competition among brokers, dealers, and markets). Part of the complexity of the debates is that, to an extent, the goals which Congress set forth are not compatible.

8.1.4 Secondary Trading Priority Rules

To understand the functioning of the markets for the shares that are traded, it is necessary to clarify a procedural rule that surprisingly has received little attention in the consolidation/fragmentation debate: the secondary trading priority rule. Such a rule specifies the sequence in which orders are to execute when they are written at the same price (where the primary trading rule is that the best-priced orders, i.e., the lowest asks and the highest bids, execute first). Time priority is the most commonly used secondary priority rule. This rule, and other possible rules, are defined as follows:

1. *Time.* An order that enters the limit-order book earlier has priority over an equally priced order that enters the limit-order book later.
2. *Size.* A larger order has priority over an equally priced order that is smaller.

3. *Public before market maker.* Orders placed by members of the public (i.e., ordinary traders or institutional traders) have priority over equally priced orders placed by market makers or specialists.
4. *Pro rata partial execution at a price.* If there is an imbalance of either buy or sell orders at a crossing price, then the orders on the smaller side of the market are entirely filled, but the orders on the larger side of the market are filled on a pro rata basis.
5. *Random selection.* Of those orders that are tied at a price, the particular orders that transact are determined randomly.

On the AMEX, public orders are executed in strict time sequence when tied according to price. The secondary rule used by the NYSE is a more complex combination of time and size priorities. The intent of the NYSE rule is essentially to minimize the number of orders on the book that a newly arrived order will execute against, and thereby to economize on the number of separate transactions, while still maintaining time priority when possible.[9]

8.2 ISSUES CONCERNING THE CONSOLIDATION/FRAGMENTATION OF ORDERS

We certainly expect that permitting brokers to make off-exchange markets for 19c-3 stocks would, at least to some extent, increase fragmentation. Would this be bad or would there be compensating benefits? To answer this question, we must identify the effects of fragmentation. To this end, we consider the eight issues listed at the beginning of this chapter.

8.2.1 The Maintenance of Price Priority

The primary rule of order execution is that the best-priced orders (the highest bids and the lowest asks) execute first. The desirability of this primary priority rule has been unquestioned; it follows from basic notions of fairness and economic efficiency.

A formal demonstration that violation of price priority reduces market quality is given by Cohen-Conroy-Maier (1985) [CCM]. CCM assume a continuous auction market with Poisson arrival of limit and market orders. They introduce fragmentation by splitting the order flow randomly between two markets. The result is that a limit order coming to either market must wait a longer time, on average, before it can execute (i.e., transact). Since some investors will cancel their limit orders if they do not execute promptly (or switch from a limit-order strategy to a market-order strategy), this will result in a thinner market, with greater price volatility, larger spreads, and so on.

One of the most interesting implications of the CCM model concerns fragmented markets of different sizes. When one of the markets initially gets a larger proportion of the order flow, the expected waiting time before an order executes in the larger market is less than in the smaller market. This is the formal counterpart of the old axiom, "order flow attracts order flow." It suggests that investors will shun the smaller market, unless it offers compensating advantages.

Initially, the greatest concern about off-board trading was that it could result in violations of price priority (or overreaching, as the execution of poorer- instead of better-priced orders is called). The extent to which overreaching would indeed be a problem in a fragmented system depends on the quality of intermarket linkages, on the effectiveness of order exposure, and on the quality of market surveillance which is possible in such a system. Currently, it does not appear that overreaching is a major problem and, even if it were to be one, it should be technically solvable. Indeed, if price priority were not maintained, it is doubtful that investors would let their orders be directed to any but the largest of the fragmented markets (since the CCM model shows that orders have the best chance of executing in the largest pool). Hence the smaller markets would disappear. Therefore, we do not feel that overreaching is a major issue concerning the *inherent* desirability or undesirability of consolidating the order flow.

8.2.2 Secondary Priority Rules

Virtually no consideration has been given in the consolidation/fragmentation debates to the desirability of instituting reasonable secondary trading priority rules to determine the sequence of execution for orders placed at the same price. A major reason for this is that the desirability of having orderly secondary priority rules has not been adequately understood.

In Section 8.1.4 we presented several alternative secondary priority rules. Of these rules, the one that appears to be the most desirable and that is most commonly used is time priority (i.e., orders tied at a price are executed according to the time of their arrival, with the orders placed earliest executing first). In the discussion that follows, we focus on the time priority rule.

It is clear that to maintain time priority across all orders tied at a price, the order flow has to be consolidated (perhaps electronically) in a single limit-order book where the individual orders are time dated. But is it desirable to enforce time priority? Unfortunately, this is a complex issue.

There are two ways to approach the issue. The first is to consider the impact of the time priority rule on the order flow itself, and the second is to take the order flow as given and to examine the impact of the time priority rule on the order execution and market clearing process. We note a few considerations that pertain to the first (but leave a formal analysis for future research), and summarize the formal analysis of CCM which relates to the second.

The time priority rule is expected to affect the order flow in at least two ways. First, it gives traders an incentive to transmit their orders to the market earlier. Because of the advantages in a gaming situation of having the other players go first, it is desirable to have some reward built into a system for those players who actually do make the first move. Second, when time or other secondary priorities are followed, some traders may have an additional incentive to better their prices so as to increase the probability of order execution. That is, individuals who in any trading session believe that they will not effectively compete according to the secondary priority rule will tend to compete more actively in relation to the primary rule (price priority). This response would also be desirable: "better" prices imply narrower spreads, thicker markets in the neighborhood of the clearing price, and hence less volatile markets.

Treating the order flow to the market as given, CCM use computer simulation to analyze the impact of a time priority rule, vis-à-vis random selection, on the order-execution, market-clearing process. As in their earlier analytical model, CCM assume Poisson arrival of limit and market orders, but in the simulation they are able to add the realistic assumption that limit orders are withdrawn if they do not transact within a constant, predetermined length of time.[10] The simulation compares two markets, both observing price priority and having discrete prices (e.g., prices in multiples of eighths). In one market it is assumed that time priority is strictly observed, while in the other market any of the existing limit orders tied at the best price is randomly matched with an incoming counterpart market order.

In this model, violation of time priority results in:[11]

1. An increase in the bid-ask spread (the specialist sets the market quotes more frequently and there are fewer public limit orders within the specialist's quotes)
2. A reduction in the expected waiting time for limit orders to execute
3. A reduction in the probability that a limit order will execute before it is withdrawn (from 88 to 83% in the runs reported)

While reduction in a limit order's expected waiting time is a benefit of violating time priority, it is purchased at the cost of reduced limit-order-execution probability and wider spreads.

We therefore conclude that violation of time priority will indeed cause a deterioration in the quality of a market, and that one advantage of a consolidated trading system is that it will enable the institution of a reasonable secondary priority rule. Of course, instituting and enforcing a secondary priority rule is not costless.

Given the desirability of time priority to limit-order placers, the question must be raised whether investors will give their orders to a market that does not offer time priority. For example, the NYSE offers partial time priority: Why would an investor let his limit order be placed on a smaller market (such as a regional exchange or a brokerage firm's in-house execution system), knowing that it would be less likely to execute? The answer has to be "not unless the regional exchange or the brokerage firm offers traders compensating advantages."[12] Whether the market as a whole is sufficiently compensated depends on the resolution of the remaining issues raised in this section.

8.2.3 The Consolidation of Information concerning the Order Flow

As discussed in Schreiber-Schwartz (1985, 1986), a primary function of a trading system is to find the prices at which trades are made. This function exists because, as shown by the theoretical analysis of Ho-Schwartz-Whitcomb (1985) and as implied by the empirical analysis we have discussed in Chapter 7, transaction prices generally differ from Walrasian equilibrium prices, even in markets composed of a large number of atomistic traders.

Several of the major design features of a trading system are best understood in relation to the price discovery process. These include the special opening procedures used by the exchanges, the imposition of trading halts following the advent of major news, some features of the operations of the stock exchange specialists, and the extensive information systems which have been created to provide rapid dissemination of last-transaction prices and current market quotes.

The consolidation of information concerning the order flow is an integral part of this process of finding, as efficiently as possible, the desired Walrasian prices. In part, consolidation in this regard is simply the physical pooling of prices on a consolidated trading tape and in a consolidated quotations system, so that public traders might write their orders in relation to current market information. Beyond this, the pooling of information enables professional traders (most important, the stock exchange specialists) to know the order flow better, and accordingly to set more appropriate quotes; these quotes in turn transmit better signals to the public traders.

The physical consolidation of orders in a market center and of traders on a trading floor contributes in two ways to the consolidation of market information. For one thing, it enables the market makers to see limit-order sizes and prices away from the market (as we discuss in Chapter 9, the information contained in a consolidated limit-order book does have economic value). Second, to the extent that information on market conditions is conveyed by factors other than the price and size of orders (e.g., if the mood, expression, and tone of traders also matters), then direct, interpersonal communication has value and might be most efficiently achieved by the physical consolidation of traders on a trading floor. The value of such interpersonal communication has to be weighed against the cost efficiencies and rapid, broad access to market information provided by automated trading (Chapter 3). Presumably, competition in market architecture among market centers will determine the appropriate balance.

Thus far, the debates concerning the consolidation/fragmentation issue have devoted only scant attention to the consolidation of information, and to its contribution to the efficiency of the price discovery process. This omission, which in part is explained by the difficulty of understanding the complexities of the securities markets, can be critical. The quality of the markets might be impaired if, in the process of bolstering intermarket competition by fragmenting the order flow, the informational content of the order flow is obscured.

8.2.4 The Public Goods Nature of Services Provided by a Securities Exchange

Securities exchanges provide a number of services in addition to the physical handling and matching of orders. These include:

1. *Price discovery.* As discussed in Section 8.2.3, a primary function of an exchange is to discover the prices at which trades are made. These prices then serve as important signals to other traders, and are often used for price basing (e.g., assessing option prices) and asset evaluation (e.g., determining the net asset value per share of mutual funds) in other markets.
2. *Price stabilization.* As we discuss in Chapters 4 and 9, an important aspect of exchange operations is the stabilization of price fluctuations over brief periods of time. The provision of stabilization services results in a more orderly market, to the benefit of all risk-averse traders.
3. *Market surveillance (stock watch).* A major part of exchange operations is to oversee market operations to guard against manipulation, fraud, exploitation, and other violations of the "rules of the game."
4. *Quality certification.* Exchanges provide a certification of soundness of brokerage firms and, because of their listing requirements, a signal regarding the quality of listed securities.

Following the discussion of CMSW (1982), each of these factors can be considered a public good–type externality from the viewpoint of individual traders. The reason is that, in placing their orders on the market, individuals do not take account of the fact that their own participation helps to provide these services to the investment community at large. In addition, the commission dollars obtained by an exchange can in part be viewed as a tax receipt which funds the provision of communal services. Therefore, if in following their own private interests individuals are led to transact off-board, the supply of these public good–type services by the exchange will be impaired, to the detriment of all.

In the debate concerning interdealer competition, it has been assumed that traders will want to have their orders routed to the exchange markets or off-board, depending on the relative costs of the broker-dealer services. Bloch-Schwartz (1978a, 1978b) have argued, however, that this is an oversimplification. That is, even if the explicit transaction cost is the same for the two alternatives, traders may have an incentive to seek in-house executions. Bloch-Schwartz argue that the formation of fragmented in-house queues provides a way for individuals to jump ahead vis-à-vis a common queue, a phenomenon that they call queue gaming.[13] From an aggregate point of view, such queue gaming is not desirable: on average, traders cannot gain and, in the process of trying, they are led to bypass the exchange system and thereby to cause the provision of exchange services to be suboptimal for all.

8.2.5 Interdealer Competition

The major argument that has been advanced in favor of allowing off-board trading is that such trading will strengthen competition in the market for dealer services. As such, the intent is the same as with negotiated brokerage commissions: to reduce the cost of trading. The SEC intended that the greater interdealer competition would result in a reduction of bid-ask spreads and greater market depth (i.e., in more shares being offered at the market quotes).

These effects would be desirable, but there are further questions to which answers are not at all obvious: (1) How much will competition be increased? (2) How much might market spreads thereby be reduced? (3) What effects other than spread reduction might attend the enhanced competition?

There is no doubt that greater interdealer competition will reduce dealer spreads.[14] However, the debate on this score has mistakenly tended to view the stock exchange specialist as a monopolist, and hence has generated an exaggerated impression of the extent to which off-board trading may indeed strengthen competition. Stock exchange specialists, as an integral part of the agency-auction market, face competition from public traders who convey limit orders to the market, and who have their orders worked on the floor by floor traders. These orders (limit and discretionary) are not inconsequential competition.[15] Furthermore, the specialists face competition from the floor traders themselves. Therefore, while allowing off-board trading will no doubt add additional competitive pressures to the market, the change might not be as dramatic as many participants in the debate seem to have expected.

With regard to any reduction in spreads that might attend increased competition among dealers, we call attention to the distinction we made in Chapter 5 between individual dealer spreads and the market spread (i.e., the inside quotes). So long as the market is not made by a single monopoly dealer, the market spread generally reflects the quotes of two different dealers or limit-order traders. Therefore, reducing individual dealer spreads per se need not reduce the market spread, although on expectation such a reduction would follow. The important point to note is that if individual spreads are wide but individual quotes are not identical, the inside spread can be relatively tight, and strengthening competition may reduce it only minimally.

The source of our concern that other effects might attend increased competition in the market for dealer services is the fact that there is a second market involved: the market for the securities that are traded. Strengthening competition in the market for dealer services might indeed reduce bid-ask spreads; however, if it fragments the trading market, it can cause a deterioration in the quality of the prices which are set for the securities themselves (as discussed in Section 8.2.3 above). That is, there may be a trade-off between the size of the spread and the location of the quotes.[16] Because investors ultimately care about the net prices that they pay and receive, it is not at all clear that increased competition in the market for dealer services will result in an overall increase in transactional efficiency for traders.[17]

8.2.6 Intermarket Competition

Competition for the order flow involves not just the setting of competitive quotes by dealers and others who submit limit orders, but also the institution of more attractive trading systems by rival market centers. Curiously, while the debates have focused on interdealer competition (where the realized gains in recent years have been minimal), the most notable occurrence is that the existence of multiple, interlinked market centers has of late resulted in strong intermarket competition (and the gains have been sizable).

Intermarket competition has been highly visible in relation to the introduction of new products such as options and futures contracts [see Silber (1981)]. Of equivalent importance, although somewhat less flashy, has been the introduction of new trading systems. For instance, SCOREX was introduced by the Pacific Stock Exchange in part to counter the competitive power of the NYSE specialists; but the introduction of SCOREX also provided further motivation for the NYSE to improve its OARS system, and to introduce Super-DOT.

Such intermarket competition is desirable with regard to the dynamic efficiencies of the marketplace. Smidt (1985) asserts that substantial inertia (due in part to the reluctance of professionals to learn a new technology) and the considerable difficulty of suddenly changing a complex technology have retarded the evolution of the securities markets. Only by intermarket competition will the markets achieve an efficient structure.

In one respect, however, intermarket competition might adversely affect the quality of the market. Currently, some third-market firms have put competitive pressure on the NYSE to extend trading hours and to curtail trading halts following the advent of major news.[18] Schreiber-Schwartz (1985) assert that the extension of trading may not be desirable if the incremental costs of keeping the system open longer hours are not, for the entire market, justified by sufficiently higher revenues, and if investors are given insufficient time to digest news before trading is resumed. Of course, it can be countered that, in the long run, if investors lose because trading becomes "too continuous," they will concentrate their trading and the market arenas will readjust their hours. However, the learning process takes time and resources, and if temporally concentrated trading creates benefits which cannot be charged for (as Schreiber-Schwartz would assert), intermarket competition may have some costs as well as the clear benefits which we have noted.

8.2.7 The Disparate Needs of Different Traders

It is inevitable that, to some extent, the market will be fragmented because different traders, primarily on the basis of their size, operate differently in the marketplace. That is, the needs and incentives of the large institutional traders differ from those of the small retail customers. That is why, in the current system, small orders are being increasingly transacted semiautomatically via systems such as OARS, DOT, and SCOREX; intermediate-sized orders are commonly "worked" in the crowd on the exchange floor by floor traders; and the largest block trades are typically negotiated off the floor in the upstairs market. Because these multiple trading systems do not assure that secondary trading priorities are satisfied, some of the adverse effects of fragmentation discussed in Section 8.2.2 above will occur.

Thus, a degree of market fragmentation is a costly by-product of the operational flexibility that should be built into a system. Effectively integrating the diverse needs of various types of traders into a unified market system will represent a continuing challenge to the designers of trading systems.

8.2.8 Fairness

One of the most important aspects of a trading system is that it be viewed as being fair by the professional and public traders who participate in the market. The importance of the fairness issue transcends the question of equity itself. That is, if any appreciable subset of traders believes that they consistently obtain inferior executions vis-à-vis other traders, these disgruntled traders might significantly reduce their participation in the market. As a direct consequence, trading volume would be reduced, the price of shares would be depressed, and the benefits to the economy of the secondary markets would be reduced. Furthermore, thinner markets would result in wider bid-ask spreads (Chapter 5), more protracted price adjustment delays (Chapter 6), and inflated stock price volatility (Chapter 4). All three of these latter results would in turn lead to further reductions in market participation and to a further decline in the quality of the marketplace.

The question, therefore, is whether or not the consolidation of orders results in a more orderly, and therefore fairer, market system. The answer is not unambiguous; however, it is clear that rules can be imposed and enforced in a consolidated system which cannot be maintained in a fragmented system. For instance, secondary priority rules can be specified for a consolidated system whereas essentially random selection is, virtually by definition, the only possibility for a fragmented system. Furthermore, market surveillance is far more efficient in a consolidated system. It should also be noted that the access of all participants to market information and to a broad market exposure of their orders may be more likely in a consolidated market. On the other hand, the dynamic efficiencies might be greater in a fragmented system because of the greater degree of competition and technological innovation among market centers which such a system implies.

8.3 INTEGRATING THE ARGUMENTS

To date, consolidating the opinions of experts concerning the fragmentation issue has proven to be considerably more difficult than consolidating the order flow itself. This is hardly surprising. The issues are complex, the outcome is of great importance, and (as can be seen from the list of issues we have discussed) the arguments do not all go in the same direction. Our purpose in this section is to pull the various arguments together, and to present a position regarding the debate.

The first issue we discussed was the maintenance of price priorities. The arguments here favor consolidation, but there is no inherent reason for price priority to be violated by the type of fragmentation implied by off-exchange trading if appropriate intermarket linkages, order exposure, and surveillance exist. Thus, while price priority is of practical importance, we do not give it much weight in reaching the position we present here. For similar reasons, this also is true of our last issue (fairness).

The arguments related to the next three issues—the maintenance of secondary priority rules, consolidation of information on the order flow, and the public-goods nature of various exchange services—all favor consolidation of the order flow. We find the arguments here to be very compelling. Further, we see no way that, in light of them, the desired features of a consolidated system could be replicated in a fragmented system.

The arguments related to the next three issues—interdealer competition, intermarket competition, and the disparate needs of different traders—support a fragmented system. Of the three, we find intermarket competition to be the most compelling argument, both conceptually and in light of recent experience. However, as we suggest below, each of these attributes can be achieved to at least some degree in a consolidated system.

With regard to interdealer competition, we stress that the exchange markets should continue to maintain their position as agency-auction markets where the flow of public limit orders is a primary source of liquidity. By encouraging the public to trade via limit orders, and by reducing restrictions on the access of dealers and other professional traders to the trading system, we anticipate that workable competition between market makers could be adequately achieved in a consolidated system.

With regard to intermarket competition, we hope for three things if markets become more consolidated than they are now: (1) that competition for the order flow which occurs between different instruments (i.e., futures versus options versus equities) may itself be effective in keeping the market centers from stagnating technologically; (2) that the pressures and inherent profitability of an ever-increasing order flow will continue to propel the markets ahead; and (3) that intermarket competition may be maintained by different types of securities being traded under different systems, and by different issues being traded in different markets (i.e., some equity shares are exchange-listed, and others are traded OTC).

With regard to the disparate needs of different traders, we know of no reason why sufficient flexibility could not be built into an essentially consolidated system. We believe that, eventually, this flexibility will be achieved through the widespread adaptation of computer technology to the trade execution–price determination process. With automated trading, it may be possible to increase the extent to which secondary priorities are observed (thus increasing effective consolidation) while still meeting the different needs of a variety of traders.

Thus we conclude that, on balance, all trading in a security should be consolidated in a single market. Market centers could compete for the listing of issues and brokers for the agency orders of investors. This conclusion is harmonious with a theme we pursue throughout this book: thicker markets are better markets, because they have smaller bid-ask spreads, lower volatility of prices, and faster adjustments of price to new information.

However, this choice is not ours to make, and full consolidation of trading is not a policy option that currently is being actively pursued. The immediate public choice is whether to protect the current national-regional exchange domination of trading in listed stocks or to increase the number of markets by encouraging off-board trading. Our analysis suggests that the multiple-exchange option (which is less fragmented) is to be preferred.

However, it does not necessarily follow that merely permitting off-board trading will automatically lead to greater fragmentation. Our analysis of the effect of violating price and time priorities suggests that investors will generally prefer to send their limit orders to the more concentrated market.[19] The possible exception occurs when the smaller market can stimulate a greater flow of market orders by guaranteeing immediate execution at the best price across the markets. To date, the attractiveness of this queue gaming appears not to have overcome the cost to brokerage firms of providing it. Whether or not extending Rule 19c-3 to all stocks would change this picture is a question we hope the SEC will not attempt to answer.

NOTES

1. For further background, particularly on the recent regulatory history, see Schreiber-Schwartz (1985).
2. The reader who is interested in the earlier debate concerning the CLOB should see

Mendelson-Peake-Williams (1979), Sametz (1979), Davant (1979), Kolton (1979), and Palamara (1979).

3. For further discussion, see Williams (1985).
4. The American Stock Exchange has a similar restriction, AMEX Rule 5. A broker can "cross" one customer's sell order with another customer's buy order off-exchange if this is to the advantage of both. However, this is unlikely to result in an in-house trading system unless the broker can also act as principal, as we note in Chapter 2.
5. An order exposure rule would require that (some or all) orders be exposed on all competing markets before a broker-dealer could trade against them (see SEC Release 19372). The purpose is to ensure that agency orders held in-house transact at the best possible price or (if they are limit orders) have the highest probability of transacting. When the exchanges proposed specific order exposure rules for 19c-3 stocks, several brokerage firms asserted that they would result in cumbersome, slow, and costly transactions.
6. Cincinnati's NSTS is an experimental fully automated trading system (see Chapter 3). Davis (1985) discusses the implications of ITS and of NSTS for fragmentation.
7. The data on listings are from Wall (1985).
8. Pooling orders increases the effective thickness of the market. It has been shown that in thicker markets: (a) bid-ask spreads are expected to be smaller [Chapter 5 above and Ho-Stoll (1983)]; (b) other aspects of transaction costs are expected to be lower [Telser-Higinbotham (1977)]; (c) market prices are expected to be less volatile [Chapter 4 above, CMNOSW (1977), Telser-Higinbotham (1977), and Telser (1981)]; and (d) price-adjustment delays are expected to be shorter, which implies weaker autocorrelation and cross-serial correlation coefficients [Chapters 6 and 7 above].
9. The NYSE's secondary priority rule is incorporated in NYSE Rule 72 [see New York Stock Exchange (1982a)]. This involves a combination of what we conveniently call priority, parity, and precedence, reflecting both time and size priorities. When two or more NYSE limit orders are tied at the same price and could cross an incoming order: (a) *priority* is applied first (but for only one order), meaning that the earliest of the tied limit orders executes; (b) if there still are unfilled shares of the incoming order, then *parity* is applied, meaning that from the subset of tied limit orders which are large enough to satisfy the remaining portion of the incoming order, the earliest of that subset executes; (c) if the parity rule is inapplicable because none of the tied limit orders are large enough to satisfy the remaining portion of the incoming order, then *precedence* is applied, meaning that the largest of the tied limit orders executes (and if there is more than one such largest order, the earliest of these executes); (d) after precedence, as described in (c), is applied one or more times, as soon as there is at least one tied limit order large enough to satisfy the remaining portion of the incoming order, then parity, as described in (b), is again applied. The application of parity and precedence on the NYSE reduces the number of transactions necessary to satisfy an incoming order, while still allowing time priority to play some role.
10. The CCM queueing-theory model, used to analyze the impact of violating price priority, cannot usefully be applied to the analysis of time priority because the result is too sensitive to the assumptions made regarding the expiration of limit orders. The most reasonable assumption (withdrawal after a fixed length of time) does not lead to a tractable analytical solution.

11. The intuitive reasonableness of these results can be seen by considering the impact of violating time priority on the likelihood that a limit order will expire before it executes. In the CCM simulation model (as well as in actual securities markets), when a more recently placed limit order executes instead of an equally priced limit order that had been submitted earlier, this increases the probability that the latter order will expire rather than execute. The reduced expected waiting time for a limit order which executes results from the book being thinner (since there are fewer limit orders having priority over any particular limit order).
12. If the smaller market is a brokerage firm's in-house execution system, the compensating advantage might be a lower commission fee. If it is a regional exchange (like the Pacific with its SCOREX) or an automated order entry-display-execution system (like Instinet), the compensating advantage may be instantaneous execution of small market orders at the inside spread among markets. This increases the relative flow rate of market orders versus limit orders in the smaller market. The flow of limit orders to the smaller market should equilibrate at the point where the trade-off between waiting time and probability of execution is equivalent to that in the larger market, ceteris paribus.
13. By the analysis in footnote 12, we see that queue gaming is unlikely to be attractive unless the flow rate of market orders past the smaller limit-order queue is so great as to overcome what would otherwise be a disadvantage in waiting time and execution probability due to smaller market size. Such a high flow of market orders may occur if the in-house market (or the regional exchange or computerized trading system) guarantees immediate execution of market orders at the inside spread.
14. For theoretical analysis see Ho-Stoll (1983), and for empirical evidence see Hamilton (1978) and Cohen-Conroy (1985).
15. See Williams (1985).
16. Ho-Macris (1985) make an analogous point.
17. For further discussion, see Schreiber-Schwartz (1985).
18. For example, the *Wall Street Journal* (July 12, 1984, p. 39) stated that Jeffries & Co., a broker-dealer based in Los Angeles which is not a member of the NYSE, has become the third-market leader in trading stocks during hours when the NYSE is not open or has suspended trading.

> When the New York Stock Exchange halts trading in a listed stock—or when a company announces bad news after markets have closed—banks, insurance companies, money managers and other institutional investors know they can usually trade at Jeffries. . . . The New York Stock Exchange, however, opposes outside trading when there is news, pending or announced, that affects a stock. "We think trading should be universally suspended to give the public a chance to assess the news," an exchange spokesman says. The Securities and Exchange Commission, however, has refused the Big Board's request to impose such a ban. The Big Board late last year adopted a procedure to limit news-pending trading halts to three hours. Asked whether the change was a response to off-market trading pressure, the New York Stock Exchange spokesman says: "We certainly aren't blind to that, but the primary reason was to assure liquidity for professional investors."

19. A vivid illustration of this belief is provided in *Business Week* (July 23, 1984, p. 22):

> Once one market seems to gain preeminence over others, the process tends to feed on itself. "There is a natural tendency for financial markets to concentrate," says Roger F. Azar, president of the Paris-based investment company bearing his name. "The players like to be in one place, and access to communications and information systems reinforces that." Agrees Salomon's Siegel [Martin J. Siegel, vice-president and manager of international arbitrage at Salomon Bros.]: "The tape is the best advertisement we have for the New York market. Trades beget trades."

9

THE DESIRABILITY AND FEASIBILITY OF SUPPLEMENTARY STABILIZATION*

The basic function of a stock exchange is, of course, to make a market by bringing orders together so as to determine which sets of orders execute, and at what prices. In so doing, the spatial concentration of orders provides a considerable degree of natural stabilization of prices. However, nearly every stock exchange assumes an obligation to provide *supplementary* stabilization. This takes various forms on stock exchanges around the world:

1. *Maximum price-change limits with trading halts.* These rules are most common on exchanges with poor on-line price information (such as closed-book periodic call markets). They serve to "protect" market order traders against their own folly and to invite stabilizing speculation.
2. *Refusal to accept destabilizing orders from certain participants on the trading floor.* According to the weak-form efficient market hypothesis, such rules as the tick test should not be necessary, but they do serve to reassure the investing public of the fairness of the trading system.
3. *Temporal concentration of orders.* Batch trading (e.g., periodic calls, particularly of thinly held issues) and short trading hours serve to concentrate orders into relatively brief periods of time, which in turn may reduce volatility (as well as operating costs). However, short hours and poorly designed call systems may drive some trading off-exchange.
4. *Market makers.* Disguised subsidies such as lower transaction costs, preferred access to floor trading information, and so on, can induce professional traders to engage in greater stabilizing speculation by standing ready

at all times to buy and sell issues for which they accept designated market maker status.

5. *Affirmative obligation stabilization.* U.S. stock exchanges have specialists who, in addition to being market makers (often in competition with others), have an "affirmative obligation" (e.g., under NYSE's Rule 104) to prevent transaction-to-transaction price changes greater than specified amounts. For affirmative obligation stabilization to be meaningful, it must be unprofitable on the margin (since designated market makers and others will freely engage in stabilizing speculation up to the point where it becomes unprofitable on the margin); hence (by definition) the activity must be subsidized if it is desirable.

In this chapter, we focus on various questions concerning designated market makers and affirmative obligation stabilization. First, is there any benefit to supplementary stabilization which may justify the cost of supplying it? Supplementary stabilization is desirable only if it is a public good-type externality; we shall address this issue in Section 9.1. Second, can a market maker operating under mechanical rules engage in affirmative obligation stabilization and stabilizing speculation, and what are the effects on profitability and market performance of the kinds of regulatory parameters used by the exchanges? These issues are addressed in a simulation study reported in Section 9.2. Finally, can we create a free market in stabilization services to replace the current patchwork of direct and indirect subsidies? This policy question is the subject of Section 9.3.

9.1 IS STABILIZATION DESIRABLE?

Clearly, risk-averse investors place a positive value on reducing the volatility of their portfolios. Hence the value of any particular security is increased if its covariance with other securities in investors' portfolios is reduced. However, it does not immediately follow that *supplementary* stabilization is desirable, or that, if it is, an optimal amount will be supplied by stock exchange specialists or some other stabilization mechanism.

9.1.1 Literature on the Desirability of Stabilization

A few academicians argue that deliberate stabilization attempts in various markets may be desirable (if they are effective).[1] For example, Samuelson (1972) suggests a proof that risk-averse consumers benefit from price stability in product markets, and Pazner-Razin (1974) show that reducing uncertainty in flexible exchange rates may increase welfare if individuals are risk averse with respect to prices.[2] Hirshleifer (1971) reasons that a continuous auction security market is effectively thin at any given instant, leading to "lumpy" supply and demand; he appears to suggest that stabilization in the form of periodic calls may be desirable.

A number of academicians completely reject the idea that any stabilization effort is desirable beyond that provided freely by competing profit-maximizing speculators. Stigler (1964) reasons that because buy and sell offers may cross at prices away from equilibrium in a thin market, speculators (mainly specialists) have a profit incentive to carry inventories of stocks so that they can readily buy or sell. When equilibrium price is assumed to be subject to random shifts, Stigler reasons that speculators will try to predict its level and to adjust their buy and sell offer prices accordingly. By offering to trade to and from their inventories, they will stabilize prices[3] (although, of course, price will not stay within some arbitrary range). In competitive equilibrium, if further stabilization were to be attempted, those providing it would incur losses.

The conclusion Stigler draws (p. 130), to which Black (1971), Smidt (1971), and Logue (1975) among others also subscribe, is that "if the impacts on equilibrium are sudden and unexpected . . . the appropriate market response is an immediate and complete shift to the new price level . . . the demand for 'continuity' in a market is a demand for delay in responding to the change in demand conditions, and . . . there simply is no merit in such delay." Black adds the thought that if specialists try to stabilize price (in response to their affirmative obligation), this will allow investors with special information to earn profits at the expense of others.

9.1.2 Stabilization as an Externality

We know of no rigorous utility-theoretic proof that speculators will be led to provide exactly the optimal amount of price stabilization. Indeed, we suggest that the amount of stabilization may be nonoptimal if laws instituted to prohibit security manipulation prevent corporations from contracting for supplementary stabilization services.

Our central proposition is that a public good–type external economy is conferred on investors by speculators and others who place limit orders. This is because, under the current market system, price stabilization meets these three conditions for being a public good–type externality: (a) placing limit orders is in effect a sale of immediacy with price stabilization as a by-product;[4] (b) investors who benefit from stabilization cannot be excluded from consuming it free of charge; and (c) stabilization directly affects an argument in investors' utility functions, so it is a (Pareto-relevant) technological externality, not a pecuniary externality.

It is a well-established result of welfare economics that insufficient quantities of public good–type external economies are produced in free-market competitive equilibrium.[5] Thus while optimal quantities of the private good, immediacy, would be produced, production of the joint product, stabilization, would be suboptimal, so long as it is not possible to "internalize" the externality. However, because issuing corporations benefit from stabilization in the form of higher security prices,[6] they might, if allowed, internalize the externality and transform stabilization into an ordinary (jointly supplied) private good. Corporations would purchase the amount of supplementary stabilization which would maximize share price, and hence in a perfect market optimal quantities would be produced.[7]

Governments, however, generally prohibit or restrict stabilization contracts between issuing corporations and potential stabilizers because of the fear of stock manipulation. Thus actual security markets are prevented from providing optimal quantities of supplementary stabilization. We may view the various supplementary stabilization arrangements of stock exchanges (specialist "continuity" obligations, call markets, maximum allowable daily price changes, etc.) as substitutes for free-market stabilization contracts between corporations and stabilizers.

These arrangements have two major defects (at least as they operate on the NYSE and AMEX): (1) All NYSE and AMEX stocks are stabilized, regardless of whether the issuing corporations wish it or not (short of not listing its stock in the first place, a corporation has no say in determining the level of stabilization). Call markets and maximum price change rules also stabilize all securities, regardless of the corporations' wishes. (2) Specialists are compensated for their trading losses from stabilizing thin securities in part by commissions and in part by trading profits on thick securities.[8] This causes investors in thick securities to subsidize investors in thin securities, a result of dubious desirability. Despite these defects, elimination of the exchanges' stabilization arrangements without simultaneous provision for a free market in supplementary stabilization might make security markets less efficient (although the theorem of second best prevents a rigorous conclusion to this effect).

One may question how much supplementary stabilization is optimal, and even whether the present system provides too much. Certainly, no stabilization system with finite resources can, or should, prevent major price adjustments. However, if the only direct stabilization is provided freely as a by-product of immediacy, a small increment of its production would likely be quite inexpensive relative to its worth. In any event, the mechanism which we shall propose in Section 9.3 will enable the preferences of consumers of stabilization to be revealed through the market.

9.2 SIMULATION OF STABILIZER ACTIVITIES

This section presents a simulation model of a continuous auction security market where quotes are primarily set by the limit orders of public traders, but where stabilization efforts and speculative trading based on knowledge of the limit-order book affect the market's performance characteristics. Our broad goal is to demonstrate both the feasibility of simulating a complex trading environment and of using simulation to gain insight into a variety of policy issues.

Many aspects of complex auction markets where market quotes may be set both by public and dealer limit orders have not been amenable to mathematical modeling or multivariate statistical analysis. Thus some researchers, beginning with Stigler (1964) and West (1970), have turned to simulation. Garman's (1976) computer simulation was used to model the market bid-ask spread in an environment where quotes are set by competitive traders. Our earlier simulation [CMSW (1978b)] explored serial correlation patterns in an "atomistic" continuous auction exchange having no stabilizers, arbitrageurs, or large traders.[9] More recently, Hakansson-Beja-Kale (1985) have simulated a call market environment to examine the feasibility of automating the specialist function.

The types of market participants incorporated in our simulation include both small and large investors (analogous to public and institutional investors, respectively), pure stabilizers (who use mechanical rules in attempting to keep transaction-to-transaction price changes from being too large), and speculating stabilizers (who, like stock exchange specialists, formulate trading strategy based on knowledge of the limit-order book). We are interested in determining how various regulatory and decision parameters affect stabilizer-speculator behavior; how, in turn, such behavior impacts on market performance characteristics (price volatility, bid-ask spreads, and serial correlation of returns); and the profits or losses the stabilizer-speculator realizes as a result of his efforts.

It is reasonable to expect that, because of the way in which he enters quotes, the stabilizer-speculator will reduce spreads and price volatility; however, his impact on serial correlation is not so transparent ex ante. Furthermore, it is not clear without the simulation that the pure stabilizer will be profitable, or how much more profitable the speculating stabilizer might be. To the extent that prices bounce between the bid and ask and show little or no trend over time, the stabilizer-speculator would realize profits by earning the spread on each round trip.[10] However, because price-continuity requirements force the stabilizer to trade against market movements, his function might prove to be unprofitable.

Empirical data concerning stock exchange specialist profitability do not measure the inherent profitability of the pure market-making function, since specialists earn commissions on trades in which they participate as brokers rather than principals. Further, they are likely to realize trading profits as a result of their face-to-face interactions with other market participants. By simulation, we eliminate these confounding elements, and determine whether monopoly knowledge of the limit-order book, used in a mechanical manner and applied with the exchange restrictions imposed on the stabilizer, can in itself be profitable.

While we have attempted to be reasonably realistic concerning the "market architecture" of a continuous auction, in several respects our model falls short of a fully realistic description. We have not incorporated professional traders who would implement the complete array of arbitrage mechanisms implied by the efficient markets hypothesis. Although the arrival of orders in our model is consistent with both liquidity and informational motives, some aspects of informational trading are intentionally excluded.[11] Furthermore, we treat only one security, rather than a more comprehensive trading arena, so that market movements which would cause trading in one security to influence others are omitted. But we have attempted to use reasonable numerical values in the simulation and our findings should be robust across a wide range of input parameter values since they are based on ceteris paribus comparisons.

9.2.1 The Model and Its Theoretical Foundations

Investors may seek to trade by placing either limit or market orders. A market order will execute immediately by crossing the counterpart market quote. A limit order will enter the limit-order book and remain until it is executed or canceled. Strict price and time priority rules are followed by public limit orders. Trades occur when a newly generated order crosses an existing limit order.

In conformity with the returns generation process modeled in Chapter 4, orders arrive at the market according to a Poisson process;[12] thus the length of time between order arrivals is determined by random draws from an exponential distribution. The mean arrival rate of orders in the runs reported here is 36 orders per day. There is an equal probability of an order being a buy or a sell. When generated, each limit order is randomly assigned an expiration date from an exponential distribution. However, a limit order is deleted from the book if it transacts before the assigned expiration date. In the runs reported here, the mean of the distribution of expiration dates is two days.

Public orders are from both "individual investors" and "institutional investors," with the relative mix being variable. In the runs reported here, on average 70% of the orders were placed by individual investors, and 30% by institutional investors.

The basic trading unit in the simulation is one round lot (100 shares). Each investor's order may be for any integer number of round lots. For an individual investor, the order size is determined by a random draw (rounded to an integer) from an exponential distribution whose mean is two lots; for an institutional investor, the order size is determined by a random draw (rounded to an integer) from a gamma distribution whose mean is seven lots.[13]

As is the case in actual security markets, there is only a discrete (but denumerably infinite) set of possible prices for a security. The results presented are based on simulation runs in which prices are quoted in mills ($0.001). Quoting prices in mills rather than in eighths eliminates the need for price-level corrections because, for all essential purposes, market characteristics are then independent of the levels of prices (generally $50 to $100 per share) used in the simulation.[14]

In an order's limit price is equal to or better than the counterpart market quote, then (part or all of) that order is considered a market order; it is crossed with the counterpart quotation, and a transaction immediately occurs. Because of the range of sizes attached to orders, a relatively large incoming order may be executed against several counterpart orders on the book.[15]

In the simulation, order prices are generated by random draws from a returns-dimensioned distribution which is linked to the current market bid-ask quotes. That is, the current quotes are used as reference prices to convert a returns-dimensioned number into the price of a new order. Using an underlying returns-dimensioned distribution to generate prices avoids artificially building negative serial correlation into the returns series, and/or the possibility of negative prices, which would result from a fixed distribution of *dollar* prices or price changes. As the quotes move from one price level to another in the course of a simulation run, the returns-dimensioned distribution remains fixed (except for minor changes associated with variations in the size of the market spread). Thus there is no underlying tendency for price trends either to continue or to reverse themselves, or for trading volume either to accelerate or to decline. In other words, the entire process, as it works itself out, is essentially independent of the level or change in the level of prices.

The returns distribution [depicted in Figure D.1 (Appendix D) and referred to as the yawl distribution due to its resemblance to the two-masted sailboat] has a double triangular configuration.[16] This shape is consistent with the analysis in Chapter 5 of an investor's order-placement strategy and the existence of the market bid-ask spread. The main feature of the yawl distribution is that the density function goes to zero as (e.g., for sell orders) x approaches the market bid from above, and then jumps to a local maximum at the market bid. This reflects the fact that, because of the "gravitational pull" effect, an investor will never place a limit order infinitesimally close to a counterpart quote already established on the market.

Although we do not model order-placement motives explicitly, the ex post pattern of prices generated by the simulation is implicitly consistent with orders being induced by the following motives: changing trading tactics,[17] liquidity needs, and informational change. The procedure by which prices are assigned to orders in the simulation is consistent with the Grossman-Stiglitz (1976) model in which any change in the current market quotes signals informational change. Because of the use of trading tactics, the existence of liquidity trading, and the "stickiness"[18] of the limit-order book, any quote change is a noisy signal. By always linking the returns-dimensioned yawl distribution to the current market quotes, we implicitly assume that overadjustments on average balance underadjustments, and hence that quote changes are an unbiased signal of informational change. As in Grossman-Stiglitz, this would be consistent with rational expectations and the random walk of stock prices.

9.2.2 Simulation Results

We performed three sets of simulation runs under three alternative degrees of stabilization intervention: a pure market without stabilizer, a pure (or mechanical) stabilizer, and a speculating stabilizer. The three types of markets are defined, and the results for each are given below. Our aim is not to distinguish three actual markets (since the first two types do not, and perhaps could not, exist); rather it is to determine the ceteris paribus impact on market performance characteristics and stabilizer profitability of the various stabilization functions performed by specialists. And it is not the absolute magnitudes of the numbers generated by one simulated market, but the relative magnitudes across markets that matter.

9.2.2.1 Pure market without stabilizer. As a baseline for our analysis of the impact of the pure and speculating stabilizers, we first examine how the market would function when orders are submitted by only individual and institutional investors. These "pure-market" results are shown in the top row of Table 1.[19]

The pure-market results conform to our a priori expectations. The standard deviation of daily returns is greater for transaction returns than for quotation (i.e., market ask) returns as the model of Chapter 4 predicts.[20] All first-order serial correlation coefficients of returns are significantly negative (at the 95% confidence level), regardless of whether returns are computed on a transaction-to-transaction or on a daily basis, and they are more negative for transaction returns than for market ask returns.[21] These relationships result from the sticky limit-order book and the nonzero bid-ask spread.

9.2.2.2 Market with a pure stabilizer. We here consider what we call a pure stabilizer [analogous to a Hakannson-Beja-Kale (1985) mechanical specialist] who is charged with maintaining price continuity—that is, with keeping transaction-to-transaction price changes from being "too large." The maximum allowable price change in the simulation is proportional to the price level. Let D denote the input parameter (1/8, 3/8, and 5/8) which sets the maximum allowable price change from one transaction to the next. When the last-transaction price is P (dollars per share), then the maximum allowable price change is $(D \times P)/75$ (dollars per share). When either a market sell or buy order would result in a price change exceeding the maximum allowable change, the stabilizer enters his own buy and/or sell limit orders inside the public quotes.[22] When the stabilizer so intervenes, the market spread cannot exceed twice the amount of the maximum allowable price change. On the other hand, the pure stabilizer intervenes on one or both sides of the market only when necessary, so the spread (as given by public limit orders) may be smaller.[23]

In the simulation, the pure stabilizer never submits (or maintains) any limit order that does not set one or the other side of the market quotes. Also, the pure stabilizer never submits orders in larger amounts than one round lot; if his order executes, he may enter another order before the next portion of any public order is permitted to execute.[24] Furthermore, the pure stabilizer must always give way to equally priced public limit orders (i.e., time priorities apply only to public limit orders).[25]

Maximum and minimum inventory limits (±500, ±1000, ±2000, or ±10,000 shares)[26] are imposed on both pure and speculating stabilizers,[27] implicitly representing the amount of available capitalization. If the pure stabilizer is at his maximum long (short) inventory limit, he may still set the ask (bid) market quote, but he will not be able to set the bid (ask). In such cases, the trans-

TABLE 1 Summary of simulation runs

Nature of Market			Market Performance Characteristic								
			Stabilizer's Normalized[a]:			Standard Deviation of Daily		First-Order Serial Correlation Coefficients			
								Transaction to Transaction		Daily	
Type of Stabilizer or Speculator in the Market	Inventory Limit (Shares)	Maximum Allowable Price Change[b] (dollars/share)	Profit (dollars/day)	Std. Dev. of Profit[c] (dollars/day)	Percentage Spread (%)	Trans. Returns ($\times 10^{-2}$)	Market Ask Returns ($\times 10^{-2}$)	Mkt. Ask Returns	Trans. Returns	Mkt. Ask Returns	Trans. Returns
None	N.A.[d]	N.A.	N.A.	N.A.	0.766	1.44	1.27	−0.09**	−0.20**	−0.20**	−0.24**
Pure Stabilizer	±1000	1/8	−74 **	13	0.262	0.90	0.87	0.34**	0.40**	−0.05	−0.08**
		3/8	13	14	0.462	1.17	1.10	0.11**	0.15**	−0.12**	−0.16**
		5/8	31 *	17	0.600	1.27	1.16	−0.00	−0.00	−0.09**	−0.17**
	±10,000	1/8	−103	138	0.256	0.85	0.83	0.36**	0.42**	−0.11**	−0.13**
		3/8	18	181	0.463	1.17	1.10	0.11**	0.14**	−0.10**	−0.14**
		5/8	10	111	0.580	1.27	1.17	−0.00	−0.00	−0.12**	−0.19**
Speculating Stabilizer	±1000	1/8	77 **	14	0.250	0.79	0.77	0.29**	0.35**	−0.07*	−0.10**
		3/8	269**	20	0.445	0.97	0.89	0.05**	0.09**	−0.07*	−0.13**
		5/8	330**	21	0.563	1.06	0.94	−0.03**	−0.05**	−0.10**	−0.19**
	±10,000	1/8	162	104	0.217	0.68	0.65	0.31**	0.37**	−0.03	−0.07*
		3/8	720**	140	0.407	0.89	0.81	0.06**	0.09**	0.02	−0.05*
		5/8	522**	145	0.526	0.96	0.87	−0.03**	−0.05**	0.01	−0.08**

[a]Normalized to an average price of $75 per share.

[b]At a price of $75 per share. At a price of $*P* per share, the maximum allowable price change is $P/75$ times the listed parameter.

[c]Standard deviation of the sample mean of daily profit, based on a sample size of 1000 days.

[d]N.A., not applicable.

*Significantly different from zero at a 95% confidence level.

**Significantly different from zero at a 99% confidence level.

action-to-transaction price change may exceed the maximum allowable price change, and the spread may exceed twice the maximum allowable price change.

For each simulation run, we compute the sample mean, standard deviation, and coefficient of variation of the pure stabilizer's daily trading profit. To measure daily trading profit, we calculate the change in value of the pure stabilizer's inventory at the end of each day and add it to his end-of-day cash holdings. We value his inventory at either the best *public* bid or ask price, depending on whether the stabilizer is long or short, respectively. The change in the value of inventory plus cash from the end of one day to the end of the next then represents the pure stabilizer's trading profit for that particular day.

If the market maker were not attempting to act as a pure stabilizer, but instead were seeking only to earn a profit from the dealership function, we would expect that, on average, his gross profit (before carrying costs, etc.) would be the spread on each share involved in a round-trip transaction. On the other hand, the pure stabilizer will suffer inventory valuation losses from trying to stabilize transaction-to-transaction prices, because he loses when price happens to trend in either direction. On balance, whether the pure stabilizer is profitable or unprofitable must be determined by simulation.

Rows 2 through 7 of Table 1 show the effects of varying the stabilizer's maximum allowable price-change parameter and inventory limits on his profitability and on the market performance characteristics. The (normalized) average daily profit of the pure stabilizer clearly depends upon the maximum allowable price change. The smaller the price change parameter, the more often he is forced to trade in a fashion that outweighs his dealership profit, and the less profitable the stabilizer tends to be.[28] For the smallest maximum allowable price change of 1/8, the pure stabilizer is unprofitable. This result is particularly interesting because in all previous published work, the stabilizer was assumed to be inherently profitable since he makes the spread on each round trip (the academic literature has tended to ignore the cost to the stabilizer of the continuity requirement).

Increasing the pure stabilizer's inventory limits from ±1000 to ±10,000 shares has a much bigger impact on the standard deviation than on the average value of daily profit. The reason is that with larger limits, the swings in inventory valuation become larger, and the volatility of this component of daily profit outweighs the volatility of the trading gains or losses component of profit.

For all combinations of inventory limit and maximum allowable price change that we ran, the pure stabilizer reduced the average percentage spread substantially below its pure market level. As the maximum allowable price change becomes smaller, a greater degree of spread reduction is achieved. There is also a tendency for larger inventory limits to lead to greater spread reduction, but the degree of spread reduction is less sensitive to the inventory limit than to the maximum allowable price-change parameter. The reason for these findings is straightforward. For smaller maximum allowable price changes, the pure stabilizer will try to keep a narrower spread. As his inventory limits increase, he is less often prevented from entering stabilizing limit orders.

The pure stabilizer also reduces the standard deviations of both daily transaction and daily quotation returns below what they are in a pure market. The size of the reduction depends upon the maximum allowable price-change and the inventory-limit parameters, in much the same manner as does the extent of spread reduction. The smaller the maximum allowable price change, the greater the reduction in the standard deviation of daily returns. The maximum allowable price-change parameter has a bigger impact on returns variance than does the inventory-limit parameter.

The pure stabilizer also impacts on the first-order serial correlation coefficients of returns. The serial correlations of transaction-to-transaction returns, which were significantly negative in the pure market, become significantly positive for maximum allowable price changes of ⅛ and ⅜, for both large and small inventory limits. However, the serial correlation coefficients of daily returns, which were significantly negative in the pure market, remain significantly negative with the pure stabilizer, although their magnitude is reduced.

As discussed in CMSW (1978b), the main reason for transaction-to-transaction returns based on transaction prices being more negatively serially correlated than transaction-to-transaction returns based on market ask prices is that transaction prices tend to bounce between the market bid and ask. The pure stabilizer, by reducing the percentage spread, also reduces the negative component of serial correlation compared to the pure market. In addition, positive serial correlation is introduced into transaction-to-transaction returns (calculated from either quotation or transaction prices) because the pure stabilizer breaks an unacceptably large price change into a sequence of smaller changes, all going in the same direction. For smaller maximum allowable price changes, the percentage spread will be smaller (which reduces negative correlation), and the pure stabilizer will more often break large orders into a series of smaller transactions. This explains why the pure stabilizer can change the negative serial correlation of transaction-to-transaction returns that exists in a pure market into positive serial correlation, and also why the serial correlation coefficients of transaction-to-transaction returns become more positive, the smaller the maximum allowable price change. The size of the pure stabilizer's inventory-limit parameter has less of an impact on serial correlation than does the maximum allowable price-change parameter.

The stabilizer's breaking up of larger orders into a series of smaller orders with positively correlated price changes is entirely a within-the-day phenomenon in the simulation. This cannot introduce positive serial correlation into daily returns, and indeed we observe none. The reason that the negative serial correlation coeficients of daily returns are smaller with the pure stabilizer than in a pure market is due only to the reduction in percentage spread by the pure stabilizer.

9.2.2.3 Market with a speculating stabilizer. Like the pure stabilizer, the speculating stabilizer is required to limit the size of transaction-to-transaction price changes. While doing so, the speculating stabilizer attempts to use his knowledge of the limit-order book in order to earn trading profits. In effect, on the basis of the limit-order book, the speculating stabilizer attempts to predict the likely direction of future price movements, and he positions himself to trade in a way that takes advantage of these predictions.

The speculating stabilizer does so in the following manner. First, he defines a "relevant range," which is a percentage price range around the mean of the public bid-ask quotes. Within this range, he compares the total number of shares offered and bid for by the public. If in the relevant range there are bid (ask) limit orders for enough more shares than there are ask (bid) limit orders, then he predicts that the price is likely to rise (fall). This is because the preponderance of limit bids (asks) tends to keep price from falling (rising). "Enough more" is defined by another input parameter that we call percentage imbalance. As the percentage imbalance becomes smaller, the signal is more apt to be triggered, but it is more likely to be a false signal.

It is not obvious a priori what pair of parameter values for the relevant range and percentage imbalance would permit the speculating stabilizer to operate most profitably. We show in Table 1 the results when the speculating stabilizer has a relevant range of 1% and a percentage imbalance of 55%. These particular values were obtained by searching over a grid of values (using in all cases an inventory limit of ± 1000 shares and a maximum allowable price change of 3/8) for the pair that gave the most profitable performance.[29]

We impose the same inventory limits and time priority rule on the speculating stabilizer as on the pure stabilizer. Also, we explicitly impose a tick-test rule analogous to that faced by an NYSE specialist: the speculating stabilizer cannot buy (sell) shares whenever he would be doing so at a price higher (lower) than the last transaction price.[30] The tick test prevents the speculating stabilizer from intensifying a limit-order imbalance by trading against the weak side of the book.

Subject to his inventory constraints, the speculating stabilizer, like the pure stabilizer, must keep both sides of the market quotes no more than the maximum allowable price change from the last-transaction price. But unlike the pure stabilizer, the speculating stabilizer may *choose* to set one of the market quotes closer to the last-transaction price in order to increase the likelihood that he will either buy or sell shares. For instance, if the speculating stabilizer predicts that price is more likely to rise than to fall, he will position his limit order(s) so as to be more likely to buy than to sell shares.[31] Because the speculating stabilizer uses an a priori reasonable rule to predict the direction of likely price change, we expect him to be more profitable than the pure stabilizer, ceteris paribus.

We expect that specialists on the NYSE and AMEX act more like our speculating stabilizer than our pure stabilizer, since they undoubtedly profit from their monopoly knowledge of the limit-order book. However, our speculating stabilizer model clearly is not a complete portrayal of the decision rules used and information flows obtained by NYSE and AMEX specialists.

Rows 8 through 13 of Table 1 show the impact on market maker profitability and market performance characteristics of replacing the pure stabilizer with a speculating stabilizer. As expected, the speculating stabilizer turns out, ceteris paribus, to be substantially more profitable. Indeed, in all six rows shown for the speculating stabilizer, average profit is positive, and in five of the six rows it is significantly different from zero. As was the case with the pure stabilizer, increasing the speculating stabilizer's inventory limit increases the standard deviation of profit more than it increases average profit, which is indicative of a decreasing return-to-risk ratio. We would expect that the less stringent the stabilization requirement (i.e., the greater the maximum allowable price change), the more profitable the speculating stabilizer would be; this clearly is the case for the lower inventory limit, but it is not necessarily true for the higher inventory limit.[32]

The speculating stabilizer reduces the percentage spread and the standard deviation of daily returns to a greater extent than does the pure stabilizer.[33] The pattern of first-order serial correlation coefficients shown in Table 1 for the speculating stabilizer is reasonably similar to the pattern for the pure stabilizer. Most interestingly, we find that the speculating stabilizer is not only able to profit from his knowledge of the limit-order book, but is also able to produce a more desirable market in terms of the performance characteristics we have considered.

9.3 CONCLUSIONS AND POLICY PROPOSALS

Much debate over the design of a national market system has focused on two proposed developments: computerizing the trading process, and consolidating and displaying price information. These are desirable developments toward which we think security markets are heading. However, the role of a market maker qua stabilizer is an equally important issue. In this section, we will first summarize our major substantive findings, and then present various policy proposals for improving the effectiveness of supplementary stabilization.

9.3.1 Desirability of Stabilization

While there has been considerable controversy concerning the desirability of supplementary stabilization, we feel that some of the central issues have not been addressed. There has been little sentiment among academicians that the provision of supplementary stabilization services is, per se, desirable, and a very strong conviction on the part of many that it is not.

We have argued that stabilization is a public good-type external economy to investors. While competition among investors in a security transfers the benefits of stabilization to the issuing corporation (i.e., internalizes the externality), current restrictions on corporation-stabilizer contracts preclude a free market in supplementary stabilization; this results in nonoptimal amounts being supplied. We view the various existing supplementary stabilization arrangements (which permit corporations little choice as to the desired amount of stabilization, and impose intercorporate transfers) as imperfect substitutes for free-market contracts between corporations and stabilizers. It is not clear whether they presently lead to too much stabilization or to too little. However, as we pointed out in Chapter 8, if brokerage firm in-house trading grows under an expanded Rule 19c-3, the existing stabilization system will wither and there will certainly be too little.

9.3.2 Effectiveness of the Specialist as a Stabilizer

In order to answer the empirical question of whether specialists actually stabilize those thin securities where their efforts are largely concentrated, in Chapter 4 (Sections 4.6 and 4.7) we compared the determinants of returns volatility on the NYSE and AMEX (specialist exchanges) and the TKYO and RIO (nonspecialist exchanges). Our major finding, a negative elasticity of returns variance with respect to market value for the nonspecialist exchanges and a significantly larger elasticity for the specialist exchanges, is consistent with the hypothesis that specialists reduce the variance of thinly held securities.

9.3.3 Simulation of Incentives for and Effects of Stabilization

In order to study the effects of different types and levels of stabilization on the stabilizer's profit and on such market performance characteristics as spreads, returns variances, and serial correlation patterns, we developed a simulation model of a continuous auction market. Both individual and institutional investors are included, and there is a variety of order sizes with which market participants attempt to transact. One version of the market has no stabilizer present, while other verisons have either a pure or a speculating stabilizer.

By contrasting runs that are in all respects identical except for the existence and nature of the stabilizer, we find that, compared to the pure-market case, each type of stabilizer reduces spreads and returns variances. Moreover, stabilization combined with speculation based on knowledge of the limit-order book leads to greater improvement than does pure stabilization alone.

It is generally believed that stock exchange specialists realize positive profits. However, since actual specialists realize returns from a number of sources, their overall profitability should not be taken as evidence that stabilization per se is profitable. By simulation we are able to separate the components of the stabilizer's profit (e.g., we have excluded commissions and any trading profit that might be derived from face-to-face contact), and find that stabilization per se can be unprofitable. With relatively tight maximum allowable price changes, pure stabilization is definitely unprofitable, and it is only marginally profitable for larger maximum allowable price changes (because then the stabilizer's dealership profits from the spread outweigh his stabilization losses).

Our simulated pure stabilizer and speculating stabilizer are, of course, entirely mechanical. That is, no human judgment or intuition is used by our programmed stabilizers. Yet the mechanical stabilization rules do reduce spreads and returns variances. At a minimum, mechanical rules analogous to those programmed in our simulation would improve the performance of an electronic system. The literature, however, has given scant thought to including a stabilization function in the design of electronic trading systems.

9.3.4 Proposals for Effective Stabilization

Creation of a Free Market in Stabilization Services. The central implication of our model of stabilization as an externality is that the listing corporations are the ultimate beneficiaries of stabilization efforts and that stabilization is for them an ordinary private good which they would buy in optimal quantities, were they free to do so. Thus we present the following proposal to create a free market in stabilization services:

1. The listing corporation should make the decision as to whether and to what extent its security should be stabilized, and should itself pay for stabilization. In essence, the corporation should choose from a set of alternative surveillance parameters. The fee that it pays would be a function of the choice and the corporation's value of shares outstanding.
2. To avoid the possibility of stock manipulation, the listing corporation should contract for stabilization with the exchange rather than directly with stabilizers. The exchange should be responsible for choosing stabilizers and regulating them.
3. The listing corporation's payment to the exchange for stabilization services should be directly linked to the cost of stabilization. This would eliminate the intercorporation subsidies inherent in the present U.S. system.
4. The stabilization function should be separated from the trade execution function. Unbundling the functions would permit payment for stabilization to be directly associated with the cost of providing it and could make stabilization an option which the issuing corporation may select or reject.

Selection and Compensation of Stabilizers. The central feature of the selection and compensation system should be periodic competitive bidding for the job of stabilizing a given security. Each bidder would state a price for meeting certain performance standards set by the exchange's contract with the listing corporation. The security should not necessarily be allocated or reallocated to the lowest bidder. Rather, it would be advisable to give weight to qualifications, experience, and success in prior stabilization contracts. An attractive feature of periodic reallocation by competitive bidding is that permanent monopoly profits would not be possible.

If stabilizers were expected to trade for their own accounts, a major part of the stabilization payment would be compensation for losses the stabilizer would expect to make on his transactions. Alternatively, the stabilization account might belong to the listing corporation (although it would be outside its control). In this case, the stabilizer would contract to manage this account according to certain specifications, including approximate losses. A major difference between these two alternatives is in who bears the risk of actual supplementary stabilization losses that diverge from their expected value.

Single Stabilizer, Multiple Market Makers. While we believe that all traders ought to have equal access to the limit-order book and should be free to make any trades they wish (including stabilizing trades), we suggest that paying multiple supplementary stabilizers for a security would be inefficient because of the "free rider" possibilities inherent in the production of stabilization. With multiple stabilizers, it would be difficult to distinguish each individual's product and hence to determine the extent to which each contributes to total production. Thus the efforts of the better stabilizer could give a "free ride" to the poorer one, resulting in a suboptimal production of stabilization. For this reason, it would be difficult to compensate separate stabilizers properly, or to enforce responsibility for stabilization. Hence each security should have but a single stabilizer.

Public Access to the Limit-Order Book. On the AMEX and NYSE, only the specialist in a security may see the limit-order book for that security. This has been widely criticized as a source of special information, and hence monopoly profits, for specialists. Our simulation results clearly demonstrate how the specialist can profitably use such information for speculation, and that this reduces volatility. Thus opening the book will force a change in the method of compensating specialists. However, we believe that this would be desirable on its own merits.

General access to the limit-order book might reduce investors' uncertainty about the strength of demand for a security, making them more likely to enter orders, and might cause speculators to provide more stabilization by entering additional limit orders. Interestingly, Tokyo and Rio both have semiopen books,[34] and CNOSW (1976) have shown that, ceteris paribus, variance is not greater on these exchanges. It may be that public access to the book on these exchanges causes a variance reduction which, on average, is comparable to that realized on the U.S. exchanges by specialists intervening primarily in the markets for thin securities.

Accommodating the Stabilization System to Anticipated Security Market Developments. Suppose that automation rapidly and radically transforms the structure of stock markets, as we predict in Chapter 3. Will the current supplementary stabilization system survive? Can any form of supplementary stabilization coexist with fully automated trading?

The answer to the first question is probably "no." An open limit-order book will eliminate one of the specialist's current sources of trading profits. More important, if OTC trading continues to weaken the smaller exchanges, and if Instinet or its competitors provide an attractive medium for trading 19c-3 stocks, all of the specialist's current revenue sources will be threatened, and affirmative obligation stabilization will be the first to go.

If this happens, the only way stabilization can be delivered is by what we have suggested is the best way: let the issuing corporation pay for it and decide how much to buy. Organizing and supervising this function would provide a role for the exchanges and their specialists in what might otherwise be, for them, a grim future.

NOTES

*The principal sources of the material in this chapter are K. J. Cohen, S. F. Maier, R. A. Schwartz, and D. K. Whitcomb, "The Impact of Designated Market Makers on Security Prices: II. Policy Proposals," *Journal of Banking and Finance*, Vol. 1, 1977, pp. 236–247 (by permission of North-Holland Publishing Company, Amsterdam); and K. J. Cohen, S. F. Maier, R. A. Schwartz, and D. K. Whitcomb, "A Simulation Model of Stock Exchange Trading," *Simulation*, Vol. 41, 1983, pp. 181–191. The study reported in Section 9.2 was partially funded by grants from Duke University.

1. Baumol (1965) states a concern that specialists may destabilize prices by mistiming their interventions. Our empirical results in Chapter 4 (Sections 4.6 and 4.7) appear to allay this concern, although they do not, of course, prove that the interventions are cost effective.
2. However, Pazner-Razin show that some who are risk averse with respect to wealth may be risk loving with respect to prices, so their welfare result is not universal.
3. This line of reasoning is part of the general view, identified most strongly with the "Chicago School," that speculation, whether it be in securities, commodities, or foreign exchange, is appropriately stabilizing; see, for instance, Telser (1959) and Friedman-Roosa (1967). Other academicians, while accepting that speculation is usually stabilizing, assert there are instances where it can be destabilizing [see, e.g., Williamson (1973)].

   It should be noted that any investor who enters limit orders rather than market orders so as to get a better price provides some degree of immediacy and price stabilization. Also, the concept of selling from inventory should be interpreted broadly here, since specialists and others can sell short and hence need not actually have shares in order to "sell from inventory."
4. Both immediacy and stabilization are jointly supplied Lancaster (1966)-type characteristics of limit orders (although the placers of limit orders may not regard themselves as sellers of either). Nonetheless, immediacy is an ordinary private good-type characteristic (for which some investors will pay and others will charge) that should be optimally supplied in a competitive economy.
5. See Whitcomb (1972) for a model of the production of public good-type externalities and a demonstration (under certainty) that competitive equilibrium violates the Pareto optimality conditions when such externalities are present. No rigorous examination of Pareto optimality conditions has been conducted for the case where the presumed externality is price stabilization.

6. A well-known result from the option-pricing literature [see, e.g., Galai-Masulis (1976) and Copeland-Weston (1979, Chap. 16)] is that a decrease in the variance of the rate of return on a firm's assets will decrease its stock price; this follows from viewing the equity in a levered firm as a call option on the firm's assets written by bondholders and exercisable by the shareholders by repaying the debt at maturity. This result is in no way inconsistent with our assertion that a decrease in the variance of the rate of return on a firm's shares may increase share price. The direction of causality between asset returns variance and share returns variance is logically one way, so a reduction in share returns volatility would have no effect on the value of the shareholders' option on the firm's assets. In a frictionless world, the value of a firm's shares would be determined solely by the value of the shareholders' option on assets; with friction, the behavior of the share market also affects share price.
7. Since stabilization and immediacy are joint products, the optimal quantity of each is the joint optimum such that the cost of an increase in the joint activity level exceeds the combined benefit of the increments of the two products. However, as is the case with any joint product, too much of one and too little of the other may be produced relative to the optimum under a technology of separate production.

   Inherent in the public good nature of stabilization (to investors) is the fact that all investors in a given security receive the same amount. Thus investors who are highly risk averse or undiversified (and who thus receive the greatest benefit from a given amount of stabilization) may retain some consumer surplus on the margin in equilibrium. However, so long as the aggregate benefit to all investors from an increment of stabilization is less than the cost of producing it, additional stabilization would not be optimal and the issuing corporation would only reduce its share price by contracting for more.
8. Note that transactions undertaken solely to provide *supplementary* stabilization must on expectation be unprofitable for both thick and thin securities.
9. See Appendix D.2 for a comparison of the results of our two simulation models.
10. Conroy-Winkler's (1981) model of a monopoly dealer's use of limit-order-book information demonstrates that the dealer profits from the spread. However, this model assumes that all public orders must be transacted against dealer quotes (as in the London but not the New York or American stock exchanges) and includes neither public trades that are informationally motivated nor dealer stabilization responsibilities. Conroy-Winkler (1985) relax the monopoly dealer assumption and demonstrate that the dealer will be less profitable when his quotes can be preempted by public limit orders.
11. We do not explicitly model (a) sequential arrival of information, as analyzed by Copeland (1976) and Jennings-Starks-Fellingham (1981), which would imply that following an underlying informational shift, there would be nonindependent order arrival, accelerated order flow, and accelerated withdrawal of old limit orders; (b) changing the probability of buy (versus sell) orders; (c) closing the market when there is a major news event; (d) putting out a quote indication when informational change leads to buy-sell imbalances; or (e) special beginning-of-day, end-of-day, day-of-week, or weekend effects, such as those analyzed by French (1980), Oldfield-Rogalski (1980), Garbade-Sekaran (1981), and French-Roll (1985).

    The procedure we have followed has the attractive property of being consistent with informational change without building into the returns series serial correlation patterns due to the information dissemination and adjustment process. Also, we did not have to incorporate traders who, in real markets, would take advantage of such correlation patterns and arbitrage them away. As a result, our simulation enables us to isolate those correlation patterns that are due only to the mechanics of the trading process itself.

12. Since at most one limit order can arrive at any instant of time, a trade will not be triggered by two new orders crossing.
13. See Appendix D.1 for an explanation of this and other aspects of the simulation.
14. The one exception is the stabilizer's average profit (and its standard deviation). On each round trip, the stabilizer's return depends on the absolute dollar size of the spread, which itself is proportional to the price level. Consequently, we normalize the daily profit measure to what it would be if the average price level of the run were always $75 (the base price) by multiplying the average daily profit of the stabilizer by the average price level divided by $75. A similar adjustment is made for the standard deviation of daily profit.
15. For a numerical illustration of this point, contrast Examples 1 and 2 in Appendix D.3.
16. Appendix D.1 provides some details of the operation of the yawl distribution and how it is parameterized.
17. As the bid-ask spread changes, the yawl distribution automatically adjusts to reflect the investor's changing preference between limit and market orders. Consistent with Chapter 5, the wider (narrower) the spread, the greater (smaller) the percentage of limit orders that will be generated.
18. Limit orders are "sticky" in the sense that they are not instantaneously revised when investors' underlying trading propensities change.
19. To get some feel for the absolute dollar spreads represented by the range of percentage spreads shown in Table 1, note that at a stock price of $75 per share, percentage spreads of 0.766% and 0.217% correspond to absolute dollar spreads of $0.575 and $0.163.
20. For compactness, in Table 1 we report some statistics only for market ask returns, and not for market bid returns. The standard deviations and serial correlation coefficients based on market bid returns are similar, and the interpretations of our results would not differ if the statistics were based on market bid prices.
21. The serial correlation patterns observed in our simulation runs may be unrealistic to the extent that they are not mitigated by the trading of arbitrageurs. The efficient markets hypothesis implies that in actual markets arbitrage activities by professional investors would reduce any resulting net nonzero serial correlation to unprofitable levels.
22. See Example 3 in Appendix D.3.
23. See Example 4 in Appendix D.3.
24. See Example 5 in Appendix D.3.
25. See Example 6 in Appendix D.3.
26. In almost all cases, the market performance characteristics are monotonic functions of the magnitude of the inventory-limit parameters. Hence, for compactness, Table 1 reports only the results for inventory limits of ± 1000 shares (which we regard as a low limit) and $\pm 10{,}000$ shares (a high inventory limit).

27. Amihud-Mendelson (1980), Bradfield (1980), Ho-Stoll (1981), and Mildenstein-Schleef (1983) have shown that the market maker's behavior depends on his inventory position.
28. The apparent exception is that for inventory limits of ±10,000 shares, the pure speculator's average daily profit goes down from $18 to $10 when the maximum allowable price change increases from 3/8 to 5/8. However, the difference in these profit levels is not statistically significant, given their large standard deviations.
29. Values searched were relevant ranges of 1, 2, and 5%, and percentage imbalances of 52, 55, 60, and 65%.
30. The way in which the pure stabilizer enters limit orders to set the bid and/or ask quotes implicitly ensures that he conforms to the tick-test rule.
31. See Examples 7 and 8 in Appendix D.3. Any buy or sell order submitted by the speculating stabilizer is for one round lot, but he may enter additional limit orders as soon as his previous limit order has transacted (which is analogous to the way we treat the pure stabilizer).
32. However, for the higher inventory limit the difference between the average daily profit of $720 for a 3/8 maximum allowable price change and $522 for a 5/8 maximum allowable price change is not statistically significant.
33. As expected, we also see that both the percentage spread and returns variance are smaller with a speculating stabilizer in comparison to the pure market.
34. On the Tokyo Stock Exchange the book is open to everybody on the floor, and the full array of bid and ask prices and the associated quantities are displayed (however, the nonfloor public is not effectively provided with this information). On the Rio de Janeiro Stock Exchange, a computerized data-information system, implemented in 1972, makes available the 10 best bid and the 10 best ask prices (but not the associated quantities) to brokers and, through them, to the public.

CONCLUSION

As any professional trader will tell you, the securities markets are highly complex institutions. Accordingly, security market microstructure is an intricate and multifaceted subject. In the last decade, a growing number of academicians have turned their attention to this new field of financial economics, and a richer understanding of these markets is now beginning to emerge. Nonetheless, there remains a great deal which we still do not know.

What makes the subject so complex? Fundamentally, two factors combine to complicate life: the dynamic instability of investor trading propensities, and the fact that trading is not a costless process. That is, investor demand propensities shift rapidly under a barrage of information and changing prices. It is as if, compared to other markets, time has sped up. As a result, the need for investors to adjust their share holdings is ever present. However, trading friction makes perfect adjustments virtually impossible. Because trading is not a costless process, investors submit only a limited number of orders at any moment in time, and there is a maximum frequency with which they change their orders and/or participate in another round of trading.

Consequently, when investors do come to the market, they employ strategy in making their trading decisions. They must answer such questions as: Should a market order or a limit order be placed? Or should the order be worked in the crowd? How often should an order be submitted? Should an order be submitted at the market opening, the market close, or during the trading day? What price should be put on an order and what size should it be? To which market center should the order be conveyed? Much of the difficulty of understanding competition in the securities markets stems from the complexities of these strategy decisions, particularly as they are made in the context of specific trading systems and in relation to investor expectations of what market-clearing prices will be.

Economic analysis, though inextricably concerned with the meeting of buyers and sellers in a marketplace, has by and large abstracted from the nitty-gritty of actual markets. That is, only scant attention has been given to the real-world problems associated with trading, and to the real-world processes by which prices are set in actual markets. The reason is that economists have usually found it convenient to assume implicitly that trading is a frictionless process. Accordingly, there has been insufficient realization that the prices established in markets will differ from their theoretically desirable values, even when markets are competitive (i.e., composed of a large number of atomistic traders). Furthermore, it has generally not been recognized that the buy/sell orders of traders are endogenous to the market system, and hence that market outcomes are not independent of institutional arrangements.

It is not surprising that the first, and thus far only, industry to be analyzed intensively from a microstructure point of view should be the securities industry. As we have noted, it is the rapidity with which market conditions change, along with the frictions involved in trading, that have magnified the problems of the market process for the securities industry. Moreover, this industry in particular has historically fed the intellectual appetite of economists. Furthermore, it has generated a voluminous amount of data. In addition, along with its varied assortment of intriguing problems, the securities industry has experienced a remarkable amount of change in the last decade. These factors have combined to provide a spur for many studies.

The industry today is very different from what it was just 10 years ago. The importance of the trading desk has increased dramatically within the brokerage houses [see Falk (1985)]. The clublike atmosphere of the NYSE has all but disappeared. The various exchange markets are far more closely tied together by electronic linkages. New challenges to the supremacy of the NYSE are developing, not only from a much improved OTC system, but also from the expanded market-making operations of firms such as Instinet.

In addition, the pressure of an ever-increasing order flow is now constantly hovering over the market. Daily trading volume on the NYSE averaged 20.9 million shares in 1977. It averaged 86 million in 1983. On August 18, 1982, daily volume for the first time exceeded 100 million shares; 129 million shares traded on the peak volume day of 1983. On August 3, 1984, 236 million shares changed hands. The NYSE is now thinking ahead to the day when it will be asked by the market to handle 500 million shares or more. Where will the process end? Will the current and proposed systems be able to meet the challenge?

New products have been introduced at a remarkable rate in recent years: futures and options on stock indexes and subindexes, interest-rate futures and options, foreign-exchange-rate futures and options, and commodity options. New systems have been introduced: ITS, DOT, OARS, Super-DOT AUTO-PER, SCOREX, PACE, CAES, SOES, and so on, through an endless stream of acronyms. The use of electronic technology is now expanding from the relatively modest order-routing and information-dissemination functions, to trade execution itself. Traders can now enter orders directly from their homes via the electronic darling of the 1980s, the personal computer. And, before long, there will be on-line, 24 hour-per-day international trading.

These technological and product changes are accompanied by, and will induce, substantial changes in the nature of competition among market centers and market participants, and in the price-formation process. Understanding and helping to give direction to these changes represents a major challenge to microstructure economists.

One change in the industry will, however, force a broader set of financial economists to be concerned with microstructure issues: as a by-product of the increasing application of computer technology in the industry, very short-period data (daily prices, intraday prices, and even transaction-to-transaction prices) are becoming available in quantity in machine-readable form. As this occurs, the short-period prices are increasingly being used in empirical studies, especially to estimate the parameters of the market model. Short-period price movements, however, are far more affected by the market's microstructure than are the longer-period changes used predominantly in the past. Understanding this, adjusting for the microstructure effects, and therefore properly assessing the informational content of security prices will become increasingly important to researchers in the future.

In one area of financial economics in particular, a better knowledge of the market's microstructure would clearly help: understanding the small-firm effect and calendar effects. That is, it has been widely observed [see, e.g., Banz (1981), Reinganum (1981), Roll (1981), Brown-Kleidon-Marsh (1983), Keim (1983), and Schwert (1983)] that smaller companies tend to have larger risk-adjusted returns, especially in January [see Keim (1983)], and that returns are systematically different over weekends than day-to-day [see French (1980) and French-Roll (1985)]. Are these real effects that can be explained by underlying economic factors excluded from our asset-pricing models, an anomaly that results from the way in which returns and risk are measured, or an indication of market inefficiency? At present, we cannot be sure. But more to the point here, we will not know until we have a fuller understanding of the small firm and calendar effects in light of such issues as the impact of the bid-ask spread on the measurement of security returns, the impact of trading and price-adjustment delays on the measurement of beta, the real-world processes by which information is reflected in security prices, and the relationship between these microstructure factors and a firm's market size.

In the first chapter of this book, we presented an overview of the microstructure literature. Clearly, the literature extends to a number of areas which we have only touched on here. Some of the more important of these include: the processes by which information is generated, disseminated through the investment community, and then reflected in security prices; rigorous models of the determination of optimal dealer quotes; and the markets for related instruments, such as options and futures. Also, there are important issues which the literature itself is just now beginning to deal with, including: comparative analysis of alternative trading arrangements such as call market versus continuous market systems, specification of the order-placement strategies of individual traders, and an assessment of the desirability of maintaining orderly secondary priority trading rules in a consolidated market.

Our own work has focused primarily on trading in a continuous double-auction market such as the NYSE, where the interaction of the public order flow, along with the specialist, makes the market for individual stocks. In examining such a market, we have largely been concerned with the returns generation process as it relates to the volatility of security prices, to the size of bid-ask spreads, and to the existence and impact of serial and cross-serial correlation in security returns. Our treatment of the issues involved can be viewed in relation to six considerations: the institutional validity of our basic model development, the impact of friction, the impact of market thinness, the impact of investor trading strategies, the use of simulation analysis to study complex market relationships, and the development of policy implications concerning systems design and market structure. We next review each of these issues in a bit more detail.

Institutional Considerations. As we have noted, microstructure analysis in many ways represents a brave attempt to study, and to incorporate into formal analysis, the specific institutional arrangements that make actual markets work. In light of the technical difficulties involved, it is not at all surprising that the first attempts have deviated too far from institutional realities for the sake of model simplicity. This has been true of many of the dealer-oriented studies which, while enjoying the simplicity of presenting a *monopoly* dealer model, have inadequately represented what a dealer does and the competitive environment within which he operates. This has also been true of some positions taken in the off-board trading debate, for the arguments that off-board trading restrictions are an unwarranted competitive constraint flow too simplistically, in our opinion, from standard frictionless market theory. No doubt, we have ourselves, in some respects, fallen victim to misleading simplification. However, we have started our discussion in this book with an institutional overview of the markets (Chapter 2 and 3), and trust that we have not been too unfaithful to what we have described.

The Impact of Friction. As we have also noted, it is the impact of friction (along with the instability of investor demand propensities) that fundamentally drives the problems with which microstructure analysis is concerned. In our work, we have examined the effect of trading friction in three ways. First, we have shown how, through its impact on the returns generation process, friction affects the variance of returns (Chapter 4). Second, we have shown how it affects investor trading strategies, and thus accounts for the existence of a market bid-ask spread in markets that comprise many traders (Chapter 5). Third, recognizing that friction results in trading delays and price-adjustment delays, we have reasoned that it causes prices for different securities to adjust nonsynchronously to news; hence we have shown that friction introduces serial cross-correlation into security returns, which causes short-period beta estimates to be biased (Chapter 6).

The Impact of Thinness. Our analysis of the impact of friction on the returns generation process has highlighted one important factor: a major determinant of friction's impact is the thinness of the market for a security. More specifically, our theoretical analysis leads us to expect the following for thinner markets: greater price volatility, larger bid-ask spreads, and short-period beta estimates that are more downward biased. These properties of thinner markets not only are important in their own right, but they also give direction to the design and interpretation of empirical analysis of the behavior of security prices.

That is, examination of the relationship between a market phenomenon that results from friction (especially serial and cross-serial correlation) and thinness can show the phenomenon to be significant. Such a correlation pattern may appear to be statistically insignificant for a substantial majority of individual stocks when each is assessed separately. However, it should be considered meaningful when a significant relationship is observed, across stocks, between the correlation patterns and thinness. Furthermore, evidence on the impact of thinness on the behavior of security prices provides indirect evidence of the basic causal factor, the impact of friction, which itself cannot readily be quantified.

Our empirical tests have focused on the variance-thinness relationship (Chapter 4) and on the beta bias-thinness relationship (Chapter 7) where, for a stock, we take the value of shares outstanding as our (inverse) proxy measure of thinness. We find that thinner securities on nonspecialist exchanges (RIO and TOKYO) are more price volatile than the larger issues. On two specialist exchanges (NYSE and AMEX), we find that thinner issues are not more price volatile, but attribute this to the impact of specialists. For the NYSE and Paris Bourse, we find that the bias in short-period betas is clearly related to thinness: beta tends to be upward biased for a few large issues, is not significantly biased for intermediate-sized issues, and is generally downward biased for the relatively thin issues. These results, in conjunction with the documentation in the empirical bid-ask literature that thinner issues have larger spreads, forcefully substantiate the assertion that market thinness has a significant impact on security returns. In sum, our analysis suggests that friction in the trading process does indeed have a most consequential effect.

The Impact of Investor Trading Strategies. Thus far, there has been a pervasive tendency in the microstructure literature to take the order flow as being exogenously given. But the order flow cannot be entirely exogenous if investors use trading strategies that are dependent on market systems (e.g., on the way in which orders are handled and the rules by which they are translated into trades) and on expectations of what market-clearing prices will be (with such expectations being affected by the information systems which have been instituted). Eventually, a better understanding of the nature and impact of investors' trading strategies will shed much light on the determinants of the order flow, the operations of the market, and the dynamic behavior of security prices.

Our demonstration of the existence of the market spread is based upon an analysis of an investor's optimal order-placement strategy (Chapter 5). The use to which we put this notion is, however, limited, and the model itself does not contain an actual solution to the order-placement decision. Nonetheless, formally introducing the concept of "an optimal order-placement strategy" into the literature has opened, we believe, an important path for further analysis.

Simulation Analysis. Our study of the securities markets, while drawing from institutional observation and empirical validation, has largely been oriented to theoretical analysis. In certain respects, however, the complexity of the subject is such that rigorous theoretical modeling is not feasible, given the current state of our knowledge. Furthermore, while theory can shed much light on the nature of relationships, it typically does not yield insight into the magnitudes involved. Thus, to support our theoretical and empirical investigations, we have also presented a simulation model of stock exchange trading (Chapter 9). The model is based on our theoretical results, particularly as these relate to the returns generation process, investor order-placement strategy, and the existence of the market bid-ask spread.

Starting with Stigler (1964), West (1970), and Garman (1976), and continuing with Hakansson-Beja-Kale (1985), simulation has been found to be a useful analytical tool for studying various aspects of the securities markets. We believe that future work will demonstrate this even more clearly. Eventually, a man-machine model may be developed. Such a model would also be useful as a training device for traders. In a compatible fashion, attempts are being made by academicians to develop another tool for studying the trading environment: experimental markets. This involves the observation of simulated trading by live "volunteers," with data generated and responses recorded by computer. To date, the approach has been used primarily to study the dissemination and impact of new information [see Friedman-Harrison-Salmon (1984)].

Policy Implications. Ultimately, microstructure analysis has three fundamental purposes: (1) to shed light on the operations of the securities markets and the activities of market participants, (2) to clarify the informational content of security prices for empirical research in finance/investments, and (3) to give useful direction to those responsible for designing and regulating the markets. It is to the last of these purposes that we now turn.

In studying the markets, we have given primary consideration to two issues: the consolidation of orders and price stabilization. We have argued that both consolidation and stabilization are desirable. Furthermore, we have considered the role of the exchange system in relation to the consolidation of orders (Chapter 8) and the role of the specialist in relation to stabilization (Chapter 9).

However, other important policy issues have been touched on only tangentially in our analysis. We have not, for instance, attempted a substantive contrast of alternative trading arrangements such as call market trading versus a continuous market trading system, or exchange-based trading versus a dealer market system. Neither have we fully probed the complexities of electronic trading so as to crystallize the problems involved and to formulate an approach for solving them. These are subjects which are best left for future research.

To an extent, it is tempting to push policy analysis too far and too fast. In the complex world of the securities markets, the danger of doing so is that recommendations may be advanced which conflict with institutional realities and lack sufficient theoretical foundation. At this stage in the development of microstructure analysis, we are content primarily to have achieved a firmer understanding of the issues and problems. We trust that, eventually, more of the answers will be found.

APPENDIX A

APPENDIX TO CHAPTER 4

A.1 REASONS FOR A NEGATIVE DEMAND TO HOLD CURVE

A stock dimension for the demand curve is implicit in modern portfolio theory [e.g., Mossin (1972)], where, given initial wealth, determination of optimal portfolio weights specifies the amount of each issue to be held. We follow Mossin (1972) in taking the stock demand curve to be negatively inclined.

There is a growing literature investigating the conditions under which an individual investor's (latent) stock demand curve is negatively sloped. Fisher (1972) showed that a Slutsky equation for asset could be derived which breaks the impact of a price change on quantity into wealth and substitution effects. Epps (1975) then discussed the interpretation of these two components. A similar Slutsky equation is derived by Bierwag-Grove (1968). Royama-Hamada (1967) and Cramer (1957) also derive Slutsky equations for assets. Taken together, Epps (1975) and Bierwag-Grove (1968) show that the individual's stock demand curve is negatively sloping.

Note that under the capital asset pricing model with homogeneous expectations, one might argue that the latent market demand curve for an asset will be highly elastic. This is because, under the model, there are many substitutes for an asset, and substitution does not greatly reduce portfolio diversification. Hence all individual demand curves may be highly elastic in the neighborhood of equilibrium, and (since the elasticity of the market demand curve is the weighted sum of the individual demand elasticities of all active market participants), so too would be the market demand curve. Essentially, this is the point made by Scholes (1972). On the other hand, this need not generally be true under heterogeneous expectations (for which our model allows). In this case, the market demand curve would be more steeply (negatively) inclined, since the price of an asset must fall in order to attract additional shareholders. In other words, the elasticity of the latent market demand curve also depends (inversely) on the dispersion of the price intercepts of individual demand curves; such dispersion will in general exist under heterogeneous expectations. Furthermore, transaction costs and other trading frictions will cause the effective market demand curve to be more steeply inclined than the latent curve.

A.2 IMPACT OF AN IDIOSYNCRATIC TENDER ON THE QUOTATION PRICE RELATIVE

Assume that for any particular security, an investor generates at most one idiosyncratic tender per trading day. Let these tenders be determined overnight (i.e., after the market's close and before the next trading day's opening). Hence the most recent price information investors have for determining their tenders is the set of closing quotes for the last trading day. On the basis of these quotes, investors determine both the estimated dollar value of their trades and the actual number of shares to be bought or sold. These tenders are then entered as market orders at random points of time during the next trading day. Note that l, the length of the interval over which returns are measured, is a behaviorally determined parameter which cannot arbitrarily be varied, and our assumptions are plausible only when l is relatively short. Nonetheless, the variance results derived here could be extended to measurement intervals of varying length by applying the time-variance relationship [see Schwartz-Whitcomb (1977a)].

Now suppose that during any trading day of length l there are $n_I(t)$ idiosyncratic tenders. $n_I(t)$ is a Poisson-distributed random variable with mean and variance each equal to λl. These tenders may be ordered according to the time at which they reach the market, so that s is the sth tender to reach the market during the day, where $s = 1, \ldots, n_I(t)$. Y_s and Z_s are the sth independent draws of the random variables Y and Z during day t. We assume that Y_s and Z_s are independent for all s.

The price that investors use between trading days to translate the dollar value of idiosyncratic tenders into number of shares tendered is P_0, the security's closing quotation price for the previous trading day. Letting ΔN_s be the number of shares in the sth tender (positive if a buy order, and negative if a sell order), we have

$$\Delta N_s = \frac{Y_s Z_s}{P_0} \tag{A.1}$$

To model the price change generated by the tender of ΔN_s shares, we make two (somewhat artificial) assumptions: (1) the effective demand-to-hold curve is linear in the neighborhood of equilibrium,[1] and (2) the elasticity of demand at equilibrium remains constant during a trading day as the demand curve shifts. In Figure A.1, panel A, we illustrate the impact of a tender to sell ΔN_s shares (the analysis would be symmetrical if the tender was to buy ΔN_s shares). Given the B_{s-1}^E curve, it is clear that price must fall to P_s in order to absorb the tender, and that this generates a price change of $\Delta P_s = P_s - P_{s-1}$.

Figure A.1, panel B, shows the effective demand-to-hold D_{s-1}^E associated with the trade curves of panel A. The point elasticity of demand of D_{s-1}^E at P_{s-1} is[2]

$$\eta = \frac{\Delta N_s/N}{\Delta P_s/P_{s-1}} \tag{A.2}$$

because (1) the slope of D_{s-1}^E in panel B is equal to the slope of B_{s-1}^E in panel A, (2) the initial price is P_{s-1} for the N shares outstanding, and (3) the curves are linear. Rearranging, we can express the percentage price change generated by the idiosyncratic tender as

$$\frac{\Delta P_s}{P_{s-1}} = \frac{1}{\eta}\frac{\Delta N_s}{N} \tag{A.3}$$

Substituting Eq. (A.1) into Eq. (A.3), we have

$$\frac{\Delta P_s}{P_{s-1}} = \frac{Y_s Z_s}{\eta N P_0} = \frac{Y_s Z_s}{\eta V} \tag{A.4}$$

where we let $V = NP_0$ represent the market value of the security. From Eq. (A.4) we can write

$$\frac{P_s}{P_{s-1}} = 1 + \frac{Y_s Z_s}{\eta V} \tag{2}$$

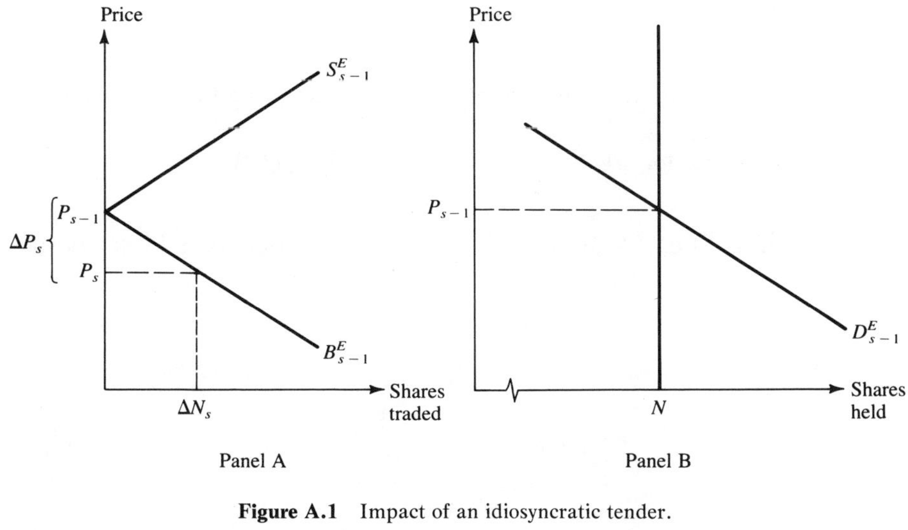

Figure A.1 Impact of an idiosyncratic tender.

Equation (2) gives the desired result, a depiction of the impact of an idiosyncratic tender on the security's quotation price relative.

A.3 THE QUOTATION PRICE RETURN DURING PERIOD *t*

It is shown in Parzen (1962) that the sum of two independent compound Poisson processes is also a compound Poisson process. Hence the combined effect of both aggregate and idiosyncratic shifts in the demand curve can be viewed as a compound Poisson process.

Let $n_A(t)$ be the number of aggregate shifts in the demand curve during a trading day of length l. $n_A(t)$ is a Poisson-distributed random variable with mean and variance each equal to Υl. Let $n(t)$ be the total number of shifts in the demand curve. Then

$$n(t) = n_I(t) + n_A(t) \tag{A.5}$$

is a Poisson-distributed random variable with mean and variance each equal to $(\lambda + \Upsilon)l$.

During a day there will be $n(t)$ changes in quotation price, generating the sequence $P_0, P_1, \ldots, P_{n(t)}$.[3] The ratio of quotation prices for the entire day can be expressed as the product of quotation price ratios traced out during the day:

$$\frac{P_{n(t)}}{P_0} = \frac{P_1}{P_0} \cdot \frac{P_2}{P_1} \cdots \frac{P_{n(t)}}{P_{n(t)-1}} \tag{A.6}$$

Substituting Eqs. (2) and (3) into (A.6), reordering the terms in the numerator and denominator of the right-hand side of Eq. (A.6), and using Eq. (A.5), we have

$$\frac{P_{n(t)}}{P_0} = \left[\prod_{s=1}^{n_I(t)} \left(1 + \frac{Y_s Z_s}{\eta V}\right)\right]\left[\prod_{s=1}^{n_A(t)} (1 + U_s W_s)\right] \tag{A.7}$$

Taking logarithms of both sides of Eq. (A.7), and using Eq. (1), we obtain

$$r_t^Q = \sum_{s=1}^{n_I(t)} \log\left(1 + \frac{Y_s Z_s}{\eta V}\right) + \sum_{s=1}^{n_A(t)} \log(1 + U_s W_s) \tag{A.8}$$

To simplify Eq. (A.8), we use the approximation [see Pierce-Foster (1956)][4]

$$\log(1 + r) \cong r \tag{A.9}$$

and write Eq. (A.8) as

$$r_t^Q = \frac{1}{\eta V} \sum_{s=1}^{n_I(t)} Y_s Z_s + \sum_{s=1}^{n_A(t)} U_s W_s \tag{4}$$

A.4 MEAN AND VARIANCE OF QUOTATION PRICE RETURNS

In order to obtain Eqs. (14) and (15) from (13), we must invoke properties of the compound Poisson process derived in Parzen (1962, pp. 128–131). In particular, we define $X_t = \Sigma_{s=1}^{n(t)} Y_s Z_s$, where $n(t)$ is a Poisson counting process with parameter ν; Y_s is the sth independent draw of the random variable Y; and Z_s is the sth independent draw from the Bernoulli random variable $Z = +1$ with probability p and $Z = -1$ with probability $1 - p$. We assume that Y_s and Z_s are independent for all s. We then have

$$E(X_t) = \nu t E(YZ) = \nu t E(Y)E(Z) = \nu t E(Y)(2p - 1)$$

$$\text{Var}\,(X_t) = \nu t E(Y^2 Z^2) = \nu t E(Y^2)E(Z^2) = \nu t E(Y^2)$$

A.5 HOMOGENEOUS EXPECTATIONS AND SEPARATION

Under homogeneous expectations, idiosyncratic tenders are generated by individual investor funds flows and changes in tastes (but not by individual reassessments of a security's value), and under separation these changes affect all securities in proportion to their weight in the market portfolio of risk assets. Hence we would have for each asset i

$$Y_i = \tilde{K} V_i \tag{A.10}$$

$$\eta_i = \eta_M \tag{A.11}$$

$$\lambda_i = \lambda_M \tag{A.12}$$

where $\tilde{K}$ is a random variable multiplicative factor identical for all assets at any moment in time, η_M is the elasticity of demand for the market portfolio,[5] and λ_M is the common arrival rate of idiosyncratic tenders.

From (A.10) we can write $E(Y_i) = V_i E(K)$, $\text{Var}\,(Y_i) = V_i^2\,\text{Var}\,(K)$, and hence

$$E(Y_i^2) = V_i^2\,\text{Var}\,(K) + V_i^2 E^2(K) \tag{A.13}$$

Substituting (A.11), (A.12), and (A.13) into (6), we obtain

$$\text{Var}\,(r_{i,t}^Q) = \frac{\lambda_M l[\text{Var}\,(K) + E^2(K)]}{\eta_M^2} + \gamma_i l E(U^2) \tag{A.14}$$

It follows immediately from (A.14) that, under homogeneous expectations and separation, the returns variance for a security is not related to the security's value of shares outstanding [except for the possibility that there is a minor relationship between $\gamma_i E(U_i^2)$ and V_i, as discussed in Section 4.4.2].

A.6 PROOFS OF ASSERTION MADE IN SECTION 4.5

We first derive the joint probability distribution of the random variables x_t that describe the time between the end of a measurement period and the last transaction (Lemma 1). We then derive Eq. (12) (Theorem 1) and Eq. (13) (Lemma 2, Lemma 3, Theorem 2, and Corollary 1) of Chapter 4. Finally, we prove that the discrepancy D, defined in Eq. (14) of Chapter 4, decreases monotonically with market value V (Theorem 3).

Lemma 1. Consider a function $g(x_{t-1}, x_t)$, where x_t is a random variable that denotes the length of time between the end of a measurement period of length l and the time of the last transaction; similarly, x_{t-1} denotes the length of time between the end of the preceding measurement period and the last transaction prior to the end of the preceding period. We then have

$$E[g(x_{t-1}, x_t)] = \int_0^\infty \int_0^l g(x_{t-1}, x_t)\lambda e^{-\lambda x_t}\lambda e^{-\lambda x_{t-1}}\, dx_t\, dx_{t-1} + \int_l^\infty g(x_t - l, x_t)\lambda e^{-\lambda x_t}\, dx_t$$

Proof. First consider the marginal probability density function $f(x_t)$ of the random variable x_t. As shown in Feller (1971, problem 7, p. 39), this distribution will approach the exponential

$$f(x_t) = \lambda e^{-\lambda x_t}$$

as the time since the process was begun approaches infinity. Since we are dealing with security markets that have been in existence for an extremely long period of time (relative to the arrival rate of transactions), we will henceforth assume an exponential distribution for the random variable x_t.

Next consider the conditional distribution of the random variable x_{t-1}, given x_t. If the random variable $x_t < l$, then x_{t-1} is independent of x_t and we have

$$h(x_{t-1} | x_t < l) = \lambda e^{-\lambda x_{t-1}}$$

In the case where $x_t \geq l$, we have that $x_{t-1} = x_t - l$, since in this situation no transaction occurred during the measurement period. Combining all these observations, we obtain our desired expectation of the function $g(x_{t-1}, x_t)$ as shown. Q.E.D.

Theorem 1

$$E(\hat{R}_T) = E(r_t^Q)$$

Proof. Since the end points of the time intervals t^*, which are defined by the x_t variables, are points at which quoted prices and transaction prices are identical, we have from Eqs. (10) and (5)

$$E(\hat{R}_T) = E\left[\frac{1}{M}\sum_{t=1}^{M} r_{t*}^T\right] = \frac{1}{M}\sum_{t=1}^{M} E[E(r_{t*}^Q | x_{t-1}, x_t)]$$
$$= E[E(r_{t*}^Q | x_{t-1}, x_t)] = E[\gamma(2p - 1)E(U)(l + x_{t-1} - x_t)]$$
$$= \gamma(2p - 1)E(U)\int_0^\infty \int_0^\infty (l + x_{t-1} - x_t)\lambda e^{-\lambda x_t}\,\lambda e^{-\lambda x_{t-1}}\,dx_t\,dx_{t-1}$$

where this last expression follows from the results of Lemma 1. Evaluating this integral and using Eq. (5), we obtain

$$E(\hat{R}_T) = \gamma(2p - 1)E(U)l = E(r_t^Q)$$

which is the desired result. Q.E.D.

Lemma 2

$$E[\text{Var}\,(r_{t*}^Q | x_{t-1}, x_t)] = \text{Var}\,(r_t^Q)$$

Proof. Following Eq. (6), we have

$$\text{Var}\,(r_{t*}^Q | x_{t-1}, x_t) = \left[\frac{\lambda E(Y^2)}{\eta^2 V^2} + \gamma E(U^2)\right](l + x_{t-1} - x)$$

In evaluating the expectation of this expression, we use the results of Lemma 1 to obtain

$$E[\text{Var}\,(r_{t*}^Q | x_{t-1}, x_t)]$$
$$= \left[\frac{\lambda E(Y^2)}{\eta^2 V^2} + \gamma E(U^2)\right]\int_0^\infty \int_0^l (l + x_{t-1} - x_t)\lambda e^{-\lambda x_t}\lambda e^{-\lambda x_{t-1}}\,dx_t\,dx_{t-1}$$

where only the first term appears, since for $x_t \geq l$ we have $x_{t-1} = x_t - l$ and $l + x_{t-1} - x_t = 0$. Evaluating this integral, we obtain

$$\left[\frac{\lambda E(Y^2)}{\eta^2 V^2} + \gamma E(U^2)\right]l = \text{Var}\,(r_t^Q)$$

where this last expression again follows from Eq. (6). Q.E.D.

Lemma 3

$$\text{Var}\,[E(r_{t*}^Q | x_{t-1}, x_t)] = 2\gamma^2(2p - 1)^2\,E^2(U)\left(\frac{1 - e^{-\mu V l}}{\mu^2 V^2}\right)$$

Proof. Following Eq. (5), we have

$$E(r_{t*}^Q | x_{t-1}, x_t) = \gamma(2p - 1)E(U)(l + x_{t-1} - x_t)$$

Theorem 1 established that

$$E[E(r_{t*}^Q | x_{t-1}, x_t)] = \gamma(2p - 1)E(U)l$$

Using these two results and the identity Var $(X \mid Y) = E\{[X - E(X \mid Y)]^2 \mid Y\}$, we have that

$$\{E(r^Q_{t*} \mid x_{t-1}, x_t) - E[E(r^Q_{t*} \mid x_{t-1}, x_t)]\}^2 = \gamma^2(2p - 1)^2 E^2(U)(x_{t-1} - x_t)^2$$

from which we obtain, by Lemma 1,

$$\text{Var}\ [E(r^Q_{t*} \mid x_{t-1}, x_t)]$$

$$= \gamma^2(2p - 1)^2 E^2(U)\left[\int_0^\infty \int_0^l (x_{t-1} - x_t)^2 \lambda e^{-\lambda x_t} \lambda e^{-\lambda x_{t-1}}\, dx_t\, dx_{t-1} + l^2 \int_l^\infty \lambda e^{-\lambda x_t}\, dx_t\right]$$

Evaluating the integral, we obtain

$$2\gamma^2(2p - 1)^2 E^2(U)\left[\frac{1 - e^{-\lambda l}}{\lambda^2}\right]$$

and on substituting $\lambda = \mu V$ we have the desired result. Q.E.D.

Theorem 2

$$E[\hat{\sigma}^2_T] \cong E[\text{Var}\ (r^Q_{t*} \mid x_{t-1}, x_t)] + \text{Var}\ [E(r^Q_{t*} \mid x_{t-1}, x_t)]$$

where $\hat{\sigma}^2_T$ is the estimator defined by Eqs. (10) and (11), and the expectation of the estimator converges to the right-hand-side components as the sample size M goes to infinity.

Proof. From Eqs. (10) and (11) we have, by definition,

$$E[\hat{\sigma}^2_T] = E\left\{\frac{1}{M - 1} \sum_{t=1}^{M} \left[r^T_{t*} - \frac{1}{M} \sum_{\tau=1}^{M} r^T_{\tau*}\right]^2\right\}$$

Since the end points of the time intervals $l + x_{t-1} - x_t$ are points at which quoted prices and transaction prices are identical, we can substitute quotation returns for transaction returns to obtain

$$E\left\{\frac{1}{M - 1} \sum_{t=1}^{M} \left[r^Q_{t*} - \frac{1}{M} \sum_{\tau=1}^{M} r^Q_{\tau*}\right]^2\right\}$$

Applying the conditional expectation identity $E[X] = E[E(X \mid Y)]$ and rearranging the order of operator evaluations, we have

$$\frac{1}{M - 1} \sum_{t=1}^{M} E\left\{E\left[\left(r^Q_t - \frac{1}{M} \sum_{\tau=1}^{M} r^Q_{\tau*}\right)^2 \mid x_1, \ldots, x_M\right]\right\}$$

We now apply the identity $E[(X - Y)^2 \mid Z] = E[(X - E[X \mid Z])^2 \mid Z] + E^2[X \mid Z] - 2E[XY \mid Z] + E[Y^2 \mid Z]$, which can be derived along the same lines as Parzen [1962, Eq. (2.29), p. 55], to obtain

$$E[\hat{\sigma}_T^2] = I_1 + I_2 + I_3 + I_4$$

where

$$I_1 = \frac{1}{M-1} \sum_{t=1}^{M} E\{E[(r_{t*}^Q - E[r_{t*}^Q | x_{t-1}, x_t)^2 | x_{t-1}, x_t]\}$$

$$I_2 = \frac{1}{M-1} \sum_{t=1}^{M} E\{E^2[r_{t*}^Q | x_{t-1}, x_t]\}$$

$$I_3 = -\frac{2}{M-1} \sum_{t=1}^{M} E\left\{E\left[r_{t*}^Q \frac{1}{M} \sum_{\tau=1}^{M} r_{\tau*}^Q | x_1, \ldots, x_M\right]\right\}$$

$$I_4 = \frac{1}{M-1} \sum_{t=1}^{M} E\left\{E\left[\left(\frac{1}{M} \sum_{\tau=1}^{M} r_{t*}^Q\right)^2 | x_1, \ldots, x_M\right]\right\}$$

We now consider each of the four components in turn. Following Parzen [1962, Eq. (2.23), p. 55], we have

$$I_1 = \frac{1}{M-1} \sum_{t=1}^{M} E[\text{Var}\,(r_{t*}^Q | x_{t-1}, x_t)]$$

$$= \frac{M}{M-1} E[\text{Var}\,(r_{t*}^Q | x_{t-1}, x_t)]$$

Similarly, the second component also simplifies to

$$I_2 = \frac{M}{M-1} E[E^2(r_{t*}^Q | x_{t-1}, x_t)]$$

In considering the third component, it is helpful to separate the returns relating to a single period and those relating to multiple periods

$$I_3 = -\frac{2}{(M-1)M} \sum_{t=1}^{M} E\left\{E[(r_{t*}^Q)^2 | x_{t-1}, x_t] + E\left[r_{t*}^Q \sum_{\substack{\tau=1 \\ \tau \neq t}}^{M} r_{\tau*}^Q | x_1, \ldots, x_M\right]\right\}$$

It is convenient to write $I_3 = I_{31} + I_{32}$, where

$$I_{31} = -\frac{2}{M-1} E\{E[(r_{t*}^Q)^2 | x_{t-1}, x_t]\}$$

$$I_{32} = -\frac{2}{(M-1)M} \sum_{t=1}^{M} E\left\{E\left[r_{t*}^Q \sum_{\substack{\tau=1 \\ \tau \neq t}}^{M} r_{\tau*}^Q | x_1, \ldots, x_M\right]\right\}$$

We postpone further consideration of I_{32} until after we examine I_4. I_4 can be separated into a return for only one period and products of two period returns as follows:

$$I_4 = I_{41} + I_{42}$$

where

$$I_{41} = \frac{1}{(M-1)M^2} \sum_{t=1}^{M} E\left\{E\left[\sum_{\tau=1}^{M} (r_{\tau*}^{Q})^2 | x_1, \ldots, x_M\right]\right\}$$

$$= \frac{1}{(M-1)M} E\left\{\sum_{\tau=1}^{M} E[(r_{\tau*}^{Q})^2 | x_{\tau-1}, x_\tau]\right\}$$

$$= \frac{1}{M-1} E\{E[(r_{\tau*}^{Q})^2 | x_{\tau-1}, x_\tau]\}$$

and

$$I_{42} = \frac{1}{(M-1)M^2} \sum_{k=1}^{M} E\left\{E\left[\sum_{t=1}^{M} \left(r_{t*}^{Q} \sum_{\substack{\tau=1 \\ \tau\neq t}}^{M} r_{\tau*}^{Q}\right) | x_1, \ldots, x_M\right]\right\}$$

$$= \frac{1}{(M-1)M} \sum_{t=1}^{M} E\left\{E\left[\left(r_{t*}^{Q} \sum_{\substack{\tau=1 \\ \tau\neq t}}^{M} r_{t*}^{Q}\right) | x_1, \ldots, x_M\right]\right\}$$

We are now in a position to combine $I_{31} + I_{41}$ and $I_{32} + I_{42}$ to obtain

$$I_{31} + I_{41} = -\frac{1}{M-1} E\{E[(r_{t*}^{Q})^2 | x_{t-1}, x_t]\}$$

and

$$I_{32} + I_{42} = -\frac{1}{(M-1)M} \sum_{t=1}^{M} E\left\{E\left[r_{t*}^{Q} \sum_{\substack{\tau=1 \\ \tau\neq t}}^{M} r_{t*}^{Q} | x_1, \ldots, x_M\right]\right\}$$

With the assumption that $x_1, \ldots, x_M$ are known, the inner expectation in this last expression can be further simplified by observing that the returns r_{t*}^{Q} and $r_{\tau*}^{Q}$ are independent:

$$I_{32} + I_{42} = -\frac{1}{(M-1)M} \sum_{t=1}^{M} E\left\{E[r_{t*}^{Q} | x_{t-1}, x_t] \sum_{\substack{\tau=1 \\ \tau\neq t}}^{M} E[r_{\tau*}^{Q} | x_{\tau-1}, x_\tau]\right\}$$

$$= -\frac{1}{(M-1)M} \sum_{t=1}^{M} \sum_{\substack{\tau=1 \\ \tau\neq t}}^{M} E\{E[r_{t*}^{Q} | x_{t-1}, x_t] E[r_{\tau*}^{Q} | x_{\tau-1}, x_\tau]\}$$

In evaluating this last expression, we must now resort to an approximation, since in general x_{t-1}, x_t and $x_{\tau-1}$, x_τ will not be independent. If we assume that the estimator $\hat{\sigma}_T^2$ has been calculated for a large sample size M, then when we examine two time periods that are not consecutive (i.e., $t \ll \tau$ or $t \gg \tau$), we find that

$$E\{E[r_{t*}^{Q} | x_{t-1}, x_t] E[r_{\tau*}^{Q} | x_{\tau-1}, x_\tau]\} \cong E\{E[r_{t*}^{Q} | x_{t-1}, x_t]\} E\{E[r_{\tau*}^{Q} | x_{\tau-1}, x_\tau]\}$$

Since most of the $M(M-1)$ products in the expression for $I_{32} + I_{42}$ will behave as though they were approximately independent, we have

$$I_{32} + I_{42} \cong -E^2\{E[r_{t*}^Q | x_{t-1}, x_t]\}$$

where the approximation improves as M gets larger.

It is convenient to write this last expression as the sum of two terms

$$I_{32} + I_{42} \cong \frac{1}{M-1} E^2\{E[(r_{t*}^Q) | x_{t-1}, x_t]\} - \frac{M}{M-1} E^2\{E[r_{t*}^Q | x_{t-1}, x_t]\}$$

If we combine the first term with $I_{31} + I_{41}$, we obtain

$$-\frac{1}{M-1} [E\{E[(r_{t*}^Q)^2 | x_{t-1}, x_t]\} - E^2\{E[r_{t*}^Q | x_{t-1}, x_t]\}]$$

$$= -\frac{1}{M-1} E[\text{Var}\ (r_{t*}^Q | x_{t-1}, x_t)]$$

If we combine the second term with I_2, we obtain

$$\frac{1}{M-1} \{E[E^2(r_{t*}^Q | x_{t-1}, x_t)] - E^2[E(r_{t*}^Q | x_{t-1}, x_t)]\}$$

$$= \frac{M}{M-1} \text{Var}\ [E(r_{t*}^Q | x_{t-1}, x_t)]$$

Combining these two expressions with I_1, we obtain

$$E[\hat{\sigma}_T^2] \cong E[\text{Var}\ (r_{t*}^Q | x_{t-1}, x_t)] + \frac{M}{M-1} \text{Var}\ [E(r_{t*}^Q | x_{t-1}, x_t)]$$

which for large values of the sample size M gives the desired result. Q.E.D.

Corollary 1

$$E(\hat{\sigma}_T^2) \cong \text{Var}\ (r_t^Q) + D$$

where

$$D = \frac{2\gamma^2(2p-1)^2E^2(U)}{\mu^2V^2}(1 - e^{-\mu Vl})$$

Proof. This result immediately follows from Lemmas 2 and 3 and Theorem 2. Q.E.D.

Theorem 3

$$\frac{dD}{dV} < 0 \qquad \text{for } V > 0$$

Proof. To examine the manner in which D depends upon V, let us rewrite Eq. (14) in the simpler form

$$D = \frac{K}{V^2}(1 - e^{-\mathrm{LV}})$$

where we have introduced the abbreviations

$$K = \frac{2\gamma^2(2p - 1)^2E^2(U)}{\mu^2} \qquad \text{and} \qquad L = \mu l$$

Note that L is clearly positive, and K is also positive whenever there is drift in the informational demand shift process.

To see how D depends on thinness, let us evaluate the limits of D as V approaches 0 and as V increases without bound. First, note that

$$\lim_{V \to 0} D = \lim_{V \to 0} \frac{K(1 - e^{-\mathrm{LV}})}{V^2}$$

is of the form 0/0. Hence, using l'Hôpital's rule, we get

$$\lim_{V \to 0} D = \lim_{V \to 0} \frac{K(1 - e^{-\mathrm{LV}})}{V^2} = \lim_{V \to 0} \frac{KLe^{-\mathrm{LV}}}{2V} = +\infty$$

Hence, as $V \to 0$, D grows without bound. Next, note that

$$\lim_{V \to \infty} D = \lim_{V \to \infty} \frac{K(1 - e^{-\mathrm{LV}})}{V^2} = 0$$

Furthermore, note that since $V > 0$, $e^{-\mathrm{LV}} < 1$; hence $D > 0$. These results imply that D is always positive, that it is very large for thin stocks, and that it becomes small for thick stocks.

Even more strongly, we can show that the size of D decreases monotonically as V increases. To establish this, it is sufficient to demonstrate that

$$\frac{dD}{dV} = \frac{K}{V^2}(Le^{-\mathrm{LV}}) - \frac{2K}{V^3}(1 - e^{-\mathrm{LV}})$$

$$= \frac{1}{V^3}[-2K + e^{-\mathrm{LV}}(K\mathrm{L}V + 2K)]$$

is always negative.

From this last expression, for $V > 0$, it is clear that $dD/dV < 0$ if and only if

$$e^{-\mathrm{LV}}(K\mathrm{L}V + 2K) < 2K$$

Let us investigate whether this last relation is necessarily valid for $V > 0$. It is equivalent to

$$-\mathrm{L}V + \log(K\mathrm{L}V + 2K) < \log 2K$$

This in turn is equivalent to

$$\log\left(1 + \frac{\mathrm{L}V}{2}\right) < \mathrm{L}V$$

Note that for sufficiently small positive values of V, the approximation for the natural logarithm given in Eq. (A.9) is valid. Applying this approximation, we have that

$$\log\left(1 + \frac{\mathrm{L}V}{2}\right) = \frac{\mathrm{L}V}{2}$$

for sufficiently small positive values of V. Clearly,

$$\frac{\mathrm{L}V}{2} < \mathrm{L}V$$

Hence, for sufficiently small positive values of V, we have proven that

$$\log\left(1 + \frac{\mathrm{L}V}{2}\right) < \mathrm{L}V$$

must hold, and hence that $dD/dV < 0$.

Our final step is to show that as V increases, the left-hand side of the last expression increases more slowly than the right-hand side; that is, that

$$\frac{d}{dV}\log\left(1 + \frac{\mathrm{L}V}{2}\right) < \frac{d}{dV}(\mathrm{L}V)$$

If we can show this, then we have completed the proof that $dD/dV < 0$. This is equivalent to

$$\left(\frac{1}{1 + \mathrm{L}V/2}\right)\frac{L}{2} < L$$

or

$$\frac{L}{2 + \mathrm{L}V} < L$$

or

$$1 < 2 + \mathrm{L}V$$

Clearly, this necessarily holds for all $V \geq 0$.

Thus we have proved that

$$\frac{dD}{dV} < 0 \qquad \text{for } V > 0 \qquad \text{Q.E.D.}$$

A.7 DETAILS OF REGRESSION STUDY

A.7.1 Empirical Definitions and Data Sources

The following empirical definitions were used.

VAR — The variance of daily returns in the first quarter of 1972. Each daily return was calculated as the log of closing price ratios adjusted for cash dividends, stock dividends, stock splits, and (for RIO and TKYO) rights issues.

FS — Floating supply, the number of shares outstanding less insider holdings[6] at the end of 1971.

P — Price per share on the last trading day in 1971, converted into U.S. dollars at the official exchange rate on that date.

V — $\text{FS} \cdot P$.

NST — The number of shares traded in December 1971.

TOR — NST/FS.

RINSH — Institutional holdings (mutual funds, pension funds, and insurance companies, but not including common trusts)[7] divided by FS.

SAV — The variance around a sales-assets trend line.

The U.S. data were obtained from the ISL and COMPUSTAT Tapes, Moody's *Stock Guide*, and S&P's *Stock Owner's Manual*. Japanese data were collected and provided by Nomura Research Institute. The Brazilian returns data were compiled by the Brazilian Capital Markets Institute (IBMEC); other data were taken from the Rio de Janeiro Stock Exchange publications *Manual do Investidor*, *Panorama 1972*, and *Boletim Diario*.

A.7.2 Results of Additional Regressions

Reg. Set C (shown in Table A.1) is a reestimation of Reg. Set A excluding the variables RINSH and LSAV, whose coefficients were insignificant in most regressions. The coefficients of the remaining variables were little changed by this omission.

Reg. Set D gives a significance test of the interexchange differences of the LTOR coefficients when LNST is accounted for separately.[8] Table A.1 shows that there are no significant difference between the TKYO and U.S. LTOR coefficients; this is consistent with the hypothesis, stated in the text, that the significant LTOR dummy coefficient in Reg. Sets A (and C) is due to a specialist effect working through LNST.

Two other results corroborate our explanation in the text for the LTOR coefficient. If the specialist intervenes to lower VAR for low TOR stocks, his own trading activity must raise these stocks' TOR above its value on a pure exchange. This would result in a smaller relative dispersion of TOR on specialist ex-

TABLE A.1 Additional Separate and Pooled Regression Results with LVAR as Dependent Variable[a]

Reg. Set	Exchange	Intercept	LV	LNST	LTOR	LP	R^2	F
C	TKYO	−5.467	−2.10		0.085	−0.499	0.360	10.17**
		(−5.690)**	(−2.630)**		(1.181)	(−3.021)**	0.676(P)	25.56**
	RIO	−5.223	−0.254		0.354	0.253	0.235	3.76*
		(−5.660)**	(−2.438)*		(−3.335)**	(1.725)*		
		(0.184)	(−0.313)		(−3.157)**	(3.477)**		
	AMEX	−5.665	0.175		0.290	−0.908	0.691	37.46**
		(9.897)**	(2.257)*		(3.508)**	(−8.397)**		
		(−0.190)	(3.252)**		(1.702)*	(−2.179)*		
	NYSE	−4.498	0.101		0.037	−0.755	0.715	41.87**
		(−8.315)**	(1.400)		(5.711)**	(−5.014)**		
		(1.030)	(3.056)**		(4.068)**	(−1.223)		
D	TKYO	−5.468		−0.210	0.295	−0.709	0.360	10.17**
		(−5.690)**		(−2.530)**	(2.573)**	(−4.931)**	0.676(P)	25.56**
	RIO	−5.223		−0.254	0.100	0.001	0.235	3.76*
		(−5.660)**		(−2.438)*	(−1.208)**	(0.013)*		
		(0.184)		(−0.313)	(−2.994)**	(4.796)**		
	AMEX	−5.665		0.175	0.115	−0.733	0.691	37.46**
		(9.897)**		(2.257)**	(1.200)	(−9.711)**		
		(−0.190)		(3.252)**	(1.189)	(−0.164)		
	NYSE	−4.498		0.101	0.537	−0.654	0.714	41.87**
		(−8.315)**		(1.400)	(4.962)**	(−5.707)**		
		(1.030)		(3.056)**	(1.626)	(−0.333)		

[a] As in Table 1 of Chapter 4, beneath each coefficient is its separate regression *t* statistic, and beneath that is the *t* statistic from the pooled regression.

*Significant at the 0.05 level.

**Significant at the 0.01 level.

changes. We have observed this in our sample; although the average level of TOR is greater for TKYO and RIO, TOR's coefficient of variation on the U.S. exchanges is about half that of TKYO and about two-thirds that of RIO. Further, specialist intervention could cause TOR's elasticity with respect to NST to be smaller on specialist exchanges, since as NST falls, the natural reduction in TOR would be tempered by specialist intervention. Table A.2 shows that $\epsilon_{TOR \cdot NST}$ is indeed smaller for the U.S. exchanges than for TKYO, with the NYSE differences significant at the 0.01 level.

A.7.3 Alternative Explanation of LV Results

An alternative explanation of our results is that the VAR-*V* elasticity is not constant and that the higher observed elasticity on the U.S. exchanges comes from imposing a constant elasticity functional form. For several reasons, we reject this hypothesis: (1) Each exchange's sample was selected by stratifying on

TABLE A.2 Separate and Pooled Regressions with LTOR Dependent Variable[a]

Exchange	Intercept	LNST	*LP*	R^2	*F*
TKYO	−7.4220	0.565	0.215	0.619	40.82**
	(−14.911)**	(9.699)**	(1.355)	0.441(P)	13.69**
RIO	−7.014	0.470	0.168	0.147	2.16
	(−4.045)**	(2.011)*	(−0.845)		
	(−0.080)	(−0.080)	(−1.426)		
AMEX	−4.971	0.455	−0.041	0.292	11.09
	(−10.351)**	(4.682)**	(−0.354)		
	(3.053)**	(−0.792)	(−1.165)		
NYSE	−2.835	0.190	−0.569	0.281	10.57**
	(−4.714)**	(2.032)*	(−4.362)**		
	(5.051)**	(−2.862)**	(−3.410)**		

[a] As in Table 1 of Chapter 4, beneath each coefficient is its *t* statistic and beneath that is the *t* statistic from the four exchange pooled regression with the base exchange (TKYO).

*Significant at the 0.05 level.

**Significant at the 0.01 level.

value of shares outstanding (for RIO, value of shares traded) so as to give a wide (and, across exchanges, overlapping) range for *V*. (2) The exchanges rank AMEX, TKYO, RIO, and NYSE in ascending order of average *V*. In order for nonconstant elasticity to explain the observed results, it would thus be necessary for elasticity first to decrease and then to rise with increasing *V*. To determine whether this might possibly be the case, we segmented each exchange (except RIO, where the sample of firms was too small) into thirds based on *V* and ran Reg. Set C-type regressions on each segment. Reducing the range of *V* reduces the stability of its coefficient, but on none of the exchanges is there any apparent tendency for the L*V* coefficient to change systematically across segments. (3) As a further test of the linearity of the LVAR–L*V* relationship, we ordered the observations on each exchange by *V* and examined the regression residuals. The plotted residual pattern did not appear to suggest curvilinearity, and the residual first-order autocorrelation estimates (calculated from the Durbin-Watson statistics) did not have the positive values that would accompany such a residual pattern.

NOTES

1. In order to assert without inconsistency that each idiosyncratic tender impacts on a linear effective demand curve (as depicted in Figure A.1), new limit orders must enter the market as transactions eliminate existing limit orders. Otherwise, an ever-increasing bid-ask spread would emerge. Hence replenishment of the limit-order book is necessary in order to maintain a constant spread (which in this chapter we have assumed to be zero).
2. Note that *N* is not subscripted in Eq. (A.2) because there is no change in the number of shares outstanding. An idiosyncratic tender causes a vertical (but not parallel) shift

in the market demand to hold curve by an amount ΔP_s. The reason for the rotation is that we have assumed the demand elasticity at equilibrium to be constant during the trading day. Since

$$\eta = \frac{\Delta N/N}{\Delta P/P} = \frac{1}{N}\left(\frac{P}{\Delta P/\Delta N}\right)$$

is a constant, and since N is fixed, any change in P must be exactly matched by a change in the slope of the demand to hold curve ($\Delta P/\Delta N$).

3. We assume the parameters of the compound Poisson processes for both idiosyncratic and aggregate demand shifts to be the same throughout the trading day. This is an oversimplication, since events that lead to demand shifts can also occur when the market is closed, and this might lead to increased trading activity near the market opening and closing.
4. This approximation is valid so long as $r^2 \ll 1$. We expect this to be the case for each term on the right-hand side of Eq. (A.8). Note that the dollar value of any idiosyncratic tender Y_s will be a very small percentage of the outstanding market value of the stock V; moreover, $|Z_s/\eta|$ is likely to be on the order of magnitude of unity. Hence with regard to the idiosyncratic tender terms on the right-hand side of Eq. (11), we clearly expect that $(Y_s Z_s/\eta V)^2 \ll 1$. For an aggregate demand shift, U_s represents the relative change in quoted price caused by the sth aggregate demand shift. Thus, for example, a 20% increase or decrease in quoted price would be a very large change for a single aggregate demand shift, and this would entail a value of $U_s = 0.2$; in this example, $(U_s W_s)^2 = 0.04 \ll 1$.
5. Under homogeneous expectations and separation, the demand curve for each asset holds market share constant, which accounts for the equality of demand elasticities. Further, recognizing that the "market portfolio" is, in general, perceived by investors to be a less-than-perfect substitute for, say, a riskless asset or a Black (1972)-type zero beta portfolio, we have $|\eta_M| < \infty$.

   A further argument for the finiteness of the market portfolio's demand elasticity can be given by examining the share valuation model of Mossin (1972), which was derived under the assumption of perfect capital markets. Since idiosyncratic tenders can be argued to be caused by individual risk perception and wealth changes, which Mossin's share evaluation equation (15) shows will cause security price changes, it follows that $|\eta_M| < \infty$.
6. "Insider holdings" are defined in the United States as shares held by officers, directors, and any shareholders owning at least 10% of the outstanding stock. Insider holdings are proxied in Japan as shares held by the 10 largest shareholders, and in Brazil as shares held by the public sector, foreign owners, directors, and "large shareholders" (as determined by the RIO exchange).
7. For RIO, institutional holdings were available only for 24 large mutual funds; however, other institutional investors (such as insurance companies and pension funds) are relatively small holders of shares in Brazil.
8. The LV coefficient in Reg. Set C must equal the LNST coefficient in Reg. Set D; the LTOR coefficient in C must equal the sum of the LNST and the LTOR coefficients in D; and the LP coefficient in C must equal the difference between the LP and the LNST coefficient in D.

APPENDIX B

APPENDIX TO CHAPTER 5

In this Appendix, we restate formally and prove Propositions 1 through 4 of Section 5.3 and develop the more technical aspects of the arguments presented in Section 5.4.

SECTION 5.3

Equation (3) of Section 5.3 presents a compound Poisson process as the stochastic process that generates a sequence of market ask prices over time. This can be used to determine the probability that a limit bid order will execute during a particular time period.

Suppose that the price of the limit order to be submitted is greater than the current market bid but less than the current market ask—that is, that $P_t^{\mathrm{MB}} < P_t^{\mathrm{LB}} < P_t^{\mathrm{MA}}$. To determine the probability that the potential limit bid will execute in a time interval of length L, we must find the probability that $P_t^{\mathrm{MA}}(\Delta)$ will decrease to a price equal to or less than P_t^{LB}.[1] Therefore, let $Y(L, P_t^{\mathrm{MA}}, P_t^{\mathrm{LB}})$ be the probability that the minimum value that $P_t^{\mathrm{MA}}(\Delta)$ achieves in the interval $0 \leq W \leq L$ is equal to or less than P_t^{LB}. As P_t^{LB} approaches P_t^{MA}, we would expect the probability of the potential limit bit executing to increase, since the amount that $P^{\mathrm{MA}}(\Delta)$ would have to decline would be reduced. However, in the limit as P_t^{LB} approaches P_t^{MA} from below, without further analysis but is unclear how far the probability will rise. Therefore, let

$$\phi(L, P_t^{\text{MA}}) = 1 - \lim_{P_t^{\text{LB}} \to P_t^{\text{MA}}} Y(L, P_t^{\text{MA}}, P_t^{\text{LB}})$$

where the limit is understood to be from below. We now prove:

Proposition 1. If $P_t^{\text{MA}}(\Delta)$ is generated by the compound Poisson process of Chapter 5, Eq. (3), then $\phi(L, P_t^{\text{MA}}) > 0$ for all intervals of length $L < \infty$.[2]

Proof. Since Z_i is stochastic with mean zero, $P(Z_i \geq 0) > 0$. Furthermore, the value of the Poisson random variable $N(L)$ will be finite in any interval of length L less than infinity. Therefore, the probability of $N(L)$ consecutive Z_i observations that are greater than or equal to zero is given by $[P(Z_i \geq 0)]^{N(L)}$, which, since $N(L)$ is finite, must be strictly greater than zero. Notice that if all the Z_i observations are greater than or equal to zero, the value of $P_t^{\text{MA}}(\Delta)$ must be greater than or equal to P_t^{MA} throughout the interval $0 \leq \Delta \leq L$; thus the limit order P_t^{LB} would not have executed. This is sufficient to demonstrate the probability jump. Clearly, there are other sample paths that $P_t^{\text{MA}}(\Delta)$ could have followed which also would have failed to execute the limit order. Q.E.D.

Proposition 2. If $P_t^{\text{MA}}(\Delta)$ is generated by the Wiener process of Chapter 5, Eq. (4), then $\phi(L, P_t^{\text{MA}}) = 0$ for all intervals of length $L < \infty$.

Proof. By the reflection principle for a continuous Wiener process [see Karlin (1968), pp. 276–277] and since $\ln P_t^{\text{MA}}(\Delta)$ is driftless,

$$\begin{aligned} Y(L, P_t^{\text{MA}}, P_t^{\text{LB}}) &= \Pr\{\min_{0 \leq \Delta \leq L} P_t^{\text{MA}}(\Delta) \leq P_t^{\text{LB}}\} = \Pr\{\min_{0 \leq \Delta \leq L} \ln P_t^{\text{MA}}(\Delta) \leq \ln P_t^{\text{LB}}\} \\ &= 2 \Pr\{\ln P_{t+1}^{\text{MA}} < \ln P_t^{\text{LB}}\} = 2 \Pr\{P_{t+1}^{\text{MA}} < P_t^{\text{LB}}\} \\ &= \frac{2}{\sigma\sqrt{2\pi L}} \int_{-\infty}^{P_t^{\text{LB}}} \exp\left\{-\frac{1}{2L}\left(\frac{x - P_t^{\text{MA}}}{\sigma}\right)^2\right\} dx \end{aligned}$$

where the latter probability distribution follows from the definition of the Wiener process. Now

$$\lim_{P_t^{\text{LB}} \to P_t^{\text{MA}}} Y(L, P_t^{\text{MA}}, P_t^{\text{LB}}) = \frac{2}{\sigma\sqrt{2\pi L}} \int_{-\infty}^{P_t^{\text{MA}}} \exp\left\{-\frac{1}{2L}\left(\frac{x - P_t^{\text{MA}}}{\sigma}\right)^2\right\} dx$$

Substituting the variable $y = (x - P_t^{\text{MA}})/(\sigma\sqrt{L})$, the preceding limit equals $(2/2\pi) \int_{-\infty}^{0} \exp\{-1/2y^2\}\, dy = 2(\frac{1}{2}) = 1$. Q.E.D.

Proposition 3. If the random variable Z_i is expressed as a Bernoulli random variable, with $\Pr(Z_i = \alpha) = \Pr(Z_i = -\alpha) = \frac{1}{2}$, and if the arrival rate ν of the Poisson process $N(\Delta)$ goes to infinity, while simultaneously reducing the size of α in such a way that $\nu\alpha^2$ remains constant, the compound Poisson process approaches the Wiener process described by Eq. (4) with $\sigma^2 = \nu\alpha^2$.

Proof. This follows from the theorem that the characteristic function for the compound Poisson approaches that of the Wiener process [see Parzen (1962), p. 99].

Proposition 4

$$\frac{\partial Y(L, P_t^{MA}, P_t^{LB})}{\partial \nu} > 0 \qquad \text{for all } P_t^{LB} < P_t^{MA} \text{ and } L < \infty$$

Proof. By the Markov property of the compound Poisson process, increasing (decreasing) the order arrival rate by some factor λ is identical to increasing (decreasing) the length of time L between decision points by λ. When λ is increased, those sample paths of the process which initially satisfied

$$\min_{0 \le \Delta \le L} P_t^{MA}(\Delta) \le P_t^{LB}$$

will still continue to do so. On the other hand, some sample paths where

$$\min_{0 \le \Delta \le L} P_t^{MA}(\Delta) > P_t^{LB}$$

will now satisfy the inequality

$$\min_{0 \le \Delta \le \lambda L} P_t^{MA}(\Delta) \le P_t^{LB}$$

Therefore, $Y(L, P_t^{MA}, P_t^{LB})$ would increase for $\lambda > 1$ for all values of $P_t^{LB} < P_t^{MA}$. Similarly, $Y(L, P_t^{MA}, P_t^{LB})$ would decrease if the order arrival rate λ is decreased. Q.E.D.

SECTION 5.4

We now present the more technical aspects of the model of an investor's order-placement strategy discussed in Section 5.4. The subjectivity-determined probability distributions are specified as follows. First, the probability distribution of future market bid and ask prices is given by $h(P_{t+1}^{MA}, P_{t+1}^{MB} \mid P_t^{MA}, P_t^{MB})$, where h is a joint density function for market asks and bids (P_t^{MA}, P_t^{MB}) at time $t + 1$, given the prices at t. Consistent with random walk models of security price behavior, we condition future prices only on current prices. Consistent with Section 5.3, we let the investor's subjective probability of a limit order executing before $t + 1$ be given $p(P_t^{LB}, P_t^{MA}, P_t^{MB})$, where P_t^{LB} is the limit bid price. (Again, this is consistent with random walk theory, since we need know only current market quotes to predict whether or not the limit order will be executed.) Last, we assume that the investor determines conditional probability distributions of future prices in the event of either successful or unsuccessful limit order. That is, for a limit bid at price P_t^{LB} submitted at time t, let $k(P_{t+1}^{MA}, P_{t+1}^{MB} \mid P_t^{MA}, P_t^{MB}, P_t^{LB})$ be the joint density function of market bid and ask prices at time $t + 1$ if the limit bid executes prior to $t + 1$, and let $l(P_{t+1}^{\mathrm{MA}}, P_{t+1}^{\mathrm{MB}} \mid P_t^{\mathrm{MA}}, P_t^{\mathrm{MB}}, P_t^{\mathrm{LB}})$ be the joint density function at time $t + 1$ if the limit bid fails to execute prior to $t + 1$. Note that only three of the four subjective probability distributions h, p, k, and l can be independently determined, since by Bayes's theorem we must have

$$h(x, y \mid P_t^{\mathrm{MA}}, P_t^{\mathrm{MB}}) = p(P_t^{\mathrm{LB}}, P_t^{\mathrm{MA}}, P_t^{\mathrm{MB}})k(x, y \mid P_t^{\mathrm{MA}}, P_t^{\mathrm{MB}}, P_t^{\mathrm{LB}}) + [1 - p(P_t^{\mathrm{LB}}, P_t^{\mathrm{MA}}, P_t^{\mathrm{MB}})]l(x, y \mid P_t^{\mathrm{MA}}, P_t^{\mathrm{MB}}, P_t^{\mathrm{LB}})$$

for all possible values of P_t^{MA}, P_t^{MB}, and P_t^{LB}.

We can now give a formal statement of the model. Given observed market quotes of P_t^{MA} and P_t^{MB} and holdings by the investor of N_t shares of the security and S_t dollars in cash, at time t the investor's expected utility of terminal wealth can be written as $\psi_t = f_t(P_t^{\mathrm{MA}}, P_t^{\mathrm{MB}}, N_t, S_t)$.[3]

We now derive an expression for ψ_t in terms of the various probability assessments and costs. Write $\psi_t = \max(U_1, U_2, U_3)$, where U_1 = expected terminal utility if a market order is placed at time t, U_2 = expected terminal utility if a limit order is placed at time t, and U_3 = expected terminal utility of doing nothing at time t. More precisely, letting x and y be values for the ask and bid prices at time $t + 1$, respectively, we have

$$U_1 = \int_0^\infty \int_0^\infty f_{t+1}(x, y, N_t + \Delta N, S_t - C^M - \Delta N P_t^{\mathrm{MA}}) \cdot h(x, y \mid P_t^{\mathrm{MA}}, P_t^{\mathrm{MB}})\, dx\, dy$$

As stated in Section 5.4, we assume that the number of shares to be purchased, ΔN, is fixed. Define the function

$$\begin{aligned} U_2(P_t^{\mathrm{LB}}) = {} & p(P_t^{\mathrm{LB}}, P_t^{\mathrm{MA}}, P_t^{\mathrm{MB}}) \int_0^\infty \int_0^\infty f_{t+1}(x, y, N_t + \Delta N, \\ & S_t - C^{L1} - C^{L2} - \Delta N\, P_t^{\mathrm{LB}}) \cdot k(x, y \mid P_t^{\mathrm{MA}}, P_t^{\mathrm{MB}}, P_t^{\mathrm{LB}})\, dx\, dy \\ & + [1 - p(P_t^{\mathrm{LB}}, P_t^{\mathrm{MA}}, P_t^{\mathrm{MB}})] \int_0^\infty \int_0^\infty f_{t+1}(x, y, N_t, S_t - C^{L1}) \\ & \cdot l(x, y \mid P_t^{\mathrm{MA}}, P_t^{\mathrm{MB}}, P_t^{\mathrm{LB}})\, dx\, dy \end{aligned}$$

for all positive prices of the limit order. Then we have

$$U_2 = \max_{P_t^{\mathrm{LB}}} U_2(P_t^{\mathrm{LB}})$$

Finally, for the do-nothing option we have

$$U_3 = \int_0^\infty \int_0^\infty f_{t+1}(x, y, N_t, S_t) h(x, y \mid P_t^{\mathrm{MA}}, P_t^{\mathrm{MB}})\, dx\, dy$$

The dynamic programming recursion permits us to obtain a solution for f_t in the order $T - 1, T - 2, \ldots, 2, 1$. This is possible since we assume that the utility value for f_T is known for all values of the parameters P_T^{MA}, P_T^{MB}, N_T, and S_T. We have defined this recursion in terms of the four state variables P_t^{MA}, P_t^{MB}, N_t, and S_t. We also have two decision variables, P_t^{LB}, and the decision as to which of the three courses of action to take.

NOTES

*This is a slightly modified version of the Appendix to K. J. Cohen, S. F. Maier, R. A. Schwartz, and D. K. Whitcomb, "Transaction Costs, Order Placement Strategy, and Existence of the Bid-Ask Spread," *Journal of Political Economy*, Vol. 89, 1981, pp. 287-305.

1. For P_t^{MA} discretely greater than P_t^{LB}, the possibility of another investor submitting a limit order with a price greater than P_t^{LB} will tend only to decrease the probability of execution of the original limit order. Thus our proof of existence of the probability jump at P_t^{MA} is conservative.
2. This proposition would also hold for other stochastic jump processes where the number of price changes is finite in any finite interval.
3. Note that the investor's underlying utility function measures the utility of the wealth he will possess at some horizon T, where $T > t$. The investor will choose those decisions at times $t, t + 1, \ldots, T - 1$ which maximize the expected utility of his terminal wealth. As of time t (the investor's current decision point), viewing the expectations operator as ranging over relevant random variables pertaining to times between t and T, we define ψ_t to be the expected utility of the investor's terminal wealth. Clearly, this depends upon the assets the investor has at time t (N_t and S_t) and the current market prices at which the investor can buy or sell shares (P_t^{MA} and P_t^{MB}).

APPENDIX C

APPENDIX TO CHAPTER 6

Proof of Proposition 1

Because the spread variables $\theta_{j,t,l}$ in Eq. (2) figure in the proof of Proposition 1, we must specify them for all l:[1]

$$\theta_{j,t,0} = \begin{cases} \text{market bid-ask spread (in the returns dimension) at the time of the last transaction} & \text{if there is a transaction in period } t \text{ and the last transaction prior to the end of measurement period } t \text{ executes at the ask} \\ 0 & \text{otherwise} \end{cases}$$

$$\theta_{j,t,l} = -\theta_{j,t,0} \qquad \text{in the first period } (t + l) \text{ following } t \text{ in which a transaction occurs}$$

$$\theta_{j,t,l} = 0 \qquad \text{for all other } l$$

First Term of Eq. (3)

Applying the identity

$$\text{Cov}\,(X, Y) = E[\text{Cov}\,(X, Y \mid \phi)] + \text{Cov}\,[E(X \mid \phi); E(Y \mid \phi)] \tag{C.1}$$

with $\phi = \{\gamma_{j,t,l};$ for all j, t, and $l\}$, we obtain

$$\text{Cov}\left(\sum_{l=0}^{N} \gamma_{j,t-l,l} r_{j,t-l};\ \sum_{m=0}^{N} \gamma_{k,t-n-m,m} r_{k,t-n-m}\right)$$

$$= \sum_{l=0}^{N}\sum_{m=0}^{N} E(\gamma_{j,t-l,l}\gamma_{k,t-n-m,m}) \text{ Cov } (r_{j,t-l};\ r_{k,t-n-m})$$

$$+ \sum_{l=0}^{N}\sum_{m=0}^{N} E(r_{j,t-l})E(r_{k,t-n-m}) \text{ Cov } (\gamma_{j,t-l,l};\ \gamma_{k,t-n-m,m})$$

Now let $k = j$ and observe that by the assumption of the proposition, $r_{j,t}$ and $r_{j,\tau}$ are uncorrelated for all $t \neq \tau$. We also apply assumption A4 of Chapter 6 and for simplicity assume that the process $\gamma_{j,t,l}$ is stationary and drop the t subscript to obtain

$$\text{Var } (r_{j,t}) \sum_{l=0}^{N-n} E(\gamma_{j,l}\gamma_{j,l+n}) + E^2(r_{j,t}) \sum_{l=0}^{N}\sum_{m=0}^{N} \text{Cov } (\gamma_{j,t-l,l};\ \gamma_{j,t-n-m,m}) \tag{C.2}$$

Third Term of Eq. (3)

By assumptions A4 and A6 we obtain

$$\text{Cov}\left(\sum_{l=0}^{N} \gamma_{j,t-l,l} r_{j,t-l};\ \sum_{m=0}^{N} \theta_{j,t-n-m,m}\right) = E(r_{j,t}) \sum_{l=0}^{N}\sum_{m=0}^{N} \text{Cov } (\gamma_{j,t-l,l};\ \theta_{j,t-n-m,m})$$

Fourth Term of Eq. (3)

By assumptions A4 and A6 we obtain

$$\text{Cov}\left(\sum_{l=0}^{N} \theta_{j,t-l,l};\ \sum_{m=0}^{N} \gamma_{j,t-n-m,m} r_{j,t-n-m}\right)$$

$$= E(r_{j,t}) \sum_{l=0}^{N}\sum_{m=0}^{N} \text{Cov } (\gamma_{j,t-n-l,l};\ \theta_{j,t-n-m,m})$$

Details of Proof of Proposition 2

To derive Eq. (5), we use Eq. (3) and recognize that assumptions A3, A5, and A6 imply that we can eliminate all but the first term if Eq. (3). Then recognize that by assumption A1, Cov $(r_{j,t}, r_{k,\tau}) = 0$ for all $t \neq \tau$ and applying Eq. (C.1) as we did in Proposition 1, we obtain

$$\text{Cov } (r^o_{j,t}, r^o_{k,t-n}) = \text{Cov } (r_{j,t}, r_{k,t}) \sum_{l=0}^{N-n} E(\gamma_{j,l}\gamma_{k,l+n})$$

$$+ E(r_{j,t})E(r_{k,t}) \sum_{l=0}^{N}\sum_{m=0}^{N} \text{Cov } (\gamma_{j,t-l,l};\ \gamma_{k,t-n-m,m})$$

Since, by assumption A2, $\gamma_{j,t-l,l}$ and $\gamma_{k,\tau,m}$ are independent for all $j \neq k$, we obtain

$$\text{Cov}\,(r_{j,t}, r_{k,t}) \sum_{l=0}^{N-n} E(\gamma_{j,l})E(\gamma_{k,l+n}) \tag{C.3}$$

If we substitute Eq. (1), we obtain Eq. (5).

Proof to Support Footnote 11 (Serial Correlation in Market Model Residuals)

Let the observed market model residuals be generated in the following way:

1. An observed alpha (α_j^o) and an observed beta (β_j^o) are computed by regressing $r_{j,t}^o$ on $r_{M,t}^o$ $(= \Sigma_k\, x_k r_{k,t}^o)$.
2. The residual is computed by the formula

$$e_{j,t}^o = r_{j,t}^o - \alpha_j^o - \beta_j^o r_{M,t}^o$$

The α_j^o and β_j^o will usually be computed during a measurement period different from that used to compute $e_{j,t}^o$.[2]

The observed covariance function can now be written in terms of the defining equation for $e_{j,t}^o$ with arbitrary lag n as

$$\begin{aligned}\text{Cov}\,(e_{j,t}^o, e_{j,t-n}^o) &= \text{Cov}\,(r_{j,t}^o; r_{j,t-n}^o) + (\beta_j^o)^2\, \text{Cov}\,(r_{M,t}^o; r_{M,t-n}^o)\\ &\quad - \beta_j^o\, \text{Cov}\,(r_{j,t}^o; r_{M,t-n}^o) - \beta_j^o\, \text{Cov}\,(r_{j,t-n}^o; r_{M,t}^o)\end{aligned}$$

which shows that the correlation of market model residuals is related to the correlation of both the security and the market index.

Proof of Proposition 5

From Eq. (C.3) with $n = 0$ (i.e., contemporaneous covariance) we have

$$\text{Cov}\,(r_{j,t}^o, r_{k,t}^o) = \text{Cov}\,(r_{j,t}, r_{k,t}) \sum_{l=0}^{N} E(\gamma_{j,l})E(\gamma_{k,l}) \tag{C.4}$$

We now make use of the structure of Eq. (C.3) to eliminate the expected price-adjustment delays by adding and substracting the cross serial covariances of observed returns, Cov $(r_{j,t}^o, r_{k,t-n}^o)$ and Cov $(r_{j,t-n}^o, r_{k,t}^o)$ using (C.3), for all lags n from 1 to N. Rearranging gives

$$\begin{aligned}\text{Cov}\,(r_{j,t}^o, r_{k,t}^o) &= \text{Cov}\,(r_{j,t}, r_{k,t})\left[\sum_{l=0}^{N} E(\gamma_{j,l}\gamma_{k,l}) + \sum_{n=1}^{N}\sum_{l=0}^{N-n} E(\gamma_{j,l}\gamma_{k,l+n})\right.\\ &\quad \left. + \sum_{n=1}^{N}\sum_{l=0}^{N-n} E(\gamma_{j,l+n}\gamma_{k,l})\right] - \sum_{n=1}^{N} \text{Cov}\,(r_{j,t}^o, r_{k,t-n}^o)\end{aligned}$$

$$- \sum_{n=1}^{N} \text{Cov}\,(r^o_{j,t-n}, r^o_{k,t})$$

$$= \text{Cov}\,(r_{j,t}, r_{k,t}) \sum_{l=0}^{N} E(\gamma_{j,l}) \sum_{m=0}^{N} E(\gamma_{k,m})$$

$$- \sum_{n=1}^{N} \text{Cov}\,(r^o_{j,t}, r^o_{k,t-n}) - \sum_{n=1}^{N} \text{Cov}\,(r^o_{j,t-n}, r^o_{k,t})$$

By assumption A8 that $\Sigma_{l=0}^{N} E(\gamma_{j,l}) = 1$ for all j, we obtain

$$\text{Cov}\,(r_{j,t}, r_{k,t}) - \sum_{n=1}^{N} \text{Cov}\,(r^o_{j,t}, r^o_{k,t-n}) - \sum_{n=1}^{N} \text{Cov}\,(r^o_{j,t-n}, r^o_{k,t})$$

Proof of Proposition 6

To prove Proposition 6, first sum Eq. (8) over all k weighting by x_k to obtain

$$\text{Cov}\,(r^o_{j,t}, r^o_{M,t}) = \text{Cov}\,(r_{j,t}, r_{M,t}) - \sum_{n=1}^{N} \text{Cov}\,(r^o_{j,t}, r^o_{M,t-n}) - \sum_{n=1}^{N} \text{Cov}\,(r^o_{j,t-n}, r^o_{M,t}) \tag{C.5}$$

Next sum Eq. (C.5) over all j weighting by x_j to obtain

$$\text{Var}\,(r^o_{M,t}) = \text{Var}\,(r_{M,t}) - 2 \sum_{n=1}^{N} \text{Cov}\,(r^o_{M,t}, r^o_{M,t-n}) \tag{C.6}$$

where we define

$$\text{Var}\,(r^o_{M,t}) = \sum_j \sum_k x_j x_k \,\text{Cov}\,(r^o_{j,t}, r^o_{k,t})$$

$$\text{Cov}\,(r^o_{M,t}, r^o_{M,t-n}) = \sum_j \sum_k x_j x_k \,\text{Cov}\,(r^o_{j,t}, r^o_{k,t-n})$$

$$\text{Var}\,(r_{M,t}) = \sum_j \sum_k x_j x_k \,\text{Cov}\,(r_{j,t}, r_{k,t})$$

Now, note that by definition the right-hand side of Eq. (9) is equal to

$$\frac{\text{Cov}\,(r_{j,t}, r_{M,t})}{\text{Var}\,(r_{M,t})} \left[1 + 2 \sum_{n=1}^{N} \frac{\text{Cov}\,(r^o_{M,t+n}, r^o_{M,t})}{\text{Var}\,(r^o_{M,t})} \right] - \sum_{n=1}^{N} \frac{\text{Cov}\,(r^o_{j,t+n}, r^o_{M,t}) + \text{Cov}\,(r^o_{j,t-n}, r^o_{M,t})}{\text{Var}\,(r^o_{M,t})}$$

Now by recognizing that our stationarity assumption A1 implies that $\text{Cov}\,(r^o_{j,t}, r^o_{k,t-n}) = \text{Cov}\,(r^o_{j,t+n}, r^o_{k,t})$ and substituting Eqs. (C.5) and (C.6), we obtain

$$\frac{\text{Cov}\,(r_{j,t}, r_{M,t})}{\text{Var}\,(r_{M,t})}\,\frac{\text{Var}\,(r_{M,t})}{\text{Var}\,(r^o_{M,t})} - \frac{\text{Cov}\,(r_{j,t}, r_{M,t}) - \text{Cov}\,(r^o_{j,t}, r^o_{M,t})}{\text{Var}\,(r^o_{M,t})}$$

$$= \frac{\text{Cov}\,(r^o_{j,t}, r^o_{M,t})}{\text{Var}\,(r^o_{M,t})} = \beta^o_j$$

Proof of Proposition 7

The expected delay distribution can be defined for an arbitrary measurement interval of length L in terms of the original expected delay distribution as

$$E[\gamma_{j,t',0}(L)] = \frac{1}{L} \sum_{\tau=t}^{L+t-1} \sum_{l=0}^{L+t-\tau-1} E[\gamma_{j,\tau,l}]$$

and

$$E[\gamma_{j,t',n}(L)] = \frac{1}{L} \sum_{\tau=t}^{L+t-1} \sum_{l=LN+t-\tau}^{L(n+1)+t-\tau-1} E[\gamma_{j,\tau,l}]$$

where t' covers the original time periods from t to $L + t - 1$ (and we restore the time subscript suppressed elsewhere). As $L \to \infty$, by A8, $E[\gamma_{j,t',0}(L)] \to 1$ and $E[\gamma_{j,t',n}(L)] \to 0$ for all $n \geq 1$.

Now, by definition we have, for any L,

$$\beta^o_{j-n}(L) = \frac{\text{Cov}\,(r^o_{j,t'-n}, r^o_{M,t'})}{\text{Var}\,(r^o_{M,t'})}$$

$$= \frac{\sum_k x_k \,\text{Cov}\,(r^o_{j,t'-n}, r^o_{k,t'})}{\sum_j \sum_k x_j x_k \,\text{Cov}\,(r^o_{j,t'}, r^o_{k,t'})}$$

From the proof of Proposition 2, we recall that

$$\text{Cov}\,(r^o_{j,t'-n}, r^o_{k,t'}) = \text{Cov}\,(r_{j,t'}, r_{k,t'}) \sum_{l=0}^{N-n} E(\gamma_{j,t',l+n}) E(\gamma_{k,t',l}) \tag{C.7}$$

$$\text{Cov}\,(r^o_{j,t'}, r^o_{k,t'}) = \text{Cov}\,(r_{j,t'}, r_{k,t'}) \sum_{l=0}^{N} E(\gamma_{j,t',l}) E(\gamma_{k,t',l}) \tag{C.8}$$

Thus, $\beta_{j-n}(L)$ goes to zero for $n \geq 1$ as L increases without bound.

A similar argument shows that $\beta^o_{j+n}(L)$ and $\beta^o_{M+n}(L)$ would also go to zero for $n \geq 1$ as $L \to \infty$. Thus Eq. (9) reduces to $\lim_{L\to\infty} \beta^o_j(L) = \beta_j$ and since $b^o_j(L)$ is just the OLSE of $\beta^o_j(L)$, the proposition follows.

It should be noted that an assumption that the price adjustment begun in period t could be observed indefinitely into the future could be substituted for our assumption of a finite N as long as the price adjustment for lengthy periods was small. For example, if for any $\epsilon > 0$, no matter how small, there exists a k such that $\Sigma_{l=k}^{\infty} E[\gamma_{j,t,l}] < \epsilon$, then a similar proof could be constructed.

Proof of Proposition 8

Take the sum of Eq. (9) over all securities weighted by their participation in the market index. This yields

$$\sum_j x_j\beta_j^o = \left(1 + 2\sum_{n=1}^{N} \beta_{M+n}^o\right)\sum_j x_j\beta_j - \sum_j x_j \sum_{n=1}^{N} (\beta_{j+n}^o + \beta_{j-n}^o)$$

but

$$\sum_j x_j\beta_{j+n}^o = \sum_j x_j \frac{\text{Cov}\,(r_{j,t+n}^o, r_{M,t}^o)}{\text{Var}\,(r_{M,t}^o)} = \beta_{M+n}^o$$

and

$$\sum_j x_j\beta_{j-n}^o = \sum_j x_j \frac{\text{Cov}\,(r_{j,t-n}^o, r_{M,t}^o)}{\text{Var}\,(r_{M,t}^o)} = \beta_{M-n}^o$$

Also recognize that our stationarity assumption on the generation process implies that

$$\beta_{M-n}^o = \beta_{M+n}^o$$

Therefore,

$$\sum_j x_j\beta_j^o = \left(1 + 2\sum_{n=1}^{N} \beta_{M+n}^o\right)\sum_j x_j\beta_j - 2\sum_{n=1}^{N} \beta_{M+n}^o$$

The proposition then follows from the assumed property that $\Sigma_j x_j\beta_j = 1$.

Proof of Proposition 9

By rearranging Eq. (9), it can be shown that

$$\text{if } \frac{1}{2\beta_j}\sum_{n=1}^{N} (\beta_{j+n}^o + \beta_{j-n}^o) \gtreqless \sum_{n=1}^{N} \beta_{M+n}^o \qquad \text{then } \beta_j^o \lesseqgtr \beta_j \tag{C.9}$$

Expanding gives us

$$\sum_{n=1}^{N} (\beta_{j+n}^o + \beta_{j-n}^o) = \frac{1}{\text{Var}\,(r_{M,t}^o)} \sum_{n=1}^{N} [\text{Cov}\,(r_{j,t+n}^o, r_{M,t}^o) + \text{Cov}\,(r_{j,t-n}^o, r_{M,t}^o)]$$

$$= \frac{1}{\text{Var}\,(r_{M,t}^o)} \sum_k x_k \sum_{n=1}^{N} [\text{Cov}\,(r_{j,t+n}^o, r_{k,t}^o) + \text{Cov}\,(r_{j,t-n}^o, r_{k,t}^o)]$$

Then using Eq. (C.2) and the stationarity, we obtain

$$\frac{1}{\text{Var}(r^o_{M,t})} \sum_k x_k \text{ Cov}(r_{j,t}, r_{k,t}) \sum_{n=1}^{N} \sum_{l=0}^{N-n} [E(\gamma_{j,l+n})E(\gamma_{k,l}) + E(\gamma_{j,l})E(\gamma_{k,l+n})]$$

Now using the assumption A8 and $\Sigma_{l=0}^{N} E(\gamma_{j,l}) = 1$ to eliminate $E(\gamma_{j,0})$ from the relationship above and rearranging terms, we obtain

$$\frac{1}{\text{Var}(r^o_{M,t})} \sum_k x_k \text{ Cov}(r_{j,t}, r_{k,t}) \left\{ \sum_{n=1}^{N} E(\gamma_{k,n}) + \sum_{l=1}^{N} E(\gamma_{j,l})[E(\gamma_{k,0}) - E(\gamma_{k,l})] \right\}$$

which, when combined with Eq. (C.9), yields the desired result.

Proof of Proposition 10

Rewriting Eq. (9), we obtain

$$\beta^o_j - \beta_j = 2\,\beta_j \sum_{n=1}^{N} \beta^o_{M+n} - \sum_{n=1}^{N} (\beta^o_{j+n} + \beta^o_{j-n})$$

Expanding the last summation as was done in the proof of Proposition 9, we obtain

$$2\beta_j \sum_{n=1}^{N} \beta^o_{M+n} - \frac{1}{\text{Var}(r^o_{M,t})} \sum_k x_k \text{ Cov}(r_{j,t} r_{k,t}) \left\{ \sum_{n=1}^{N} E(\gamma_{k,t,n}) + \sum_{l=1}^{N} E(\gamma_{j,l})[E(\gamma_{k,0}) - E(\gamma_{k,l})] \right\}$$

Using this expression, we can now state the difference between $\beta^o_j - \beta_j$ and $\beta^o_i - \beta_i$:

$$\beta^o_j - \beta^o_i = -\frac{1}{\text{Var}(r^o_{M,t})} \sum_k x_k \text{ Cov}(r_{j,t}, r_{k,t}) \times \left\{ \sum_{l=1}^{N} [E(\gamma_{j,l}) - E(\gamma_{i,l})][E(\gamma_{k,0}) - E(\gamma_{k,l})] \right\} \quad \text{(C.10)}$$

where all identical terms have been canceled. [*Note:* By assumption, $\beta_i - \beta_j$ and $\text{Cov}(r_{j,t}, r_{k,t}) = \text{Cov}(r_{i,t}, r_{k,t})$ for all k.]

Since we assume that $\text{Cov}(r_{j,t}, r_{k,t})$ is positive for all k, the first half of Eq. (C.10) is obviously negative. If we can show that the term $\{\cdot\}$ is always positive, we will have established our result.

Rewriting $\{\cdot\}$ from Eq. (C.10), we have

$$E(\gamma_{k,0}) \sum_{l=1}^{N} [E(\gamma_{j,l}) - E(\gamma_{i,l})] - \sum_{l=1}^{N} E(\gamma_{k,l})[E(\gamma_{j,l}) - E(\gamma_{i,l})]$$

Substituting the identity $\Sigma_{l=1}^{N} E(\gamma_{j,l}) = 1 - E(\gamma_{j,0})$ for securities i and j in the expression above yields

$$\sum_{l=0}^{N} E(\gamma_{k,l})[E(\gamma_{i,l}) - E(\gamma_{j,l})]$$

which by algebraic manipulation is equal to

$$E(\gamma_{k,0}) \sum_{l=0}^{N} [E(\gamma_{i,l}) - E(\gamma_{j,l})] + \sum_{l=1}^{N} [E(\gamma_{k,l-1}) - E(\gamma_{k,l})] \sum_{n=l}^{N} [E(\gamma_{j,n}) - E(\gamma_{i,n})] \tag{C.11}$$

The first term of this expression is zero since

$$\sum_{l=0}^{N} E(\gamma_{i,l}) = \sum_{l=0}^{N} E(\gamma_{j,l}) = 1$$

By the assumption of the proposition, the left half of the second term is nonnegative for all securities and strictly positive for at least one value of l for each security k. The right half of the second term is positive for all values of l, since security j is assumed to have strictly greater expected price adjustment delay than security i. Thus Eq. (C.11) is positive for all values of k.

NOTES

1. An example is useful to explain our notation. Let $N = 1$, $r_{j,t} = 0$ for all t, and suppose that there is a transaction each period and the bid and ask prices are stable. Letting X represent the last transaction, a possible pattern could be:

Period:	0	1	2	3
Ask:		X	X	
Bid:	X			X

For period 0, we have $\theta_{j,0,0} = 0$; hence from Eq. (2), $r^{o}_{j,0} = 0$. For period 1, we have $\theta_{j,1,0} = S$ (where S is the spread), $\theta_{j,0,1} = -\theta_{j,0,0} = 0$; hence from Eq. (2), $r^{o}_{j,1} = S + 0 = S$. For period 2, we have $\theta_{j,2,0} = S$, $\theta_{j,1,1} = -\theta_{j,1,0} = -S$; and hence $r^{o}_{j,2} = S + (-S) = 0$. Finally, for period 3, $\theta_{j,3,0} = 0$, $\theta_{j,2,1} = -\theta_{j,2,0} = -S$; hence $r^{o}_{j,3} = 0 + (-S) = -S$.

2. α^{o}_{j} and β^{o}_{j} are treated as constants in the defining equation for $e^{o}_{j,t}$.

APPENDIX D

APPENDIX TO CHAPTER 9

D.1 DETAILED EXPLANATIONS FOR ASPECTS OF SIMULATION MODEL

Choice of Order-Size Distributions. The distributions were chosen because their shapes are reasonable in view of how these different classes of investors seek to trade. The negative exponential distribution gives the largest probability to small orders, and the probability decreases monotonically with order size. With the gamma distribution, the probability of order size is low for small orders, increases rapidly to a unique mode, and then decreases less rapidly with order size, such that the probability distribution of order size is skewed to the right.

Use and Parameterization of Yawl Distribution. The yawl distribution, depicted in Figure D.1, operates as follows. For simplicity, consider only the generation of sell orders (the mirror image distribution underlies the generation of buy orders). Each draw from the distribution is a (logarithmic) returns-dimensioned random variable x; this is translated into price (P) of the associated order using the relationship $P = P^{\mathrm{MB}} \exp(x)$ (where P^{MB} is the current market bid quotation). A draw of $x \leq 0$ is a market order that triggers a trade at a price of P^{MB}, while $x > 0$ causes a new limit order to be entered on the book at the appropriate price.[1]

The yawl distribution is parameterized so as to satisfy the following considerations: (1) in line with our model of Chapter 5, we keep the point of zero mass at the market bid, and the peak of the right-hand (limit-order) triangle over the

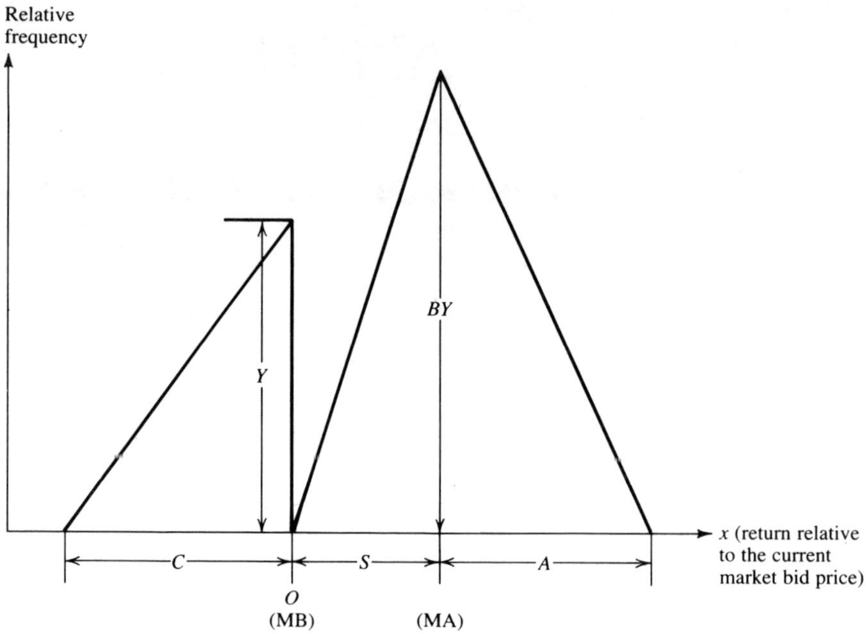

Figure D.1 Yawe distribution used to generate limit ask prices.

market ask, (2) the bid-ask spread can freely vary with the arrival of new orders, and (3) the area of the distribution equals unity.[2]

Simulation Mode. The simulation is run in a critical event (rather than a master clock) mode. A block diagram of the program structure for one complete simulation run is shown in Figure D.2. The simulation results reported here are based on 1000 trading days that follow an initial 30-day warm-up period which allows the limit-order book to be established. The probability distributions used remain constant throughout the simulation, implying that there are no special beginning-of-day, end-of-day, and so on, effects.

Preventing Empty Limit-Order Book. Because a clearing out of the limit-order book on one side or the other would be unrealistic in actuality and would cause erratic and unrealistic behavior in the simulation, we prevented this from occurring by adopting the following mechanism. If either side of the book would empty due to the execution or expiration of the last remaining public limit order, we allow the order to execute or expire, but replace it with an identical order. In the runs reported in this paper, this mechanism is used rarely.

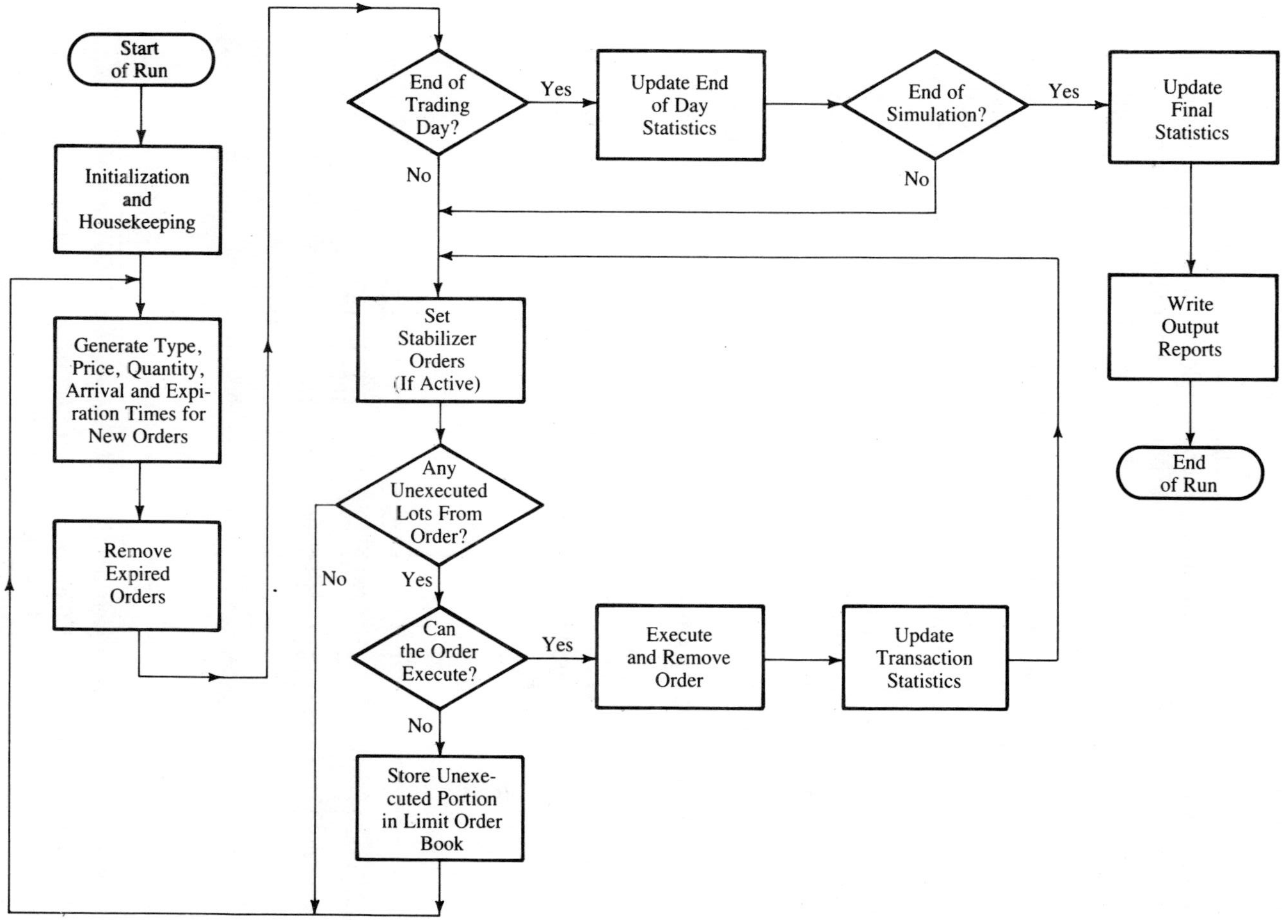

Figure D.2 Program structure for a simulation run.

D.2 COMPARISON WITH MODEL AND RESULTS OF CMSW (1978b)

In our previous simulation [CMSW (1978b)], we used a more primitive approach, in which the peak of the limit-order triangle of the yawl distribution was kept a fixed distance (0.01) away from the point of zero frequency, and hence did not in general coincide with a market quote, nor did it reflect an endogenously determined spread.

Comparing the results shown in Table 1 (Chapter 9) for the pure market with the results we previously reported for the corresponding parameter values, we find that the first-order serial correlation coefficients were more strongly negative in CMSW (1978b). The major difference between these two sets of results is that the earlier model treated an atomistic market where all trades were for only 100 shares at a time, whereas in the present model there is a distribution of order sizes. As expected, mixing both large and small orders tends to introduce positive components of serial correlation into the data (a large market order executing against a sequence of differently priced smaller limit orders causes a run of identically signed priced changes).

D.3 ILLUSTRATIVE EXAMPLES

Example 1: Sequential Execution of Large Limit Order

The limit-order book near the market quotes is shown below. (*Note*: Prices are shown in eighths for the reader's convenience, although the simulation uses prices in mills.)

	Price	Number of Shares	
	⋮	⋮	
	76	600	Sell (ask) orders
	$75\frac{1}{2}$	300	
	$75\frac{3}{8}$	100	
MA	$75\frac{1}{4}$	200	
MA	75	100	Buy (bid) orders
	$74\frac{7}{8}$	800	
	$74\frac{3}{4}$	200	
	⋮	⋮	

Buy limit order arrives: 900 at $75\frac{5}{8}$

Transaction sequence: 200 at $75\frac{1}{4}$
100 at $75\frac{3}{8}$
300 at $75\frac{1}{2}$

Remaining 300 shares of order enter limit-order book at $75\frac{5}{8}$

New quotes: MB = $75\frac{5}{8}$ (300 shares), MA = 76 (600 shares)

Example 2: Execution of Small Limit Order

Same beginning limit-order book as Example 1

Sell limit order arrives: 200 at $74\frac{7}{8}$

Transaction sequence: 100 at 75
100 at $74\frac{7}{8}$

New quotes: MB = $74\frac{7}{8}$ (700 shares), MA = $75\frac{1}{4}$ (200 shares)

Example 3: Stabilizer Intervention on Both Sides of Limit-Order Book

Intervention rule: If inventory limits permit, enter one round-lot order(s) inside quotes to prevent excessive price change (parameter).

Maximum allowable price change: $\frac{3}{8}$

Last transaction: $80\frac{1}{8}$

Quotes (public): $79\frac{1}{2}$-$80\frac{5}{8}$

Possible transaction sequences: MB: $80\frac{5}{8}$; price change = $\frac{1}{2}$
MA: $79\frac{1}{2}$; price change = $\frac{5}{8}$

Stabilizer enters: $79\frac{3}{4}$ (100 shares)–$80\frac{1}{2}$ (100 shares)

Example 4: Stabilizer Intervenes Only When Necessary

Maximum allowable price change: $\frac{3}{8}$

Last transaction: $80\frac{1}{8}$

Quotes (public) 80–$80\frac{5}{8}$

Stabilizer enters: ask $80\frac{1}{2}$ (100 shares)

Example 5: When Stabilizer Does and Does Not Intervene

Maximum allowable price change: $\frac{3}{8}$

Last transaction: $82\frac{3}{8}$

Quotes (public): $82\frac{3}{8}$ (100 shares)–$83\frac{5}{8}$ (300 shares)

Stabilizer enters: Ask $82\frac{3}{4}$ (100 shares)

Public buy limit order arrives: 500 at $83\frac{3}{4}$

Transaction sequence (seller) and stabilizer action:
100 shares (stabilizer) at $82\frac{3}{4}$
Stabilizer enters: ask $83\frac{1}{8}$ (100 shares)
100 shares (stabilizer) at $83\frac{1}{8}$
Stabilizer enters: bid $82\frac{3}{4}$ (100 shares); ask $83\frac{1}{2}$ (100 shares)
100 shares (stabilizer) at $83\frac{1}{2}$
Stabilizer enters: bid $83\frac{1}{8}$ (100 shares)
200 shares (public) at $83\frac{5}{8}$
Stabilizer enters: bid $83\frac{1}{4}$ (100 shares)

New quotes: bid $83\frac{1}{4}$ (100 shares); ask $83\frac{5}{8}$ (100 shares)

Example 6: Stabilizer Yields Time Priority

Same as Example 3 (stabilizer quotes $79\frac{3}{4}$–$80\frac{1}{2}$)

Public sell limit order arrives: 100 at $80\frac{1}{2}$

Stabilizer withdraws his sell limit order.

Example 7: Operation of Speculating Stabilizer

Maximum allowable price change: $\frac{3}{8}$

Last transaction: $53\frac{1}{2}$

Quotes (public): $53\frac{1}{8}$ (100 shares)–$53\frac{3}{4}$ (100 shares)

Speculating stabilizer predicts price is likely to rise, is not at inventory limit.

Speculating stabilizer enters: bid 100 at $53\frac{1}{4}$ if eighths (53.126 if mills)

If speculating stabilizer's order is crossed, he replaces it at same price (tick test prevents higher) until his inventory limit is exhausted or until an equal or higher-priced public bid enters.

Example 8: Limitations on Speculating Stabilizer Activities

Same as Example 7, but market bid is $53\frac{1}{2}$

No speculating stabilizer order (tick test prevents)

NOTES

1. Strictly speaking, this discussion in the case of $x \le 0$ applies only to sell orders for one round lot. When the sell order is for more than one round lot and $x \le 0$, then the following happens. Let n = the number of shares in the sell order, and let m = the number of shares sought at the current market bid price of P^{MB}. (1) If $n \le m$, then all n shares of the sell order are a market order which trades at P^{MB}. (2) If $n > m$, then m shares of the sell order are a market order which trades at P^{MB}, and the remaining $n - m$ shares become a new sell order at its previously assigned limit ask price P^{LA}; if P^{LA} is greater than the new market bid price, then the $n - m$ shares enter the limit-order book as a limit sell at P^{LA}; otherwise, the above analysis is repeated, and part or all of the $n - m$ shares will trade at the new market bid price. Thus if the size of the incoming (market) order is relatively large, so that it cannot fully execute at prices equal to or better than the designated price on that order, then the balance of that order is considered to be a limit order and is entered on the book.
2. These considerations are satisfied by setting values for only three parameters: A, the base length of the limit-order triangle to the right of the market ask; B, the height of the limit-order triangle relative to the height of the market-order triangle; and C, the base length of the market-order triangle. Two additional dimensions of the triangles shown in Figure D.1 are determined in the simulation. They are: S, the percentage spread, which establishes the base length of the portion of the limit-order triangle to the left of the market ask; and Y, which gives the actual height of the market-order (and hence also the limit-order) triangle. In each simulation run, values are assigned to the parameters A, B, and C, while S varies in accordance with the arrival of new orders, and Y varies automatically so as to ensure that the area of the yawl distribution remains unity. In the runs reported here, we assigned the following values to the yawl distribution input parameters: $A = 2.0$, $B = 1.0$, and $C = 3.0$.

REFERENCES

ALLEN, D. M., 1974. "The Relationship between Variable Selection and Data Augmentation and a Method for Prediction," *Technometrics*, 16, 124–127.

ALLEN, D. M., and F. B. CADY, 1982. *Analyzing Experimental Data by Regression*. New York: Von Nostrand Reinhold.

ALTMAN, E. I., B. JACQUILLAT, and M. LEVASSEUR, 1974. "Comparative Analysis of Risk Measures: France and the United States," *Journal of Finance*, 29, 1495–1511.

AMIHUD, Y., and H. MENDELSON, 1980. "Dealership Market: Market-Making with Inventory," *Journal of Financial Economics*, 8, 31–53.

AMIHUD, Y., and H. MENDELSON, 1985. "An Integrated Computerized Trading System," in Amihud-Ho-Schwartz (1985).

AMIHUD, Y., T. HO, and R. SCHWARTZ, eds., 1985. *Market Making and the Changing Structure of the Securities Industry*. Lexington, Mass.: Lexington Books.

BAGEHOT, W., 1971. "The Only Game in Town," *Financial Analysts Journal*, 27 (March–April), 12–14, 22.

BANZ, R. W., 1981. "The Relationship between Return and Market Value of Common Stocks," *Journal of Financial Economics*, 9, 3–18.

BARNEA, A., 1974. "Performance Evaluation of New York Stock Exchange Specialists," *Journal of Financial and Quantitative Analysis*, 9, 511–535.

BARNEA, A., 1976. "Reply: Specialists' Performance and Serial Dependence of Stock Price Change," *Journal of Financial and Quantitative Analysis*, 11, 909–911.

BARNEA, A., and D. E. LOGUE, 1975. "The Effect of Risk on the Market Maker's Spread," *Financial Analysts Journal*, 31 (November–December), 45–49.

BASU, S., 1977. "Investment Performance of Common Stocks in Relation to Their P/E Ratios," *Journal of Finance*, 32, 663–682.

Baumol, W., 1965. *The Stock Market and Economic Efficiency*. New York: Fordham University Press.

Beaver, W. L., P. Kettler, and M. S. Scholes, 1970. "The Association between Market Determined and Accounting Determined Risk Measures," *Accounting Review*, 45, 654–682.

Beaver, W. L., and J. Manegold, 1975. "The Association between Market-Determined and Accounting-Determined Measures of Systematic Risk: Some Further Evidence," *Journal of Financial and Quantitative Analysis*, 10, 231–284.

Beja, A., and M. B. Goldman, 1980. "On the Dynamic Behavior of Prices in Disequilibrium," *Journal of Finance*, 35, 235–248.

Beja, A., and N. H. Hakansson, 1977. "Dynamic Market Processes and the Rewards to Up-to-Date Information," *Journal of Finance*, 32, 291–304.

Beja, A., and N. H. Hakansson, 1979. "From Orders to Trades: Some Alternative Market Mechanisms," Chap. 7 in Bloch-Schwartz (1979).

Benston, G. J., and R. L. Hagerman, 1974. "Determinants of Bid-Asked Spreads in the Over-the-Counter Market," *Journal of Financial Economics*, 1, 353–364.

Ben-Zion, U., and S. S. Shalit, 1975. "Size, Leverage, and Dividend Record as Determinants of Equity Risk," *Journal of Finance*, 30, 1015–1026.

Bierwag, G. O., and M. A. Grove, 1968. "Slutsky Equations for Assets," *Journal of Political Economy*, 76, 114–127.

Black, F., 1971. "Toward a Fully Automated Stock Exchange," *Financial Analysts Journal*, 27, Part I (July–August), 28–35, 44; Part II (November–December), 24–28, 86–87.

Black, F., 1972. "Capital Market Equilibrium with Restricted Borrowing," *Journal of Business*, 45, 444–455.

Bloch, E., and R. A. Schwartz, 1978a. "The Battle over Rule 390," *Wall Street Journal*, September 11 (editorial page).

Bloch, E., and R. A. Schwartz, 1978b. "The Great Debate over NYSE Rule 390," *Journal of Portfolio Management*, 5, 5–8.

Bloch, E., and R. A. Schwartz, eds., 1979. *Impending Changes for Securities Markets: What Role for the Exchanges?* Greenwich, Conn.: JAI Press.

Blume, M. E., and F. Husic, 1973. "Price, Beta, and Exchange Listing," *Journal of Finance*, 28, 283–299.

Bradfield, J., 1980. "Optimal Dynamic Behavior of a Market-Maker in Choosing Bid and Asked Prices," Working Paper, Hamilton College.

Branch, B., and W. Freed, 1977. "Bid-Asked Spreads on the Amex and the Big Board," *Journal of Finance*, 32, 159–163.

Brown, P., A. W. Kleidon, and T. A. Marsh, 1983, "New Evidence on the Nature of Size-Related Anomolies in Stock Prices," *Journal of Financial Economics*, 12, 33–56.

Clendenin, J. E., 1951. "Quality versus Price as Factors Influencing Common Stock Price Fluctuations," *Journal of Finance*, 6, 398–405.

Cohen, K. J., and R. M. Conroy, 1985. "An Empirical Study of the Impact of Rule 19c-3," Working Paper, Duke University.

COHEN, K. J., R. CONROY, and S. F. MAIER, 1985. "Order Flow and the Quality of the Market," in Amihud-Ho-Schwartz (1985).

COHEN, K. J., G. A. HAWAWINI, S. F. MAIER, R. A. SCHWARTZ, and D. K. WHITCOMB, 1980. "Implications of Microstructure Theory for Empirical Research on Stock Price Behavior," *Journal of Finance*, 35, 249–257.

COHEN, K. J., G. A. HAWAWINI, S. F. MAIER, R. A. SCHWARTZ, and D. K. WHITCOMB, 1983a. "Estimating and Adjusting for the Intervalling-Effect Bias in Beta," *Management Science*, 29, 135–148.

COHEN, K. J., G. A. HAWAWINI, S. F. MAIER, R. A. SCHWARTZ, and D. K. WHITCOMB, 1983b. "Friction in the Trading Process and the Estimation of Systematic Risk," *Journal of Financial Economics*, 12, 263–278.

COHEN, K. J., S. F. MAIER, W. L. NESS, JR., H. OKUDA, R. A. SCHWARTZ, and D. K. WHITCOMB, 1977. "The Impact of Designated Market Makers on Security Prices: I. Empirical Evidence," *Journal of Banking and Finance*, 1, 219–235.

COHEN, K. J., S. F. MAIER, R. A. SCHWARTZ, and D. K. WHITCOMB, 1977. "The Impact of Designated Market Makers on Security Prices: II. Policy Proposals," *Journal of Banking and Finance*, 1, 236–247.

COHEN, K. J., S. F. MAIER, R. A. SCHWARTZ, and D. K. WHITCOMB, 1978a. "The Returns Generation Process, Returns Variance, and the Effect of Thinness in Securities Markets," *Journal of Finance*, 33, 149–167.

COHEN, K. J., S. F. MAIER, R. A. SCHWARTZ, and D. K. WHITCOMB, 1978b. "Limit Orders, Market Structure, and the Returns Generation Process," *Journal of Finance*, 33, 723–736.

COHEN, K. J., S. F. MAIER, R. A. SCHWARTZ, and D. K. WHITCOMB, 1979a. "Market Makers and the Market Spread: A Review of Recent Literature," *Journal of Financial and Quantitative Analysis*, 14, 813–835.

COHEN, K. J., S. F. MAIER, R. A. SCHWARTZ, and D. K. WHITCOMB, 1979b. "On the Existence of Serial Correlation in an Efficient Securities Market," *TIMS Studies in the Management Sciences*, 11, 151–168.

COHEN, K. J., S. F. MAIER, R. A. SCHWARTZ, and D. K. WHITCOMB, 1981. "Transaction Costs, Order Placement Strategy, and Existence of the Bid-Ask Spread," *Journal of Political Economy*, 89, 287–305.

COHEN, K. J., S. F. MAIER, R. A. SCHWARTZ, and D. K. WHITCOMB, 1982. "An Analysis of the Economic Justification for Consolidation in a Secondary Security Market," *Journal of Banking and Finance*, 6, 117–136.

COHEN, K. J., S. F. MAIER, R. A. SCHWARTZ, and D. K. WHITCOMB, 1983. "A Simulation Model of Stock Exchange Trading," *Simulation*, 41, 181–191.

COHEN, K. J., W. L. NESS, JR., H. OKUDA, R. A. SCHWARTZ, and D. K. WHITCOMB, 1976. "The Determinants of Common Stock Returns Volatility: An International Comparison," *Journal of Finance*, 31, 733–740.

CONROY, R. M., and R. L. WINKLER, 1981. "Informational Differences between Limit and Market Orders for a Market Maker," *Journal of Financial and Quantitative Analysis*, 16, 703–724.

CONROY, R. M., and R. L. WINKLER, 1985. "Market Structure: The Specialist as Dealer and Broker," *Journal of Banking and Finance*, forthcoming.

COPELAND, T. E., 1976. "A Model of Asset Trading under the Assumption of Sequential Information Arrival," *Journal of Finance*, 31, 1149–1168.

COPELAND, T. E., and D. GALAI, 1983. "Information Effects on the Bid-Ask Spread," *Journal of Finance*, 38, 1457–1469.

COPELAND, T. E., and J. F. WESTON, 1979. *Financial Theory and Corporate Policy*, Reading, Mass.: Addison-Wesley.

CRAMER, J. S., 1957. "A Dynamic Approach to the Theory of Demand," *Review of Economic Studies*, 24, 73–86.

DAVANT, J. W., 1979. "Davant on the Davant Report: The NYSE Looks at the Central Market System," Chap. 4 in Bloch-Schwartz (1979).

DAVIS, J. L., 1985. "The Intermarket Trading System and the Cincinnati Experiment," in Amihud-Ho-Schwartz (1985).

DEMSETZ, H., 1968. "The Cost of Transacting," *Quarterly Journal of Economics*, 82, 33–53.

DIMSON, E., 1979. "Risk Measurement When Shares Are Subject to Infrequent Trading," *Journal of Financial Economics*, 7, 197–226.

EPPS, T. W., 1975. "Wealth Effects and Slutsky Equations for Assets," *Econometrica*, 43, 301–303.

FALK, R., 1985. "Upstairs Trading in Securities Markets," in Amihud-Ho-Schwartz (1985).

FAMA, E. F., 1970. "Efficient Capital Markets: A Review of Theory and Empirical Work," *Journal of Finance*, 25, 383–417.

FAMA, E. F., 1976. *Foundations of Finance*. New York: Basic Books.

FAMA, E., and J. D. MACBETH, 1973. "Risk, Return and Equilibrium: Empirical Tests," *Journal of Political Economy*, 71, 607–636.

FARRAR, D. E., 1971. "Wall Street's Proposed 'Great Leap Backward'," *Financial Analysts Journal*, 27 (September-October), 14–16, 59–62.

FELLER, W., 1971. *An Introduction to Probability Theory and Its Applications*, Vol. II, 2nd ed. New York: Wiley.

FEUERSTEIN, D. M., 1972. "Toward a National System of Securities Exchanges," *Financial Analysts Journal*, 28 (May-June), 28–34, 90–91.

FISHER, L., 1966. "Some New Stock Market Indexes," *Journal of Business*, 39, 191–225.

FISHER, L., and J. KAMIN, 1985. "Forecasting Systematic Risk: Estimates of 'Raw' Beta That Take Account of the Tendency of Beta to Change and Heteroskedasticity of Residual Returns," *Journal of Financial and Quantitative Analysis*, 20, forthcoming.

FISHER, S., 1972. "Assets, Contingent Commodities, and the Slutsky Equations," *Econometrica*, 40, 371–385.

FORTE, A. J., 1976. "Profitability of Listed Securities," American Stock Exchange Memorandum.

FOWLER, D. J., and C. H. RORKE, 1983. "Risk Measurement When Shares Are Subject to Infrequent Trading: Comment," *Journal of Financial Economics*, 12, 279–284.

Fowler, D. J., C. H. Rorke, and V. M. Jog, 1984. "A Bias Correcting Procedure for Beta Estimation in the Presence of Thin Trading," Working Paper, Faculty of Management, McGill University.

Francis, J. C., 1975. "Intertemporal Differences in Systematic Stock Price Movements," *Journal of Financial and Quantitative Analysis*, 10, 205-220.

Franks, J. R., J. E. Broyles, and M. J. Hecht, 1977. "An Industry Study of the Profitability of Mergers in the United Kingdom," *Journal of Finance*, 32, 1513-1525.

French, K. R., 1980. "Stock Returns and the Weekend Effect," *Journal of Financial Economics*, 8, 55-69.

French, K. R., and R. Roll, 1985. "Stock Return Variances: The Arrival of Information and the Reaction of Traders," Working Paper, University of California, Los Angeles.

Friedman, D., G. W. Harrison, and H. W. Salmon, 1984. "The Informational Efficiency of Experimental Asset Markets," *Journal of Political Economy*, 92, 349-408.

Friedman, M., and R. V. Roosa, 1967. *The Balance of Payments: Free versus Fixed Exchange Rates*. Washington, D.C.: American Enterprise Institute.

Friend, I., 1979. "Implications of the Growth in Institutionalization of the Stock Market," Chap. 8 in Bloch-Schwartz (1979).

Fung, W. K. H., 1981. "The Empirical Properties of Alternative Procedures for Estimating Betas with Nonsynchronous Data," Working Paper, Rutgers University.

Fung, W. K. H., R. A. Schwartz, and D. K. Whitcomb, 1985. "Testing Alternative Adjustment Procedures for the Intervalling-Effect Bias in Beta Estimates Using Paris Bourse Data," *Journal of Banking and Finance*, 9, 443-460.

Galai, D., and R. Masulis, 1976. "The Option Pricing Model and the Risk Factor of Stock," *Journal of Financial Economics*, 3, 53-82.

Garbade, K. D., 1982. *Securities Markets*. New York: McGraw-Hill.

Garbade, K. D., and C. P. Sekaran, 1981. "Opening Prices on the New York Stock Exchange," *Journal of Banking and Finance*, 5, 345-355.

Garbade, K. D., and W. L. Silber, 1976. "Price Dispersion in the Government Securities Market," *Journal of Political Economy*, 84, 721-740.

Garbade, K. D., and W. L. Silber, 1979a. "Structural Organization of Secondary Markets: Clearing Frequency, Dealer Activity and Liquidity Risk," *Journal of Finance*, 34, 577-593.

Garbade, K. D., and W. L. Silver, 1979b. "Dominant and Satellite Markets: A Study of Dually-Traded Securities," *Review of Economics and Statistics*, 61, 455-460.

Garman, M. B., 1976. "Market Microstructure," *Journal of Financial Economics*, 3, 257-275.

Glosten, L. R., 1981. "Return to Information in a 'Market Microstructure' Model of Price Formation," Working Paper, Northwestern University.

Goldman, M. B., and A. Beja, 1979. "Market Prices vs. Equilibrium Prices: Returns Variance, Serial Correlation and the Role of the Specialist," *Journal of Finance*, 34, 595-607.

Goldman, M. B., and H. B. Sosin, 1979. "Information Dissemination, Market Efficiency and the Frequency of Transactions," *Journal of Financial Economics*, 7, 29-61.

GROSSMAN, S. J., and J. E. STIGLITZ, 1976. "Information and Competitive Price Systems," *American Economic Review*, 66, 246–253.

HAKANSSON, N. H., A. BEJA, and J. KALE, 1985. "On the Feasibility of Automated Market Making by a Programmed Specialist," *Journal of Finance*, 40, 1–20.

HAMADA, R. S., 1969. "Portfolio Analysis, Market Equilibrium and Corporation Finance," *Journal of Finance*, 24, 13–32.

HAMILTON, J. L., 1976. "Competition, Scale Economies, and Transaction Cost in the Stock Market," *Journal of Financial and Quantitative Analysis*, 11, 779–802.

HAMILTON, J. L., 1978. "Marketplace Organization and Marketability: NASDAQ, the Stock Exchange, and the National Market System," *Journal of Finance*, 33, 487–503.

HAMILTON, L., 1979. "Marketplace Fragmentation, Competition, and the Efficiency of the Stock Exchange," *Journal of Finance*, 34, 171–187.

HAUGEN, R. A., 1970. "Expected Growth, Required Return, and the Variability of Stock Prices," *Journal of Financial and Quantitative Analysis*, 5, 297–307.

HAWAWINI, G. A., 1977. "On the Time Behavior of Financial Parameters: An Investigation of the Intervaling Effect," Ph.D. dissertation, New York University.

HAWAWINI, G. A., 1980. "Intertemporal Cross Dependence in Securities' Daily Returns and the Short-Run Intervaling Effect on Systematic Risk," *Journal of Financial and Quantitative Analysis*, 15, 139–150.

HAWAWINI, G. A., and A. VORA, 1980. "Evidence of Intertemporal Systematic Risks in the Daily Price Movements of NYSE and AMEX Common Stocks," *Journal of Financial and Quantitative Analysis*, 15, 331–339.

HEINS, A. J., and S. L. ALLISON, 1966. "Some Factors Affecting Stock Price Variability," *Journal of Business*, 39, 19–23.

HIRSHLEIFER, J., 1971. "Reflections on the Role and Functioning of the Organized Exchanges," The RAND Corporation, Paper P-4666.

HO, T., and R. G. MACRIS, 1985. "Dealer Market Structure and Performance," in Amihud-Ho-Schwartz (1985).

HO, T., R. A. SCHWARTZ, and D. K. WHITCOMB, 1981. *A Comparative Analysis of Alternative Security Market Trading Arrangements*, New York Stock Exchange Research Report.

HO, T., R. A. SCHWARTZ, and D. K. WHITCOMB, 1985. "The Trading Decision and Market Clearing under Transaction Price Uncertainty," *Journal of Finance*, 40, 21–42.

HO, T., and H. R. STOLL, 1980. "On Dealer Markets under Competition," *Journal of Finance*, 35, 259–267.

HO, T., and H. R. STOLL, 1981. "Optimal Dealer Pricing under Transactions and Return Uncertainty," *Journal of Financial Economics*, 9, 47–73.

HO, T., and H. R. STOLL, 1983. "The Dynamics of Dealer Markets under Competition," *Journal of Finance*, 38.

IBBOTSON, R. G., 1975, "Price Performance of Common Stock New Issues," *Journal of Financial Economics*, 2, 235–272.

IBBOTSON, R., and R. SINQUEFIELD, 1982. *Stocks, Bonds, Bills and Inflation: The Past and the Future*, Financial Analysts Research Foundation Monograph No. 15, Charlottesville, Va.

JENNINGS, R. H., L. T. STARKS, and J. C. FELLINGHAM, 1981. "An Equilibrium Model of Asset Trading with Sequential Information Arrival," *Journal of Finance*, 36, 143-161.

KAHN, C. M., 1982, "Market Microstructure and Rational Expectations," Working Paper, University of Chicago Graduate School of Business.

KARLIN, S., 1968. *A First Course in Stochastic Processes*, 2nd ed., enl. New York: Academic Press.

KEIM, D. B., 1983. "Size-Related Anomolies and Stock Market Seasonality: Further Empirical Evidence," *Journal of Financial Economics*, 12, 13-32.

KLEMKOSKY, R. C., and J. W. PETTY, 1973. "A Multivariate Analysis of Stock Price Variability," *Journal of Business Research*, 1, 1-10.

KOLTON, P., 1979. "Discussion," pp. 107-110 in Bloch-Schwartz (1979).

LACHENBRUCH, P. A., 1967. "An Almost Unbiased Method of Obtaining Confidence Intervals for the Probability of Misclassification in Discriminant Analysis," *Biometrics*, 23, 639-645.

LACHENBRUCH, P. A., and M. R. MICKEY, 1968. "Estimation of Error Rates in Discriminant Analysis," *Technometrics*, 10, 1-11.

LANCASTER, K. J., 1966. "A New Approach to Consumer Theory," *Journal of Political Economy*, 74, 132-157.

LEVINE, M., 1974. *Institutional Activity and Liquidity on the New York Stock Exchange, 1869-1973*, Research Department, New York Stock Exchange.

LOGUE, D. E., 1975. "Market Making and the Assessment of Market Efficiency," *Journal of Finance*, 30, 115-123.

MCINISH, T. H., and R. A. WOOD, 1985a. "Adjusting for Beta Bias: An Assessment of Alternate Techniques," Working Paper, Pennsylvania State University.

MCINISH, T. H., and R. A. WOOD, 1985b. "Intertemporal Differences in Movements of Minute-to-Minute Stock Returns," *Financial Review*, forthcoming.

MARSH, P. R., 1979. "Equity Rights Issues and the Efficiency of the UK Stock Market," *Journal of Finance*, 34, 839-862.

MENDELSON, H., 1984. "Consolidation, Fragmentation and Market Liquidity," presented at the Conference on Trading Mechanisms in Securities Exchanges: Towards the Era of Sophisticated Automation, Tel Aviv, Israel, January 30-31.

MENDELSON, M., 1972. *From Automated Quotes to Automated Trading*, Bulletin Nos. 80-82, NYU Graduate School of Business Administration, Institute of Finance.

MENDELSON, M., J. W. PEAKE, and R. T. WILLIAMS, JR., 1979. "Toward a Modern Exchange: The Peake-Mendelson-Williams Proposal for an Electronically Assisted Auction Market," Chap. 3 in Bloch-Schwartz (1979).

MERTON, R. C., 1973. "An Intertemporal Capital Asset Pricing Model," *Econometrica*, 41, 867-887.

MILDENSTEIN, E., and H. J. SCHLEEF, 1983. "The Optimal Pricing Policy of a Monopolistic Marketmaker in the Equity Market," *Journal of Finance*, 38, 218-231.

MOSSIN, J., 1972. *Security Pricing Theory and Its Implications for Corporate Investment Decisions*. Morristown, N.J.: General Learning Press.

NEW YORK STOCK EXCHANGE, 1976. *Report of the Committee to Study the Stock Allocation System.*

New York Stock Exchange, 1982a. *Constitution and Rules*. Chicago: Commerce Clearing House.

New York Stock Exchange, September 23, 1982b. "Supplementary NYSE Comments: Monitoring of the Operation of Rule 19c-3," submitted to the SEC.

New York Stock Exchange, October 15, 1982c. "Supplementary NYSE Comments: Summary and Rebuttal," submitted to the SEC.

Ng, K. W., 1981. "Theoretical and Empirical Evaluation of Alternative Procedures for Estimating Betas on Nonsynchronous Data," Master's thesis, University of Manchester Institute of Science and Technology.

Oldfield, G. S., Jr., and R. J. Rogalski, 1980. "A Theory of Common Stock Returns over Trading and Non-trading Periods," *Journal of Finance*, 35, 729–751.

Oldfield, G. S., Jr., R. J. Rogalski, and R. A. Jarrow, 1977. "An Autoregressive Jump Process for Common Stock Returns," *Journal of Financial Economics*, 5, 389–418.

Ord, J. K., T. H. McInish, and R. A. Wood, 1984. "Trade-to-Trade Beta Estimation: Methodology and Deficiencies," Working Paper, Pennsylvania State University.

Palamara, F. J., 1979. "Discussion," pp. 104–107 in Bloch-Schwartz (1979).

Parzen, E., 1962. *Stochastic Processes*. San Francisco: Holden-Day.

Pazner, E. A., and A. Razin, 1974. "Welfare Aspects of Exchange Rate Uncertainty," *Economica*, 41, 256–268.

Pettit, R. R., and R. Westerfield, 1972. "A Model of Market Risk," *Journal of Financial and Quantitative Analysis*, 7, 1649–1668.

Pierce, B. O., and R. M. Foster, 1956. *A Short Table of Integrals*, 4th ed. Boston: Ginn.

Pogue, G. A., and B. H. Solnik, 1974. "The Market Model Applied to European Common Stocks: Some Empirical Results," *Journal of Financial and Quantitative Analysis*, 9, 917–944.

Reinganum, M. R., 1981. "Misspecification of Capital Asset Pricing: Empirical Anomalies Based on Earnings Yields and Market Values," *Journal of Financial Economics*, 9, 19–46.

Roll, R., 1981. "A Possible Explanation of the Small Firm Effect," *Journal of Finance*, 36, 879–888.

Royama, S., and K. Hamada, 1967. "Substitution and Complementarity in the Choice of Risky Assets," in *Risk Aversion and Portfolio Choice*, edited by D. Hester and J. Tobin, Cowles Foundation Monograph 19. New York: Wiley, pp. 27–40.

Sametz, A. W., 1979. "A Modest Proposal toward a National Market System—From CLUB to CLOB," Chap. 5 in Bloch and Schwartz (1979).

Samuelson, P. A., 1972. "The Consumer Does Benefit from Feasible Price Stability—Rejoinder," *Quarterly Journal of Economics*, 86, 476–493.

Saniga, E. M., T. H. McInish, and B. K. Gouldey, 1981. "The Effect of Differencing Interval Length on Beta," *Journal of Financial Research*, 4, 129–135.

Santomero, A. M., 1974. "The Economic Effects of NASDAQ: Some Preliminary Results," *Journal of Financial and Quantitative Analysis*, 9, 13–24.

Schmidt, H., 1977. "Advantages and Disadvantages of an Integrated Market Compared with a Fragmented Market," Commission of the European Communities, Approximation of Legislation Series.

SCHOLES, M. S., 1972. "The Market for Securities: Substitution versus Price Pressure and the Effects of Information on Share Prices," *Journal of Business*, 45, 179–211.

SCHOLES, M. S., and J. WILLIAMS, 1977. "Estimating Beta from Non-synchronous Data," *Journal of Financial Economics*, 5, 309–327.

SCHREIBER, P., and R. SCHWARTZ, 1985. "Efficient Price Discovery in a Securities Market: The Objective of a Trading System," in Amihud-Ho-Schwartz (1985).

SCHREIBER, P., and R. SCHWARTZ, 1986. "Price Discovery in a Securities Market: Implications for Regulation, System Design, and the Informational Content of Security Prices," *Journal of Portfolio Management*, forthcoming.

SCHWARTZ, R. A., and D. K. WHITCOMB, 1974. "Can Betas Be Estimated from Daily Data?" presented at the Center for Research in Security Prices, University of Chicago, May 1974 (available in *Proceedings of the Seminar on the Analysis of Security Prices*, 19).

SCHWARTZ, R. A., and D. K. WHITCOMB, 1976. "Comment: Assessing the Impact of Stock Exchange Specialists on Stock Volatility," *Journal of Financial and Quantitative Analysis*, 11, 901-908.

SCHWARTZ, R. A., and D. K. WHITCOMB, 1977a. "The Time-Variance Relationship: Evidence on Autocorrelation in Common Stock Returns," *Journal of Finance*, 32, 41–55.

SCHWARTZ, R. A., and D. K. WHITCOMB, 1977b. "Evidence on the Presence and Causes of Serial Correlation in Market Model Residuals," *Journal of Financial and Quantitative Analysis*, 12, 291–314.

SCHWERT, G. W., 1977. "Stock Exchange Seats as Capital Assets," *Journal of Financial Economics*, 4, 51–78.

SCHWERT, G. W., 1983. "Size and Stock Returns and Other Empirical Regularities," *Journal of Financial Economics*, 12, 3–12.

SECURITIES AND EXCHANGE COMMISSION RELEASE No. 18062, August 25, 1981. "A Monitoring Report on the Operation and Effects of Rule 19c-3 under the Securities Exchange Act of 1934."

SECURITIES AND EXCHANGE COMMISSION RELEASE No. 19372, December 23, 1982. "Proposed Order Exposure Rule 11A-1."

SECURITIES AND EXCHANGE COMMISSION RELEASE No. 20074, August 12, 1983. "Request for Comment on Off-Board Trading Pursuant to Rule 19c-3."

SHANKEN, J., 1985. "Nonsynchronous Data and the Covariance/Factor Structure of Returns," Working Paper, University of Rochester Graduate School of Management.

SILBER, W. L., 1975. "Thinness in Capital Markets: The Case of the Tel Aviv Stock Exchange," *Journal of Financial and Quantitative Analysis*, 10, 129–142.

SILBER, W. L., 1981. "Innovation, Competition, and New Contract Design in Futures Markets," *The Journal of Futures Markets*, 1, 123–155.

SMIDT, S., 1971. "Which Road to an Efficient Stock Market: Free Competition or Regulated Monopoly?" *Financial Analysts Journal*, 27 (September-October), 18–20, 64–69.

SMIDT, S., 1979. "Continuous vs. Intermittent Trading on Auction Markets," *Journal of Financial and Quantitative Analysis*, 14, 837–886.

SMIDT, S., 1985. "Can We Get There from Here?" in Amihud-Ho-Schwartz (1985).

STIGLER, G. J., 1961. "The Economics of Information," *Journal of Political Economy*, 69, 213–225.

STIGLER, G. J., 1964. "Public Regulation of the Securities Markets," *Journal of Business*, 37, 117–142.

STOLL, H. R., 1978a. "The Supply of Dealer Services in Security Markets," *Journal of Finance*, 33, 1133–1151.

STOLL, H. R., 1978b. "The Pricing of Security Dealer Services: An Empirical Study of NASDAQ Stocks," *Journal of Finance*, 33, 1153–1172.

STOLL, H. R., 1985. "Alternative Views of Market Making," in Amihud-Ho-Schwartz (1985).

STOLL, H. R., and R. E. WHALEY, 1983. "Transaction Costs and the Small Firm Effect," *Journal of Financial Economics*, 12, 57–80.

SUNDER, S., 1980. "Stationarity of Market Risk: Random Coefficients Test for Individual Stocks," *Journal of Finance*, 35, 883–896.

TELSER, L. G., 1959. "A Theory of Speculation Relating Profitability and Stability," *Review of Economics and Statistics*, 41, 295–301.

TELSER, L. G., 1981. "Why There Are Organized Futures Markets," *Journal of Law and Economics*, 24, 1–22.

TELSER, L. G., and H. N. HIGINBOTHAM, 1977. "Organized Futures Markets: Costs and Benefits," *Journal of Political Economy*, 85, 969–1000.

THEOBALD, M., 1983. "An Analytic Relationship between Intervaling and Non-trading Effects in Continuous Time," *Journal of Financial and Quantitative Analysis*, 18, 199–209.

TINIC, S. M., 1972. "The Economics of Liquidity Services," *Quarterly Journal of Economics*, 86, 79–93.

TINIC, S. M., and R. R. WEST, 1972. "Competition and the Pricing of Dealer Service in the Over-the-Counter Stock Market," *Journal of Financial and Quantitative Analysis*, 7, 1707–1727.

TINIC, S. M., and R. R. WEST, 1974. "Marketability of Common Stocks in Canada and the USA: A Comparison of Agent versus Dealer Dominated Markets," *Journal of Finance*, 29, 729–746.

TINIC, S. M., and R. R. WEST, 1984. "Risk and Return: January vs. the Rest of the Year," *Journal of Financial Economics*, 13, 561–574.

U. S. SECURITIES AND EXCHANGE COMMISSION, 1971. *Institutional Investor Study Report*, Washington, D.C.: U. S. Government Printing Office.

WALL, J. T., 1985. "The Competitive Environment of the Securities Market," in Amihud-Ho-Schwartz (1985).

WEST, R. R., 1970. "Simulating Securities Markets Operations: Some Examples, Observations and Comments," *Journal of Financial and Quantitative Analysis*, 5, 115–137.

WEST, R. R., and S. M. TINIC, 1971. *The Economics of the Stock Market*. New York: Praeger.

WHITCOMB, D. K., 1972. *Externalities and Welfare*. New York: Columbia University Press.

WILLIAMS, S. L., 1985. "The Evolving National Market System," in Amihud-Ho-Schwartz (1985).

WILLIAMSON, J., 1973. "Another Case of Profitable Destabilizing Speculation," *Journal of International Economics*, 3, 77–84.

INDEX